A SEASON
ON THE WIND

ALSO BY KENN KAUFMAN

Kingbird Highway

Flights Against the Sunset

Field Guides and Reference Books

Peterson Field Guide to Advanced Birding

Lives of North American Birds

Kaufman Field Guide to Birds of North America

Kaufman Field Guide to Butterflies of North America
   (with Jim P. Brock)

Kaufman Field Guide to Mammals of North America
   (with Nora Bowers and Rick Bowers)

Kaufman Guía de campo a las aves de Norteamérica

Kaufman Field Guide to Insects of North America
   (with Eric R. Eaton)

Kaufman Field Guide to Advanced Birding

Kaufman Field Guide to Nature of New England
   (with Kimberly Kaufman)

Kaufman Field Guide to Nature of the Midwest
   (with Jeff Sayre and Kimberly Kaufman)

A SEASON
ON THE WIND

Inside the World
of Spring Migration

KENN KAUFMAN

Houghton Mifflin Harcourt
Boston   New York   2019

For information about permission to reproduce selections
from this book, write to trade.permissions@hmhco.com or to
Permissions, Houghton Mifflin Harcourt Publishing Company,
3 Park Avenue, 19th Floor, New York, NY 10016.

hmhco.com

Library of Congress Cataloging-in-Publication Data
Names: Kaufman, Kenn, author.
Title: A season on the wind : inside the world of spring migration /
Kenn Kaufman.
Description: Boston : Houghton Mifflin Harcourt, 2019.
Identifiers: LCCN 2018042564 (print) | LCCN 2018052904 (ebook) |
ISBN 9781328566768 (ebook) | ISBN 9781328566423 (hardcover)
Subjects: LCSH: Birds — Migration — North America. | Birds —
Effect of human beings on — North America. | Birds —
Conservation — North America. | Birds — Ohio — Magee Marsh
Wildlife Area. | Magee Marsh Wildlife Area (Ohio)
Classification: LCC QL698.9 (ebook) | LCC QL698.9 .K368 2019
(print) | DDC 598.156/8—dc23
LC record available at https://lccn.loc.gov/2018042564

Book design by Greta D. Sibley

Printed in the United States of America
DOC 10 9 8 7 6 5 4 3 2 1

CONTENTS

Prologue
Pilgrims at the Gates of Sunrise

Last night they were on the move.

They had been waiting. Yesterday and days before they had been scattered in a million hiding places, biding their time. For four days, while cold rain pelted down, they had lurked unnoticed, waiting, resting, building their strength. But yesterday the rain had cleared and a south wind had moved in. So after sunset, as the last glow died on the western horizon, they had arisen all at once. They were a multitude of independent invaders, linked by nothing but an intense awareness, taking to the sky, swarming north.

Flying through the night sky, they could see lights below, both near and distant. Vast fields of light marked Cincinnati, Dayton, Columbus, although the names meant nothing to them. Smaller patches of light glowed everywhere. But these travelers would not have considered navigating by the lights below. They looked up at lights overhead, at the stars arrayed across the black velvet dome of the sky. Those were the reliable guides. Cities, after all, might rise and fall, but the constellations overhead would persist, pointing the way for those who could read the sky.

Most humans on the ground below were utterly unaware of the abundance of life passing overhead. But this springtime movement of migratory birds was nothing new. Birds had flown north across this landscape before there were any electric lights, even before there were scattered campfires. They flew before names like "United States" and "Ohio" were first used, and before any calendars called this the second week of May. They flew before the human ideas of weeks and months were invented. The routes and seasons of their travels varied over long spans of time as sea levels rose and fell, as ice sheets advanced and retreated, but the basic movement of migration began millennia ago, its origins lost in the mist of prehistory.

In the last few centuries humans have made sweeping changes to the landscape. There is now less room for wild birds, there are fewer places for them to raise their young, and the northward spring flights are only a shadow of what they once were. But even these diminished flights are still astounding. On peak nights in spring tens of millions of birds, representing hundreds of different species, are moving north all across the continent. During the course of the season migrating birds fly over every square mile of land in North America. Some flying north, some northeast, some northwest, mostly navigating as individuals and not as flocks, they form a living, seething layer of life, far above the ground, for as long as the night lasts.

Most humans are completely oblivious to the feathered parade in the night sky. But some of us are keenly aware. We have been watching weather patterns all season, looking for nights like this with prime conditions. Last night after dark we went online to look at Doppler radar: as small as these birds are, their sheer numbers show up on weather radar, indicating to us when birds are actively moving. Later in the night we went outdoors to listen, and we could hear the occasional flight calls of small birds, drifting down from a thousand feet in the air. And before daylight this morning we headed out to the lakeshore, eager to be there at dawn, to watch for the arriving migrants.

The birds coming from the south, flying a few hundred feet up in the last hours of the night, will see hints of what lies ahead even before first daylight. Below, the velvety blackness of the land is broken only by the isolated lights around farmhouses and small towns and the larger glow from distant cities. But up ahead, moonlight or starlight glints on water, a vast swath of water stretching toward the north: humans call it Lake Erie, one of the Great Lakes. The flying birds see it miles before they reach it, and they may start to drop a little lower, as if calculating whether to end their night's journey before coming to the water's edge.

As the glow increases on the eastern horizon, the scene ahead comes into focus. Beyond the solid darkness of land, light reflects on ragged patches of water punctuated by grass and trees and dikes and roads, a broad band of waterlogged land stretching away to both the west and the east. Just beyond that is a darker line of the beach ridge, and past that ridge nothing but miles of open water.

If they had reached this point earlier in the night, the birds would have kept going, powering on across the lake. With dawn approaching, their calculation changes. If it's clear weather, the migrants can see a few islands in the lake, and probably the far shore —in most places here it's less than thirty miles across the lake to the shoreline in Ontario. But if the birds have been flying all night, most of them will stop now, dropping into cover or swooping down to fly parallel to the lake, not across it.

All over eastern North America at this moment, or at least all along the advancing edge of daylight, migrating birds are dropping out of the sky and looking for cover. In most places they are so widely dispersed that they'll go unnoticed. But here, up against the barrier of the lake, numbers build as more and more birds pause and then come down before the water's edge. In the trees, in the thickets, in the marsh edges, the arriving birds pile up. In the immediate vicinity of the lakeshore, so many small birds will concentrate that they'll be impossible to ignore.

That's why the people are heading to the lakeshore now.

The sun is just climbing above the horizon and cars are arriving in a steady stream, coming north past the woodlots and ponds of the state wildlife area, north along the low causeway that crosses the broad marsh, following the road as it turns left onto the beach ridge and enters the long, narrow parking lot between the woods and the lake. This parking lot will hold hundreds of cars — the adjacent lakeshore used to be a popular swimming beach, when the area was part of a state park — and by 10 a.m. the lot will be filled to capacity, with more vehicles parked in the grassy overflow lot to the east. All of these humans are coming here for just one reason: to witness the swarms of birds now arriving from the south.

We might expect it to look like a mob scene. But it doesn't. In the early morning light, people are scattered out all along the quarter-mile edge between the parking lot and the woods — groups of two or three or a dozen people, moving slowly, talking quietly, looking intently at the trees. A boardwalk loops through the woods, with entrances near the east and west ends of the parking lot, and some people have gone that way already, vanishing into the trees. The overall feeling is peaceful but intense, quiet but brimming with possibility.

The woods are alive with birds — but at a glance you might not notice them at all. Your eyes need time to adjust. Stop next to one of these little groups of birders and look where they're looking, listen to what they're saying.

Look: up in this maple, where pale green buds are just starting to unfold into leaves, a tiny bird is moving. It's bright yellow and gray with black stripes and white patches; someone tells you it's a magnolia warbler. It's moving about actively, too perky and alert for a bird that just spent the whole night flying, and you're trying hard to get a good look. Then you're distracted by another tiny bird behind it, dapper and dark with accents of blue, but that one is chased away by a small yellow bird before you find out its name. Someone points out a Swainson's thrush, soft brown with buff markings, hopping over the ground: "Back there, by the two white-throated sparrows." People are talking about a blue-headed vireo and a palm warbler, but you don't see where they're looking, and before you can ask, a birder just down the road calls out, "Golden-winged warbler!" Your temporary companions hurry over to look, so you join them. Everyone is focused on the same branch, so you quickly spot the warbler, a gray-and-white sprite with dashes of brilliant yellow.

Stick with this group of birders or circulate, make the loop of the boardwalk or stay on the edge, you'll just keep seeing more and more birds — only a few at a time, but they're everywhere. Small, loose groups are moving through the treetops and through the undergrowth, and flocks of other kinds are flying overhead, going east or west, paralleling the lakeshore. Sounds are everywhere, too: a few rich, mellow whistles and many light twitters, chirps, and buzzes from hidden singers. Everything is dynamic, everything is in motion. You won't see every bird here — no one will. It doesn't matter. Watch and listen. Even without knowing any details, it would be obvious that something remarkable is going on.

The details, when you learn them, are even more astonishing. If you didn't know about the popularity of bird-watching, the sheer numbers of people here might seem unbelievable. Right at the moment there's a bird festival in the neighborhood — a major one, appropriately called the Biggest Week in American Birding. But almost all the official festival activities take place several miles from here, so the vast majority of the people now at this spot on the Lake Erie shore have found their way here independently.

These people have come from everywhere. You weren't just imagining the variety of license plates in the parking lot, the variety of accents and languages on the boardwalk. Most people here today are from Ohio or adjoining states, but others have come from New York, California, Florida, and twenty other states, plus Canada and Mexico. There are people here from England, Panama, South Africa, and other countries. During April and May, this spot will see human visitors from every state and up to fifty nations.

The birds they've come to see represent an even wider range. These small migrants don't wear license plates or carry passports, so it takes some study even to guess where they're traveling from and where they're going. The vast majority of these migrants are navigating solo, not in flocks, though they'll join up with other birds during their daytime stopovers. Every individual here has its own story — ten thousand separate stories in this little woodlot today, each one an epic.

Look: here's a tiny bird with a face and throat of brilliant, burning orange, set off by a sharp pattern of black. You could fall in love with it just for its Halloween colors and its alert, perky behavior. But if you know it's an adult male of a species called the blackburnian warbler, you can learn more about it. This bird just spent the winter in South America, in misty forests somewhere on the slopes of the Andes — maybe in Colombia, maybe in Peru, more than three thousand miles south of here. Early in spring it started moving north, working its way up through Central America in a series of night flights and daytime stopovers, then flying north across the Gulf of Mexico to the southern United States. Here in Ohio it's getting closer, but it still has many miles to go before it reaches its destination in some Canadian spruce forest.

That's only part of this bird's story, because last fall, of course, it had to make its way south, flying from Canada to South America. And it wasn't the first time. This bird is an adult, at least two years old. A little scrap of life weighing about half an ounce, it has probably flown across the Gulf of Mexico at least four times, spring and fall, and traveled untold thousands of miles under its own power. Now it is pushing north toward the breeding grounds, to claim a territory, find a mate, and try to raise another brood, to pass its strong and successful genes along to the next generation of blackburnian warblers.

And this is just one individual bird. That subtle olive-and-yellow sprite, called Nashville warbler for no good reason, probably spent the winter in Mexico. The flashy red-and-black scarlet tanager in the next tree has just come from somewhere in the Amazon Basin. This Cape May warbler, yellow and chestnut with lots of stripes, spent the winter in the Caribbean, perhaps in Jamaica or Cuba. And this dull brown bird in the thicket, so drab that it hardly seems to merit a second glance — that's a gray-cheeked thrush. It spent the winter in South America, probably in Brazil, and it's headed for northern Canada or maybe all the way west to Alaska, or it might even cross the Bering Strait to spend the summer in Siberia. The bird is so small, weighing barely more than an ounce; if it sat in the palm of your hand, it would feel like nothing. But it is pausing here in the middle of a journey that may touch three continents.

Thousands of birds and hundreds of birders are in the woods today, each with a story. Here are a couple of young women, perhaps in their late twenties, who appear to be new to this birding thing. They've been fumbling a bit with their binoculars, and their bird guide lies open on the boardwalk rail, as if they've been trying to figure out which birds they're seeing. Now a blazing golden prothonotary warbler is dangling from a twig just a few feet in front of their faces. Their eyes shine with delight and wonder, as if they're witnessing a miracle. And in a way they are.

In the confluence of the watchers and the watched this morning, humans and birds arrived here under different circumstances. Birders came to this exact spot intentionally. Whether they live nearby or on another continent, they are in Ohio today by design. This morning they may have considered other birding hot spots along the lakeshore before deciding to come to this place, the Magee Marsh Wildlife Area. But it was a conscious choice.

For the birds there is less choice and more chance. Their migration is a compromise between will and wind, a compromise between their intended route and the vagaries of weather. These songbirds are too small to fight the wind for long, so they literally go with the flow, waiting for calm weather or for winds that will help them move in the right general direction. Those that survive the journey will eventually make it to their destinations with pinpoint accuracy, but on the way they may experience setbacks and detours. Large waterbirds like cranes and geese may have traditional migratory stopovers that they use for generations, but small songbirds can't be so picky, and they must find stopover habitat wherever they happen to be when the sun comes up. On a given spring morning, many will happen to be at this spot on the Lake Erie shore.

So here we are, humans and birds, in the same place. We're arriving at the same time, but the journey here has been profoundly different. For humans, travel has never been easier and safer than it is now. For songbirds, it's more dangerous every year.

When a bird is resident on its territory, it learns many details useful for survival, including where to find food and water, what dangers to expect, and where to go for shelter if threatened. A bird traveling through unfamiliar country knows none of those details. A long-distance migrant must contend with a remarkable number of hazards. During its nighttime flights, a sudden storm could prove fatal, especially if the bird is flying over open water. During its daytime stopovers, it is at risk from a multitude of unfamiliar predators, from hawks and snakes and weasels to prowling pets. It's no wonder that, according to some studies, a songbird is fifteen times more likely to die during migration than during its long stays in its summer and winter territories.

Against all odds, these birds must make their long journeys or perish in the attempt. People may imagine them to be cheery little songsters with the freedom to roam the world, but in fact they're driven by instinct that burns with white-hot intensity, locked in a pattern that leaves no room for choice. Time after time they fling themselves into the air for another long flight or gamble with their lives on a risky daytime stopover. None of them will die of old age. They'll just keep on performing herculean feats over and over until that moment when weakness or lack of attention or bad luck takes them down.

For songbirds, then, travel is dangerous, and becoming more so. Their journeys already push the limits of what is possible. The precise timing of migration of each species has been honed by natural selection over hundreds of generations, threading every needle to hit the sweet spot in the season, not too early, not too late: early enough to claim a prime nesting territory, but not too early for food to be available. Now, however, the season is becoming more unpredictable. Extremes of weather are becoming more extreme, and more frequent. In at least some places spring is arriving earlier, and the migration of songbirds isn't keeping up; the birds are missing the optimum timing that worked for their ancestors. The very basis of their aerial existence is changing. These birds live on the wind, and the wind is failing them.

A rapidly changing climate will affect most living things on Earth, but none are as vulnerable as the birds that migrate long distances. Their survival depends on precise conditions of habitat and season at a whole series of locations — breeding grounds, wintering grounds, and stopover sites in between — and on weather conditions that allow them to make the journeys between these sites. Damage or remove any one of these elements and the birds will be in trouble.

Most people now understand that climate change is being driven by the greenhouse effect, the buildup of certain heat-trapping gases in the atmosphere, largely from the burning of fossil fuels and other activities related to energy production. Serious efforts are under way to curtail these kinds of air pollution by phasing in clean sources of energy. But in a grim irony, some of the most promising sources of otherwise green energy are disastrous for migratory birds if they're put in the wrong places.

So the birds are caught in the middle. They are collateral victims, hammered first by the damage that humans have done and then by our fumbling attempts to fix that damage.

For the small feathered travelers before us now, dropping out of the sky and pitching into treetops on the edge of Lake Erie, these large concepts would have no meaning. Their blazing focus is on the here and now: this tree, this branch, this moment. They'll be with us only a short time, regaining strength, before they take to the wind and push northward. The instinct that drives them allows no compromise. Whatever the obstacles, whatever the odds, each small bird plays out its part in the ancient cadence of life, risking everything to return to the breeding grounds one more time.

1

The First Migration

During the first few years here, I must have been asked a thousand times, "Why would you move to Ohio?"

To understand the significance of that question, you have to know who asked it.

The questioners, without exception, were birders. Yes, bird-watchers, bird enthusiasts, bird freaks. For most of my life, most of my friends have been people keenly tuned in to the sprawling diversity of feathered creatures. These people not only notice that distant speck in the sky but also recognize it as a red-tailed hawk. These people miss the dialogue in a movie because they are so busy identifying the birdcalls dubbed into the soundtrack. These people are intensely aware, but aware in ways that can be unnerving for anyone else. These are *my* people. When they asked a question like that, they meant it in a specific way. It wasn't about Ohio. What they meant was, "Why would you move away from Arizona?"

We birders have our own geography. Our map of the world is illuminated by the peaks and valleys of birding potential. On the birders' map, cities like Paris and London might fade into gray anonymity, while a landfill in Texas or a nameless riverbank in Brazil shines like a beacon. On the birders' mental map of North America, southern Arizona is a fabled destination. Every birder dreams of going there. I had lived there for years, and all my friends knew it and wondered why I would leave.

I had been in Arizona a long time. As a teenager, hitching rides around North America in pursuit of birds, I had gone to Arizona and fallen in love with the state immediately. The rugged canyons had an irresistible wild beauty, and the birds were unlike those anywhere else, with many tropical types barely slipping above the border. It seemed magical. When I moved there, every birder I knew was jealous: "Wow! Arizona! I saw thirty new birds in my first hour there! You're so lucky to get to see those birds all the time!"

Of course they were right, in a sense; it *is* a lucky thing to get to see *any* bird all the time. But when you live there and you've seen them every day for ten years, they no longer seem so unusual. After thousands of repetitions, the exotic becomes the familiar. A Mexican jay in Arizona is not intrinsically more special than a blue jay in New Jersey. It's the expected local thing, and it's beautiful, but it's no longer exotic.

Try as I might to explain that to people, I could see them shaking their heads with doubt, and then they would ask again. "Why would you move from Arizona to Ohio?"

For some questioners, all I had to do was to point to Kimberly. They would look at her, this amazing and smart and beautiful woman, and they would nod their heads. Yes, that explains it; I moved to be with her.

But that wasn't really a complete answer. Kimberly was not nailed down here. When she and I were first getting together, both of us recovering from sad and awkward divorces, we could have moved anywhere. I was a freelance writer and artist, and I could have made my living anyplace with an Internet connection. We wound up here, forty miles from her former home and two thousand miles from mine, because she had a connection to the bird migration in northwestern Ohio.

The migration — that was the thing. That was the deciding factor.

Birds move. That's part of their appeal. Birds move in quick and unpredictable ways, and that must have been part of what pulled my attention to them in childhood. After all, children are naturally drawn to things that move, and all children will love animals and birds if they are given the right exposure. I was lucky: sparrows and grackles on the lawn, seen up close, were so vividly and intensely and shockingly alive that I was captivated by their every motion, fascinated for life.

But beyond the fact that birds move, there is the added appeal that they *move* — across landscapes, across continents, beyond horizons. That fact took a powerful hold on my imagination when I was nine or ten years old, reading about birds in detail for the first time. Some of our summertime backyard birds, chipping sparrows and catbirds and the like, might pick up in fall and fly south to another state or another country. I read about these birds and pored over maps and globes, trying to grasp some idea of the distances involved, while the birds expanded my concept of the world.

The more I read, the more astounding it all seemed. Ten thousand kinds of birds in the world, and more than five thousand of them performed some kind of seasonal movement. Billions of individual birds on the move twice every year, in spring and fall. Some birds moving only a few miles, including uphill or downhill, with the seasons. Others moving a few hundred miles to get to a more favorable climate for the winter, and still others going thousands of miles. Seabirds flying from one ocean to another, land birds flying from one continent to another, the skies of the whole planet seething with small travelers, numbers beyond counting, miles beyond anything I could imagine.

I was still trying to wrap my head around these things when I started traveling myself, in my late teens. Hitchhiking across the continent gave me plenty of time to think about distances and about the challenges of travel. Hitching rides all the way from Montana up to Alaska and back was a challenge, but I knew that some thrushes and warblers would fly from central Alaska all the way to Brazil. Some plovers would fly from the North Slope all the way to the southern tip of South America. Arctic terns might fly from the northernmost islands of the Canadian Arctic archipelago, just a few degrees from the North Pole, all the way to the edge of the Antarctic. Such epic journeys spanned the globe. Nothing on this planet, aside from the craziest humans, ever traveled as far as the birds.

These travels of birds were so hard to observe directly. Most of the small birds traveled on a broad front, spanning much of the continent; they were not following narrow "highways in the sky." So even in vast numbers, they were so spread out that their journeys were not obvious.

Standing on roadsides, waiting for rides and thinking about birds, I dredged up factoids from geography class and tried geeky calculations. What if a million migrating sparrows dropped into the state of Kansas at the same time? Would anyone see them? Kansas covers about 80,000 square miles, so a million sparrows would amount to only about twelve per square mile. Or one for every fifty acres. Bump it up to 10 million migrating sparrows and you'd still have only one per five acres. Would anyone in that five-acre block happen to see that one bird? I concluded that an enormous movement of migratory songbirds, tens of millions sweeping across the continent, could go largely unnoticed.

But I kept watching. As I traveled around North America and then the world, I watched for migration, or signs of it. In the jungle in Costa Rica in December, I might see a colorful songbird called a chestnut-sided warbler, and I could read that it was found there only during winter. In a coastal woodlot in Louisiana in April, I might see chestnut-sided warblers again, and I could read that they showed up there only during brief times in spring and fall. Then in June along a leafy stream in eastern Canada I might see the same kind of warbler and read that it was only a summer resident there. So I was seeing hints that the birds had traveled but missing the experience of seeing the migration itself.

This was the paradox I faced in my unrequited fascination with winged migration. Tremendous numbers of birds were traveling vast distances, navigating with remarkable precision, performing astonishing feats of endurance as they spanned the globe . . . it was a huge phenomenon, but mostly invisible. It would become visible only in places where quirks of geography forced the birds to concentrate in unusual numbers.

So after I settled in Arizona, where seasonal movement of birds was never an obvious thing, I made repeated trips out to other places in the world where I thought I might catch it in the act — places where the migration itself might be visible.

For several years my friend Victor Emanuel and I taught an annual workshop on spring migration on the upper Texas coast, east of Houston. Throughout the week, throughout our days in the field and our evening classroom sessions, we were watching the weather, watching the radar, trying to predict when the next big flight would arrive.

There are always scads of birds on the upper Texas coast, but our focus was on the trans-Gulf migrants, birds flying north across the Gulf of Mexico from the Yucatán Peninsula. These migrants included a wide variety of songbirds and others that had wintered in the tropics, from southernmost Mexico to South America, powering north through Central America in spring until they came to the Yucatán Peninsula's northern edge. After pausing and waiting for the right weather, these migrants would leave the Yucatán at dusk and fly north overnight across the Gulf. The crossing would take an average of eighteen hours, bringing them to the Gulf Coast of the United States around the middle of the next day—but if they arrived in good weather, many would keep flying for another two or three hours, going fifty to one hundred miles inland before putting down. Only a minority would settle immediately in isolated woodlots out among the coastal marshes.

But if those northbound migrants happened to run into bad weather before they reached the coast—if they hit storms and rain over the Gulf, or along the immediate coastline—the equation would change. In those conditions, migrating birds would come down at the first opportunity, in the phenomenon called a "fallout." Struggling against rain and wind, fighting for survival, songbirds would come in low off the Gulf, pitching into the first line of trees or patch of bushes or even landing on the beach. Savvy birders, seeing fallout conditions develop, would drive out to these coastal spots and watch in awe as exhausted migrant birds filled the trees.

A true fallout was a bittersweet paradox: good for birders, bad for birds. It gave us unparalleled close views of these small travelers, but we knew we were seeing the survivors of a stressful event. We knew that other birds would have perished before reaching shore. So with our workshop groups we were prepared to witness the concentration of birds resulting from a fallout, if one occurred, but we couldn't bring ourselves to hope for one.

A different kind of concentration featured in the passage of birds along the coast of China, around the town of Beidaihe, where I spent a month one autumn to witness the migration of Asian birds.

Birds moving south out of the Russian Far East in fall, out of the whole vast wilderness of eastern Siberia, and headed to Southeast Asia for the winter, had two possible routes. They could make long, long overwater flights, or they could detour far to the west to stay over land, to go around the westernmost extension of the Yellow Sea. Apparently great numbers of them took the latter route and came down the coast past Beidaihe. Expat British birders living in Hong Kong had pioneered the birding possibilities at Beidaihe, mapping out the approach for foreign visitors. In the month I was there, from early September to early October, two American friends and I observed birds every day from dawn to dark.

It was a magical experience. This was just before the great explosion of economic growth in China, so even though Beidaihe is considered a resort town for the Chinese, it wasn't too crowded, and traffic consisted mostly of bicycles and buses. We stayed at the one hotel in town that could legally accommodate foreigners, we rented bicycles for a dollar a day, and we explored every inch of habitat within about a seven-mile radius along the coast.

Out at first light every morning, watching sunrise colors paint the clouds over the Yellow Sea, we greeted a morning of endless possibilities. Small birds would be moving in the dawn, songbirds called pipits and wagtails flying south along the coast in a high, bounding flight, announcing their identities with sharp callnotes. Every little ravine and vacant lot along the shoreline would hold a new cast of characters every day, new songbirds from Siberia that had arrived overnight. There were treasures enough to keep us occupied for hours, or we could ride our rented bikes out to the estuaries to see what new sandpipers or plovers had just hauled in from the tundra. As the day warmed, the birds of prey would start to move, harriers gliding past on their long wings, sparrowhawks hugging the treetops and moving on in bursts of speed. Every day was a parade of wonders. A handful of young European birders came through Beidaihe that fall, all of them just exploring by bicycle as we were, and we compared notes in the evenings. We all had the sense that we were on the cutting edge, learning things about migration on the China coast that no one had ever known.

Then there was Veracruz, far down along the Gulf of Mexico, five hundred miles south of the Texas border. For several weeks in fall, hawks pour through in what has come to be called "the river of raptors." Now, most kinds of hawks in North America are not long-distance migrants: they may stay in one area all year, or migrate a short distance, say from central Canada to the central United States. But there are a few striking exceptions, such as Swainson's hawk and Mississippi kite, that fly all the way to South America in autumn. Although other birds take part in the movement, raptors make up the bulk of the flight in Veracruz.

It's not easy for raptors to hunt while they're traveling; they can't just fatten up on abundant tiny insects or seeds, as a songbird might. They may go days without eating, so they conserve energy as much as possible. Aside from the speedy falcons, most go out of their way to avoid crossing open water, where they would have to flap continuously to stay aloft. Instead they seek out routes with natural lift — especially thermals, columns of warm, rising air above sun-heated flatlands. Across open country the hawks circle and rise high on a thermal, then set their wings and glide south to the next thermal, traveling for miles without flapping their wings at all.

Vast stretches of North America are suitable for creating thermals, allowing these hawks to migrate south on a wide front. But in eastern Mexico the broad coastal plain along the Gulf gradually narrows until finally, in the state of Veracruz, there's a point where the mountains come down almost to the shore, leaving a flat gap only a few miles wide. Through this gap, the raptors from more than 6 million square miles of land come pouring southward in the fall, with seasonal totals running into the millions of birds.

One of the best vantage points was the roof of the Hotel Bienvenido in the town of Cardel. When I was there, the site was manned by counters from the conservation organization Pronatura, sitting up there every day in fall to tally the hawks. Six stories above the busy streets, these confident, barefoot young men would lean back in their chairs to scan the northern horizon, spotting distant hawks long before any of the visiting birders did. When a spiral of hawks began to rise on a distant thermal, the counters would lean forward, peering through binoculars, and then start rapid-fire bursts on their clickers to tally the various species. We would follow the line of their binoculars to find the hawks and watch as each swirling vortex of raptors climbed the sky and then broke off to glide southward, many coming right over our heads.

One October day we were at another site, at the village of Chichicaxtle, for the dedication of a new hawk-watch tower. It was a big deal. The governor of the state of Veracruz came to officiate, arriving by helicopter on the adjacent soccer field. The ceremony was under way, the governor was partway through his remarks, when the heavens opened up — not with rain but with birds.

The sky was alive. All over the northern horizon, distant and close, at least half a dozen spirals of hawks went swirling up on thermals: slow, ponderous tornadoes of hawks. From the top of each vortex hawks poured out in lines, their wings half furled, in long, slow glides toward other columns of hawks rising to the south of us. Rivers of hawks, thousands upon thousands of birds, swept over our heads. Their lines mingled and crossed, new columns formed before our eyes, and it seemed that every part of the sky was exploding with circles and streams of hawks. Everyone, including the governor, was staring at the sky. Even the seasoned counters were looking around with dazed eyes and fumbling to keep up. We later heard the tally for the day came to more than 400,000 hawks, and we could have believed the number was even higher.

That kind of thing could happen only in a place where migrants were concentrated by geography in an extreme way — where a continent's worth of migrants were forced into a corridor a dozen miles wide. But as I traveled I saw many places that served to concentrate migrating birds to a lesser degree. In Southeast Asia in early spring, taking a boat upriver through the rainforest to Taman Negara, I saw how swallows were massing all along the river, staging for their flight to the north. In Africa in late fall, staying at a lodge in the hills of Tsavo National Park, I was amazed when a wet, foggy night brought a fallout of migrating songbirds to the lodge lights. Disoriented in the mist, thrush nightingales, whitethroats, and other migrants came out of the darkness to circle the glare of the lights. Even though it was late November, these birds from Europe and northern Asia were still on their way southward through Kenya, stealth migrants revealed only when unique conditions pulled them out of the night sky.

Then there was Central Park, that manmade wilderness in the middle of Manhattan. For years I did editing work for the National Audubon Society, and whenever I went to its headquarters in New York I would take time to visit the park, often leading an Audubon group. Practically any morning in spring or fall, Central Park revealed a rich assortment of migratory birds. I could picture how they had arrived, too: at first light, many nocturnal migrants would be over the New York City region, looking down at square miles of gray concrete. In that cityscape, the green parks would shine like beacons for tired songbirds, and they would converge on the parks from miles around — especially the big, verdant rectangle of Central Park. If we went there and searched with care, we'd get a sampling of the parade of birds that had passed overhead during the night. Hemmed in by skyscrapers and awash with traffic noise, Central Park was still an astonishingly good place to witness bird migration in action.

After all of these trips I would go home to Arizona. I loved many things about the desert Southwest, to be sure, and I hadn't thought actively about leaving. It was a fine region for studying nature. But at the back of my mind was always the sense that I had let myself down by abandoning my youthful focus on bird migration.

Yes, migratory birds moved through Arizona. Sometimes artificial ponds in the desert held numbers of shorebirds that were just passing through. Sometimes in late summer, high in the mountains, mixed flocks of songbirds moved through the tall pines, and I knew that some of these birds had come from the north. But the visible migration that had captured my imagination on trips around the world was rarely more than a rumor in Arizona. Year after year, it seemed my dreams of migration were drying up and dying in the desert wind.

Then I met Kimberly. After that, nothing in my life would be the same.

Our backgrounds were wildly different, but our hearts responded to the same things. Kimberly had not come to an interest in birds as early in life as I had, but she had fallen just as hard. By the time we were getting acquainted, Kimberly was working as a research tech in spring and fall, banding migratory songbirds for a bird observatory in northern Ohio.

I had heard about the legendary concentrations of migratory birds around western Lake Erie. I had even gone to see them. On the Canadian side of Lake Erie, at Point Pelee, Ontario, I had taught several birding workshops over the years. People had told me that places on the Ohio side of the lake could be just as good, especially in the region around Magee Marsh.

I had even heard about the bird observatory where Kimberly worked. At least, I had heard its name—Black Swamp Bird Observatory—but somehow I hadn't connected it to the Lake Erie migration. I didn't know that the famous Magee Marsh was just a tiny remnant of a vast wetland formerly known as the Great Black Swamp, the source of the observatory's name. Not knowing this connection, I imagined an observatory stuck in some godforsaken swamp, far from any bird action. I imagined researchers slogging through this black swamp, hoping to find birds to study. I had no idea that the Black Swamp Bird Observatory sat at the heart of an astonishing hot spot for migration.

Even after I knew the connection, it took me a while to grasp what that could mean. When Kimberly and I realized we were seri-

ous and we wanted to be together, we talked about various places
we might live. We talked about Florida, Texas, California — all famous destinations for birding and nature. Finally it dawned on me:
*Hey, listen up. For years you've said you wanted to experience bird mi-
gration. Your new girlfriend works in a place that's famous for it. Why
not just move there?*

So I did.

Even as I was in the process of moving, I still didn't realize the
extent to which my life was changing. I assumed that I would just
continue working on the same kinds of projects that had occupied
my time in Arizona but that when I wanted a break, I could run out
and look at some migratory birds. It sounded so simple.

I had no idea just how much the phenomenon of spring migration would come to dominate my waking hours and even my
dreams. I had no idea how much I still had to learn. My new companions in Ohio, having seen my bird books and my magazine arti-
cles for years, assumed that I must already have a solid background
in this aspect of birds' lives. But by coming to the epicenter of
spring migration I was really throwing myself back to square one,
and I was going to have to start learning the basics all over again.

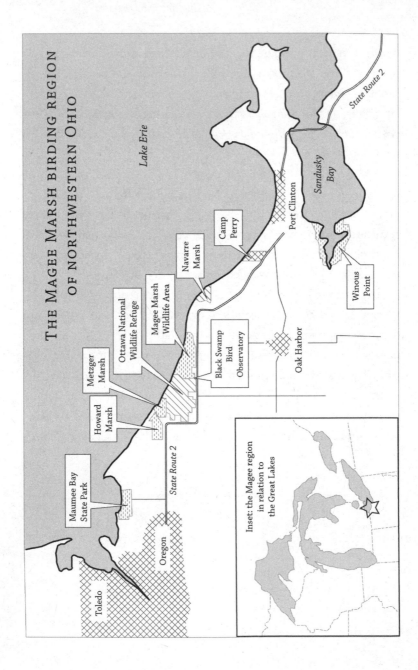

2

Wilderness and Waterfowl

For years I ignored the upper Midwest. Born in Indiana, moved away at the age of nine, I had traveled the globe with an assumption that everyplace else in the world must be more interesting. Ohio barely registered in my awareness. I'd gone to speak in Ohio a few times, at bird festivals and public programs, and I thought I knew enough about it.

I was wrong.

On a map of North America, the region looks even flatter than it is in real life. The Great Lakes — splayed along the United States–Canada border for a thousand miles — look like odd-shaped cardboard cutouts on the map, flat and dead. But that's an illusion. In reality the Great Lakes make up a living, flowing watershed. Rivers flow into all of them, and the western lakes flow toward the east. Waters from Lake Superior and Lake Michigan move eastward into Lake Huron, and from there they flow south through little Lake

St. Clair and south again through the Detroit River into Lake Erie. Wide and shallow, Lake Erie angles toward the east-northeast. Its waters drift imperceptibly in that direction until they pour into the Niagara River and plunge over Niagara Falls, quickening eastward through Lake Ontario, to empty into the mighty St. Lawrence River and flow hundreds of miles northeastward into the Gulf of St. Lawrence and the open Atlantic. So regardless of first impressions, the heart of this region is a vast waterway in constant motion.

For now we'll stick with Lake Erie. Down at its southwestern corner, the city of Toledo perches on the edge of the Maumee River where it empties into the lake. Toledo's population is down from the prosperous peak that it enjoyed when manufacturing was stronger; this is one of the cities dismissed with the "rust belt" label by those who haven't been here. The city still has some remarkable cultural advantages for its size, things established when the money was better, like an outstanding art museum and a superb park system. Today, though, we're leaving the city, heading out to areas ten to forty miles farther east, where the real story takes place.

If you didn't read the signs along the road, you wouldn't guess that the highway paralleled the edge of a huge lake, passing vast acreages of low, marshy land. Going east out of Toledo, State Route 2 stays one to four miles south of the Lake Erie shoreline. Leaving Toledo and its satellite city of Oregon, Route 2 runs past strip malls and businesses and box stores, finally breaking out into farm country. The land is flat as a table, all brown and gray and tawny yellow on this winter day, the fields a patchwork of corn stubble and soybean remains and fallow weeds. It could be any farmland anywhere.

But the signs tell a different story. MAUMEE BAY STATE PARK.

MEINKE MARINA. BAIT AND TACKLE. MALLARD CLUB MARSH. Bays and marinas and marshes, all off to the left, off the north side of the highway. LITTLE CEDAR POINT WILDLIFE REFUGE. HOWARD MARSH. METZGER MARSH WILDLIFE AREA. The highway zags to the south, then east again, making wide, sweeping curves so the truckers won't have to slow their big rigs. OTTAWA NATIONAL WILDLIFE REFUGE. MAGEE MARSH WILDLIFE AREA. Clearly there must be wildlife around, and marshes, even if we're seeing only soybean fields from the highway. BLACK SWAMP BIRD OBSERVA-TORY. Bookmark that one; we'll come back to it later.

The signs continue as we keep driving east. TURTLE CREEK AC-CESS. TOUSSAINT WILDLIFE AREA. INLAND MARINA. WILD WINGS MARINA AND DOCKS. HAPPY HOOKER BAIT & TACKLE. We still can't see Lake Erie, but we see more wet woodlots, more roadside water. The highway skirts past the cooling tower for a nuclear power plant, past a mostly empty business park, and then past a mili-tary reservation, Camp Perry. There are bridges over the Toussaint River and the Portage River, with wide marshy margins. Signs point off to towns with waterside names: Oak Harbor, Port Clin-ton. We can't ignore the proximity of big water.

Finally, after the highway has made another wide southward swing around the town of Port Clinton, it arrows straight south over a long, long bridge and causeway across Sandusky Bay. The bay, two miles wide and ten miles long, is open to Lake Erie at its eastern end and extends at least six miles west of this bridge, put-ting Port Clinton on a peninsula. It's the first real view of Lake Erie water that we've had.

And looking up the bay from the top of the bridge, to the west, we see something interesting: there are very few buildings near the water. Looking at night, we would see very few lights.

This is odd if we stop to think about it. Waterfront property is valuable and sought-after. Lake views and bay views should demand high prices. Why is the bay not lined with expensive houses?

There's a reason. And there's a reason why we saw all those signs along Route 2 pointing to parks and wildlife refuges — north of the highway, toward the lake, toward what should be the most valuable real estate. To understand it, we have to step back and look at the history of the land here.

At one time this landscape was covered by a huge wetland. The Great Black Swamp, it was called. A hundred miles long and twenty to forty miles wide, occupying a shallow depression left over from the last ice age, it carried a slow, oozing flow of water east-northeast from parts of Indiana and Ohio into Lake Erie. The swamp may have been called "black" either for the deep black mud or for the sense of menace that the place exuded, but the combination of these two elements kept settlers out for a long time. Native Americans from at least ten different tribes understood the secrets of the swamp, and they traveled there and hunted there, but most whites stayed out.

Into the 1830s, long after Ohio gained statehood and towns and farms spread across the landscape, travelers still detoured around the Great Black Swamp. Early attempts at roads across it mostly failed, as horses and wagons sank into the muck. Soldiers and settlers who survived crossing the swamp described it as "my great terror" and "the home of Satan."

From the viewpoint of a naturalist, of course, this hellhole would have been a paradise. After the surrounding territory had been beaten down to bland farm fields, the Great Black Swamp still stood as a wilderness. Streams, swales, low quagmires choked

with maple and buttonbush, higher spots crowned with towering cottonwoods and sycamores and beeches, a vast hodgepodge
unmapped and unmappable, it must have been a wonder. Wildlife was abundant. Not only were there otters and mink and bea-
vers and white-tailed deer, but herds of elk roamed here, too. Black
bears wandered through the swamp all summer and denned up on
higher ground in winter.

Wolves were also here. Yes, the land that's now the humdrum
Midwest had wolves once, beautiful savages, free and wild. Even
after they had disappeared from most of Ohio, packs of wolves
ranged through the Black Swamp and the surrounding territory.
The spine-tingling music of their howling would rise at night, a
paean to the vanishing wild. People raised on fairy tales were afraid
of the wolves, and that fear may have been one more factor to keep
settlers out of the Black Swamp for a time; but it also made them
more determined to conquer the swamp, and they chipped away at
its edges, shooting and trapping all the predators whenever they
could. When the last wolf died, the wilderness died, too, and the
spirit of the land was forever diminished.

The Great Black Swamp also died. Once humans worked out
the methods, it didn't take long for them to drain most of it. The
slow, gradual seepage of water from Indiana east through the
swamp and out into Lake Erie was channelized and accelerated.
The process took almost forty years, from the 1850s to the 1890s,
but people essentially drained the whole thing. Deep ditches still
line most of the main roads here, deep and wide enough in places
to swallow a truck. They are reminders of the effort it took to
empty the swamp and the effort that it still takes, to this day, to
keep it emptied.

Ecologists make a distinction between swamp and marsh: a swamp has woody plants like trees and shrubs, while a marsh features low plants like grasses, reeds, and cattails. Most of this region was indeed a wooded swamp, but at its eastern end, approaching the lakeshore, it opened up into wide marshes that stretched from horizon to horizon.

And those marshes were legendary.

The western Lake Erie marshes were at least as wondrous as the Black Swamp, a vast wetland, perfect for waterfowl throughout the late fall and early spring. At one time these marshes must have erupted with clouds of ducks. On November mornings, against that wide-open sky, the flights of wild ducks must have been extraordinary: thousands upon thousands of mallards, pintails, wigeons, black ducks, canvasbacks, bluebills, and so many more, flocks moving in every direction, flocks of dozens or scores or hundreds in high, swift flight, filling the sky in a spectacle that no one living today has ever seen. Native Americans came here to hunt the ducks, of course, and wild predators stalked the marsh, but they could not even begin to blunt the overwhelming abundance of waterfowl. Predation was always a natural part of the equation, and never a problem, so long as the ducks had plenty of habitat. This marshy paradise must have seemed like a scene straight out of Eden, while it lasted.

Marshes and swamps differ in their plant life, but they're pretty much the same when it comes to draining and destruction. The western Lake Erie marshes, like the Black Swamp, were systematically drained. The resulting flat farmland crept toward the lakeshore like an inexorable tide.

Improbably, though, the destruction was halted before it was complete. There's a singular reason that some of the best marshes were saved. One reason, two words: duck hunters.

It sounds blunt and oversimplified to say it, but from the viewpoint of wildlife, farmers and merchants and developers almost wrecked this land. The duck hunters saved it.

Some readers may be put off immediately. Hunting is a divisive topic. The division is rooted in geography to some extent. I have many friends in large cities like New York and Boston who regard hunting as a barbaric practice, a horrifying holdover from the Stone Age. They can't understand how anyone could do it. On the other hand, I have many friends in rural areas who regard hunting as a normal part of life. In some regions of farms and woods and small towns, such as where I live now, most of the men and many of the women go hunting at least occasionally, just as their fathers and grandfathers did. They obey the game laws, they eat what they shoot, and they can't understand how anyone could object.

I'm in the middle between these viewpoints. I've never gone hunting. On the other hand, I have caught fish and eaten them — and how is that different? — and I haven't turned vegetarian, so I'm still eating meat at least occasionally. It would be hypocritical for me to take an antihunting stance.

And from the standpoint of conservation, in America today, hunters and their organizations are extremely influential. If we think in terms of protecting whole populations rather than individuals, hunters are in the forefront of ensuring the survival of species.

Among the hunting community, those who hunt ducks and geese make up a special breed. For one thing, hunting waterfowl is typically more expensive than hunting other kinds of small game. If you live in the country, you might be able to shoot rabbits or squirrels by walking out to the back forty. But hunting waterfowl involves more effort, equipment, and expense. It may require a blind, chest waders, full camouflage, decoys, a retriever, often a boat of some kind, and access to good wetland habitat. The habitat can be one of the most challenging requirements. After centuries of draining and destruction of marshes and swamps, natural wetlands are scarce. It's possible to restore lost wetlands or create new ones by building dams and impoundments, installing canals and gates and pumps, but it's expensive. In general, where good duck-hunting habitat exists in the Midwest today, someone is spending a lot of money to maintain it.

And in northwestern Ohio, people spent a lot of money to save that habitat in the first place. All along Lake Erie, all around Sandusky Bay, individuals and groups purchased marshland to save it from draining, turning the rescued marshes into duck-hunting clubs. It was a heroic effort and it happened just in time.

The Winous Point Shooting Club was established on Sandusky Bay in 1856, just about the time that the draining of the Great Black Swamp was picking up speed. Winous Point was a club for successful gentlemen from the start; some of its early members served in cabinet posts under Lincoln and other United States presidents. Today, as the largest and oldest private hunting club in northwestern Ohio, it is also the most exclusive. Annual dues are outside the reach of most people. Its total membership is limited to fewer than thirty people at a time, and when there is a vacancy, someone must receive a unanimous vote of the current members in order to join.

I had a rare look behind the scenes when a member of Winous Point invited me to come out and join him for a morning's hunt. Deke is a towering figure in the Toledo area, a captain of industry, a major supporter of the arts and culture and wildlife conservation throughout the region; his father was a member of Winous Point, and he carries on the tradition. I barely knew him at the time, but he had heard that I was researching the history of habitat preservation in northwestern Ohio, and he graciously offered me an up-close look at the place where it all started. I could not pass up this opportunity to learn more about the club.

It was a weeknight toward the end of duck season, in December, and only a couple of other members were there, out-of-state executives on brief vacations. Deke showed me around the main clubhouse, rustic but elegant, with wood paneling on the walls and collections of mounted ducks and antique decoys from the 1800s. We looked at ledgers that tracked how many ducks and geese had been shot, by the day, back to 1874. John Simpson, the current manager of Winous Point, showed us maps of the whole property. The marshes are divided into more than two dozen impoundments, ranging from forty to four hundred acres, each with its own management plan. While some other duck clubs in the area plant crops and then flood the fields, Winous Point sticks with native marsh plants and manages the area for all native wildlife, not just game species. The shooting club has a parallel organization, the Winous Point Conservancy, supporting research into every aspect of marsh ecology. John and Deke talked with pride about projects to support populations of king rails, sedge wrens, Blanding's turtles, and other species that have no connection to ducks other than sharing some of the same habitat. These people, I had to admit, were conservationists in every sense of the word.

Late in the evening we went into the central hall for the traditional choosing of each man's hunting site for the next morning.

On a map John Simpson pointed out the marsh units available and talked in detail about the conditions of each and ducks that had been using each area. Then the men drew numbers to see who would get first choice.

Up long before dawn, we motored across an arm of the bay in the dark, hiked over a dike, and then continued by punt boat into the impoundment. The two punters — members of a group of expert local outdoorsmen who are universally respected by all the wealthy club members — propelled us silently through the shallows to the blind, hidden in the edge of tall cattails. Deke and the punters arranged the decoys in front of the blind; the setup had to be perfectly natural and random, because wild ducks are smart and wary, put off by anything that looks suspicious. Dressed in chest waders and heavy parkas, we were all in full camouflage from head to toe, all to avoid giving away our presence.

As the sky melted from black to gray, as the first hint of dawn began tinting the clouds on the eastern horizon, the marsh began to wake up. We could hear the gabbling of ducks and geese far in the distance and the occasional splash of a muskrat, but no sound that betrayed the existence of human civilization. The scene out in front of us could have been plucked from the distant past, from a thousand years ago, for all that we could see. Then the first flights of ducks started to cross our line of sight, high and wild against the streaks of pink and purple brightening the eastern sky, and we tensed up as we waited for some of those ducks to come in close.

Among my friends there are some, I know, who would have found that situation unbearable. Even if they got as far as sitting in the blind, at the last moment they would have felt driven to leap up and shout, causing the ducks to veer off out of range. They may be disappointed that I didn't do that. Instead I sat there taking it in, watching the drama play out.

Wild ducks don't die of old age. Even those that make it to adulthood must watch constantly for foxes, mink, coyotes, hawks, eagles, falcons, and owls. They may evade such predators, but they have no ready defense against silent killers like botulism. As a way to die, a clean quick shot seems more humane than being dragged into the marsh and ripped apart by a fox or wasting away under the limp paralysis of disease. That was what I repeated to myself while I watched from the blind.

If you're of a different persuasion you will never understand, and I may not totally understand it myself. But after being in the blind with Deke, I came away convinced that he loved the wild waterfowl. I had the same sense about the punters who took us across the bay predawn, and the other hunters I'd met the night before, and the managers of Winous Point. They loved the ducks as the central element of the whole experience. It was a dry-eyed and unsentimental kind of love, but it translated into a fierce determination to protect these wild marshes, to honor 150 years of traditions, to ensure the survival of waterfowl in healthy numbers for future generations.

Whether the birders like it or not, it's a fact that our birding today in northwest Ohio rests on a foundation of habitat built by duck hunters. Magee Marsh Wildlife Area, famous around the world as a place to see warblers and other songbirds, was saved from farming and development because it was a duck club before it was turned over to the state of Ohio. The same is true of other lesser known but equally valuable birding sites, such as the Pipe Creek, Metzger Marsh, and Mallard Club Marsh wildlife areas. Ottawa National

Wildlife Refuge, a huge tract next door to Magee and managed by the federal government, has a similar history.

This is all common knowledge around here. Local birders certainly know it. Professionals with the federal and state wildlife agencies all know it. Most of the latter come from backgrounds more aligned with hunting and fishing than with birding, but they acknowledge the connection.

Over the last few decades, one person has been an essential link between the wildlife professionals and the birders in this region: my friend Mark Shieldcastle. He grew up hunting and fishing with his father in central Ohio, and by the late 1970s he was working for the state Division of Wildlife as a wetlands biologist in the western Lake Erie marsh region. Most of his professional attention went to issues involving huntable ducks and geese, but in his spare time he was becoming keenly interested in the songbirds that thronged the lakeshore in spring and fall. He started doing research on them on his own time. By 1992 Mark was gathering so much data that he and a few friends started a new nonprofit organization, the Black Swamp Bird Observatory.

For another two decades Mark Shieldcastle continued to work full-time for the Division of Wildlife and to pour all his spare-time energy into the Black Swamp Bird Observatory. After he retired from the state job, he became the observatory's research director. By that time the observatory was well established in migration studies and was turning into a major force in the birding world and in bird conservation efforts. BSBO is an independent organization and always has been, but it can trace its genesis back to the state wildlife agency and to professionals who worked on ducks before songbirds.

The relationship between birders and hunters in northwest Ohio tends to be cordial, but it's sometimes disrupted by people from the outside who come in with antihunting rants. The disconnect seems to be rooted in a difference in focus: hunters' conservation groups emphasize the long-term survival of the species. Animal-rights groups focus on the feelings of the individual animal. Emotions make it almost impossible to reconcile the two approaches. As a person who dwells somewhere between these viewpoints, I understand.

But I also live somewhere between the shoreline of Lake Erie and the edge of Sandusky Bay. The region still has about thirty private duck clubs, protecting thousands of acres of prime wetland habitat. Thousands more acres of former duck clubs are now protected as state or federal wildlife refuges. These huge tracts have a profound influence on the region, giving it a sense of wilderness and abundant wildlife that otherwise would be long gone.

Vast acreages of official refuge land, whole square miles of marshes, meadows, and tangled woods, teem with unruly and untamed life. Take away these wild marshes and you'd be left with something like wide stretches of west-central Ohio, deserts of soybean and corn with few other living things. But the protected tracts act as reservoirs for wildlife, and animals stubbornly push out from them along the creeks, the flooded ditches, the isolated woodlots, the pocket marshes along railroad rights-of-way, any square foot that isn't paved or poisoned.

Anywhere around here, even miles from the lake, a mink may go bounding across the road or a huge snapping turtle may crawl up out of a ditch. Anywhere, a farm field flooded by rain or snowmelt may fill up with flocks of wild swans. Foxes and raccoons range everywhere across the landscape. Muskrats commute along networks of drainage ditches. White-tailed deer have become abundant, if elusive, hiding in the tiniest woodlot by day and wandering across the fields at night. Bald eagles have made a comeback in recent decades and may be seen every day of the year over the towns of Oak Harbor and Port Clinton.

It would be too much to hope that the wild wolves would come back. But in a way, in the smaller wilderness that remains, a smaller substitute wolf has arrived. Coyotes originally were native to western regions of the continent, but after the wolf was wiped out, these slightly smaller canines spread eastward to fill the vacated niche.

Experts disagree as to when coyotes reached Ohio—it may have been early in the twentieth century, or they may not have become established until the 1940s. They are definitely here now. These crafty animals are masters at staying out of sight, but they go everywhere, leaving their tracks in the wide marshes, the farm fields, the edges of towns. Uninformed people hate the coyotes as they once hated the wolves and try to kill them whenever they can, but the coyotes are wily and tough and they persist despite persecution.

Even if we go months without seeing them, we hear them late at night. When the coyotes start up, Kimberly and I always stop what we're doing, go to the windows, and listen. We love to hear them yipping and howling, taunting the farm dogs, celebrating their freedom.

The best coyote music we ever heard was one December night when we had gone outdoors to watch the Geminid meteor showers. In the sharp, cold air the stars crackled with brilliance, and we stood in silence, gazing upward. Once every few minutes another glowing meteor would blaze across the sky, and we would squeeze each other's hands and keep watching. And then somewhere out in the fields the coyotes started singing. We sensed that they were also watching the sky; their cries had a pensive, solemn tone, as if they had become the voices of the lost wilderness, the voices of Earth. Unseen in the dark they went on and on, with yips, keening howls, mournful wails, an elegy to the sky, calling down the falling stars.

3

A Broken Season

Lake Erie is the southernmost of the five Great Lakes, but in a cold winter it's the first to freeze. It is much shallower than the others, with an average depth of only about sixty feet (the other Great Lakes average more than three times as deep), so its total volume of water is much less. A larger body of water takes longer to freeze. There are times in a cold winter when Lake Superior — far to the north but huge, a quarter mile deep in places — is still a roiling wilderness of dark water, while the surface of Lake Erie is frozen from shore to shore.

It used to be the norm for Lake Erie to freeze every winter. Or so I'm told. My friend Randy has lived in the Oak Harbor area for all of his sixty-five years, except for a few years away at college, and his parents and grandparents lived here before that. He knows local history well. When Randy was a boy, Lake Erie would freeze over before midwinter.

It was no big thing then for people to go out near Port Clinton and drive onto the ice, drive several miles out to South Bass Island to visit the town there. Before the end of December, some would go out to check the thickness of the ice, determine a safe route, then mark it with brush or with discarded Christmas trees. It was a popular approach back then to take a beat-up old car and cut off the entire top half, leaving it open to the sky, and drive this across the frozen lake. If something went wrong and the ice started to give way, the open top would allow everyone to get out quickly. But such emergency escapes were seldom necessary.

In the heart of the season, ice fishermen would throng this section of Lake Erie, driving their trucks a mile or two or three out onto the frozen surface. Even if they camped on the lake, they'd have to come to shore for supplies, and most patronized the hotels and restaurants in the shoreline towns. Local businesses relied on the economic boost of the ice fishermen in midwinter. There are still fishermen out on the ice in many winters, but not all, and the season is not as long nor as consistent as it used to be. Incidents of ice shelves breaking loose and floating farther offshore, of fishermen having to be rescued by helicopter, are starting to dampen the enthusiasm for this winter tradition.

When Randy was a boy, in counties near the lake snow lay on the ground for most of the winter. No one minded. Everyone had snow tires and chains, everyone knew how to drive on snow and ice. As mass-market snowmobiles became more widely available, they became tremendously popular in this region. Today there are still plenty of snowmobiles around, but the average winter doesn't bring as many chances to use them. Today a snowfall of a few inches may be enough to cancel school for the day.

Winter, in genuine and measurable ways, just isn't what it used to be.

It still gets cold here. Even an oddly mild winter will still have stretches with single-digit readings and windchills below zero. Half-hardy birds that linger into December won't make it through the whole season; they must move out or perish. Many more birds perish in those freakish seasons when a ridge of high pressure remains over the center of North America, holding high temperatures in the West while the East is locked in a deep freeze for weeks at a time. We sit here in Ohio reading about this, trying to understand the patterns: how warmer sea temperatures in the Pacific and a loss of sea ice in the Arctic are somehow leading to brutal, killing cold here in our backyards. But whether it's a bitterly frigid season or an oddly mild one, winter is still the quiet time from the birders' viewpoint, the lull between migration seasons.

To understand winter in the region, to understand its impact, you have to look at the landscape in February. A visit in December just won't do it. Early in the season, after the first snowfalls, the woods may look as pretty as a Christmas card under their gentle blanket of snow. Trees stand elegant and newly bare against the winter sky. Out in the fields the seedheads of weeds poke up out of the snow, attracting cavorting flocks of goldfinches, and everything looks tidy and clean. It won't stay that way. As winter goes on, weather will add injury to insult, with snow falling and melting, hard freezes and abrupt thaws, ice coating and breaking the branches, and howling winds from every point of the compass. By late in the winter the woods will be bashed and trashed and broken, and it will appear that they could never be restored to their former beauty. They will be restored, eventually, but spring won't arrive in time to save the woods from an awkward period of looking defeated.

Like most people in northwestern Ohio, birders don't spend as much time outdoors in winter. There's a flurry of activity just after the first of the year, as many birders begin to keep a new year list, checking off the common winter birds on January 1. Some in Ohio make a serious attempt to see one hundred species of birds during the month of January (a total that would be an easy half-day target in May). Often they succeed, but not without a lot of driving around to chase rarities. And the possibilities are diminished further by February.

Northwestern Ohio is a region that celebrates migratory birds, and migration is the focus of this book. But I should pause a moment to salute resident birds that survive in our local climate without ever going anywhere. Consider small birds like chickadees, nuthatches, and downy woodpeckers, year-round residents of our woodlots. They avoid the rigors of travel but they endure other rigors in staying put, including wild variations in weather. Some midsummer days bring a heat index above 100 degrees Fahrenheit, ending in evenings of violent thunderstorms. Winter may bring windchills far below zero, and sudden swings from thaw to rain to deep freeze, locking everything under a coat of ice. Resident birds in the woodlots don't go anywhere, but the setting around them seems to shift back and forth between the jungle and Siberia.

Most of the land here is open farm ground. In summer much of it is green with corn or soybeans, but those fields lie open and barren in winter. Or seemingly barren; there's actually life out there. Horned larks revel in the flattest of flat land, and they're probably more numerous here today than in centuries past, when much of

Ohio was covered with forest or swamp. Flocks of horned larks forage far out in farm fields among soybean stubble or plowed-under remains of cornfields. The birds are drab and brown with touches of yellow, and with tiny black "horns" on the head that are usually invisible. The larks themselves are usually invisible, too, until they flush and circle around high, with graceful quick wingbeats and tinkling calls.

There are horned larks around at all seasons, but it's anyone's guess how many are the same individuals all year. Most likely many of the wintering birds arrive from farther north. The birds that join them in the winter fields certainly have come from that direction, because Lapland longspurs and snow buntings spend their summers in the High Arctic, more than a thousand miles north of Ohio. When they arrive here in late fall, birders may notice them along the Lake Erie shoreline — especially the snow buntings, conspicuous with their white plumage. But then the buntings and longspurs disappear into the vast square miles of bare farm fields, joining the horned larks in obscurity.

Other birds also come here from the north. Flocks of American tree sparrows are common in midwinter in counties near the lake. They're poorly named: most of them nest in Canada, not the United States, and they have no particular connection to trees; much of their summer range is north of tree line, and in winter they favor brushy field edges and thickets. They represent thousands of birds that have traveled thousands of miles to get here for the winter, but no one except the birders even notices them.

The edge of Lake Erie is central to the activity of some birds. There are gulls around through the season, and flocks of the hardier types of ducks, especially those that dive in deep water like scaups and mergansers. Even when the lake is essentially frozen over, they still find areas of open water: a few ponds fed by deep springs, warm-water outlets at power plants, some rapids on the Maumee River over by Toledo. The gulls don't need open water anyway, since they can forage at landfills or scavenge out in the fields, but they'll gather by water if it's available.

Of course some other birds remain. We'll have action outside our windows all season as long as we keep the bird feeders filled. But I get a different picture if I get out and start walking.

In the middle of February I put on my parka and muck boots and walk out the back door of our house, out in farm country north of Oak Harbor. Cardinals and house finches flee from the feeders into the hedges as soon as I step outside. But after I walk away from the yard, out along the edges of farm fields, everything descends into silence.

I may be walking half an hour without seeing or hearing a bird. I pause along the edge of a woodlot where bare black branches creak in the cold wind, but nothing else stirs. Finally, along a weed-filled ditch, I scare up a flock of six or eight American tree sparrows. They make soft musical calls as they fly up to perch on dry weed stems. These birds seldom come to our bird feeders except when there's a heavy snow; they seem to prefer the open wastes. I detour around them and keep walking.

If I trudge for a couple of miles I might see a few other birds: maybe a red-tailed hawk hunched in a distant tree, maybe a drift of juncos, little gray "snowbirds" flashing white tail feathers as they flit away. If I'm lucky, a flock of horned larks might fly high overhead, possibly with Lapland longspurs or snow buntings mixed in. But the overriding impression is that birds are scarce.

Like an icy desert, the scene has a desolate beauty. The landscape is stark but not still, bleak but not silent—not with this constant wind. The wind blasts the open ground, tugs at every exposed thing, nips at the edges of every barrier. Even when I find a sheltered spot, I hear it gusting overhead. The wind seems threatening, sinister, as if the February gales carry warnings of undefined danger to come. I look around at the horizon and find myself shivering with more than just the cold.

Ohio winters came as a shock when I first moved here from Arizona. By the third week of February, the low ebb of the birding year, it seemed there was hardly any reason to go outdoors. But then I became intrigued by the most unlikely harbinger of spring: migrating crows.

Most birders in the Lower 48 don't think of crows as being migratory at all, because they're so conspicuously present all year, their cacophonous cawing a constant background noise everywhere from countryside to city parks. But crows are oddly scarce in this part of Ohio. The landscape looks perfect for them, with farms, woodlots, and small towns, but the crows don't seem to share that perception. Around Magee Marsh, Oak Harbor, and surrounding areas, at most seasons we can go weeks without seeing or hearing a single crow. For a brief period each year, however, from mid-February to mid-March, a major migration of crows moves north through the region.

South of the lake it takes luck to notice the beginning of the movement. You have to be outdoors (or at least looking out a window) and alert when the first one or two crows pass over, silently flapping toward the north. Later in February they may be in a flock, a straggling string of a dozen or twenty or thirty, twisting across the wind. Even the bigger flocks are thinly spread over the landscape, easy to miss. But along Lake Erie, they concentrate.

Flocks that had moved north on a broad front from somewhere in the interior will pause when they get to the lake. Whether or not the lake is frozen, whether or not the land is snow-covered, the boundary of land and water is still obvious; the crows turn and move along the shoreline, heading toward the west-northwest, flying around the lake instead of across it.

If you know it's possible, you can head to the lakeshore on a day when there's any breeze from the south or southwest and see this kind of movement. The calendar says it's still hard winter, but the crows are announcing spring. And by late February they're not the only ones. From a good vantage point near the lake's edge, with a few hours of watching, you may see other birds — a lone bald eagle, a little group of horned larks, a tight cluster of red-winged blackbirds — in that purposeful, direct flight, paralleling the shoreline, that says they're actually on the move.

Living in northwestern Ohio, I've come to relish that moment in February when the season shifts. When the first migrating crow passes overhead, it signals an almost imperceptible tilt into spring. Hardly anyone but the birders will notice, but from that point on, spring is on its way: first as scattered birds, then a trickle of migrants that turns into a steady stream, then a river, a torrent of migrating birds of all sizes and colors cascading over our area, building to a crescendo during the impossible peak of May.

That feeling — knowing what's coming, waiting for it to arrive — is intoxicating. We dream about the spring rush at other times of year, impatient for it to come again.

I knew I wanted to write a book about this migration, but for a long while I was undecided about how to approach it. My first solid plan was to just write down the experience of a typical spring as

it happened — to start with the first migrating crow and then describe the key details of every single day. By focusing on the particular I would illuminate the broad patterns, and by the end of May I
would have a deep portrait of the whole grand parade of the spring
migration. That was what I thought, anyway.

At first the plan seemed to be working. But that was the year
the temperature flipped in early March, abruptly rising from a
deep freeze up into the eighties. Day after day the highs climbed
into the seventies and eighties. Day after day readings were thirty
or forty degrees above normal for the dates. All-time records fell.
Trees leafed out, flowers bloomed, insects emerged weeks early.
My daily notes began to reflect my frustration: *This is crazy. This
is ridiculous. This is nothing at all like a normal spring; there's no point
in detailing this weird year.* Finally I wrote, *I'm too late. I can't detail a
normal spring. We are never going to have a normal season again.*

I'd been aware of the issue of climate change for years, but
that was the season it became personal and visceral for me. The
news was impossible to ignore. Global average temperatures every
month were above the long-term norms, as they had been for several years running. Sea ice in the Arctic was steadily diminishing.
Ice caps in Greenland and the Antarctic were starting to shrink,
and all over the world glaciers were receding. Extremes of weather
were becoming more extreme and more frequent, with floods,
droughts, and violent storms making headlines. Denial of the facts
continued in some political circles, but the scientific community
was in widespread agreement that we were all in for a rough ride.

I stopped recording the details of that hot spring — even as the
season shifted to torrential rains, freezing temperatures in May,
and then record heat again — and started reading more about cli-

mate and projections for the future. Most analyses looked at how humans would be affected, of course, and the picture wasn't appealing, although it seemed likely that affluent societies would find technological ways to adapt to a warmer world.

But I was thinking of the impact on bird populations, and I had a sense of how it would play out, especially in regard to the spring migration.

Many of the resident birds, the ones that stayed on permanent territories all year, probably would be all right. The nuthatches and downy woodpeckers in the woodlots should be able to adapt; they already dealt with huge swings in local weather every year, and they belonged to species that thrived as far south as the Gulf Coast, so a year-round warming trend shouldn't hurt them. Our local black-capped chickadees might be replaced by Carolina chickadees, expanding from the south, but the family still would be represented. Short-distance migrants like crows and horned larks should be able to shift around to accommodate changing conditions.

But for long-distance migrants, for birds that journey between the tropics and the far north—for the birds that truly bring the magic of spring in northwestern Ohio and throughout eastern North America—these changes could be very bad news. Many of these small travelers already push the boundaries of possibility. What happens when the course becomes more challenging? What happens to trapeze artists when the poles are moved farther apart: will they still make the leap, or will they fall?

In my travels around the world I've been amazed constantly by the stubborn resilience of life, so I hold to the belief that most of these migratory species will find a way to survive. But the nature of the migration here is likely to change. The phenomenal rush of spring that captured my imagination may be unrecognizable in the future.

It won't work anymore to record the details of a "typical spring." That opportunity has passed, as every year brings new, odd variations. But what we have now, even if it's shifting, even if it's diminished, is still an extraordinary thing. We should celebrate it, revel in it, immerse our souls in the science and magic of it, before it's carried away on the wind.

4

An Ill Wind

From a distance it looks so clean. The white steel column rises above the land, straight and smooth, aiming at the sky. From the hub at the top of the column, three long, narrow blades splay out at equal angles. Seen from afar, the blades seem to turn ever so slowly, facing into the wind and tracing a lazy circle, and the whole structure seems as pure as the fluffy white clouds in the sky behind it.

If you were concerned about the effects of carbon dioxide and other greenhouse gases in Earth's atmosphere, and if you knew this structure could produce clean power by converting wind into electricity, you might see it as a miracle. You might come to regard this wind turbine as a silver bullet, a magic solution to the thorny problem of climate change. To show your support for the environment and for "green energy," you might start using stylized images of three-bladed wind turbines as symbols. These little designs would be an easy shorthand, much more recognizable than, say, a rectangle to represent a solar panel. You might start to sprinkle these happy little turbines over your publications, letterheads, websites, as a quick way of showing everyone that you care for the environment.

Furthermore, if you were associated with one of the companies cashing in on wind power — one of the big corporations collecting millions of dollars in government subsidies, tax breaks, and investments to install wind turbines — you absolutely would not discourage anyone from using these little graphics as positive symbols. All these allies in the environmental community would make your job in public relations so much easier. You wouldn't have to spend as much of your profits putting a positive spin on wind power, because eager volunteers would be doing it for you.

Up to a point, perceptions mean everything.

Descriptions of wind turbines rarely mention how big they are. Instead, in a triumph of marketing, they're classified by their capacity to produce power. That little turbine is only a 100-kilowatt machine, but this more substantial one is rated at 1.5 megawatts, and over there, that's a 3 megawatt. The underlying message is, *Just think of all that electricity. Enough to power one thousand homes.* The turbines are never described in alternate terms: *This one stands more than four hundred feet tall, from the base to the tip of the highest blade. It will dominate the skyline from five miles away. That one has blades more than 150 feet long. This turbine weighs more than 250 tons altogether — in other words, more than half a million pounds — and to give it a firm foundation, we had to blast down to bedrock and pour in almost a thousand tons of concrete. On that one, each individual blade weighs more than thirteen tons; if the blade assembly flies apart while it's turning, that blade could be thrown hundreds of yards, destroying whatever it hits.*

No, they are definitely not described in terms like that.

The way the turbines are named, by power-generating capacity, is misleading from the start. The "nameplate capacity," as it's called, is the amount of power that the turbine will produce when the wind blows at optimum speed. For example, a particular turbine rated at 1.5 megawatts may not produce that amount of power until the wind reaches twenty-seven miles per hour. At lower wind speeds, it produces less power or none at all. At wind speeds above twenty-seven miles per hour, it will continue to generate 1.5 megawatts, but only up to a certain speed — if the wind gets too strong, the turbine is supposed to shut down automatically to avoid being damaged. Because the wind isn't always blowing at optimum speed, and because of other limiting factors, the average wind turbine on land produces its nameplate capacity of power only about one fourth of the time. People in the wind industry don't deny this, but they almost always skate past this point.

Promoters of wind energy, both those who stand to profit from it and those who sincerely see it as a key to fighting climate change, tend to avoid mentioning any of its negatives. The so-called rare earths used in the motor assembly of some wind turbines have been linked to shocking levels of toxic pollution in areas where they're mined, especially in China, but proponents of wind downplay this, pointing out that many turbines don't use these elements. Massive amounts of concrete are needed to anchor the turbines, and production of all this concrete releases vast amounts of carbon dioxide into the atmosphere. Low-frequency noise from large turbines may cause chronic disturbance to people even at a distance, and the constant flicker of shadows cast by the rotating blades may cause people nearby to develop headaches, anxiety, and depression, although the wind industry has tried to minimize the importance of these claims.

Then there are the birds and bats being killed by collisions with wind turbines. Naturally, this aspect is of particular interest to my friends and me. It's also an aspect that is poorly understood by the general public. We had a firsthand look at this when the city of Oregon, Ohio, just east of Toledo and just west of our main migration hot spots, announced plans to erect large "experimental" turbines at a couple of schools.

Kimberly and I, along with Mark Shieldcastle, went to a school board meeting and a couple of city council meetings. We didn't live in Oregon, but our Black Swamp Bird Observatory had members in the city, so we had a legitimate claim to be there and to speak up.

Sitting in those folding metal chairs under the bright ceiling lights, we listened while we waited for our chance to speak. Almost all the items under discussion were small matters of purely local impact but of sincere importance to the elected officials at the front of the room and to the citizens attending. Government at the local level — that's where participation in issues and policies and actions could actually work. It didn't for us, in this case, but it was educational.

A science teacher at one of the schools was pushing the wind-power project. He was collaborating with a regional company that had offered to build the turbines and put up part of the money (the rest would come from subsidies and incentives) — in effect, the company would make a loan to cover turbine construction costs. In theory, the school district could pay it back over time with all the money it would save on electricity.

I think the science teacher was sincere in his belief that the project would be good for the schools and for the students. I also think he was in over his head. He believed the students could learn about energy issues and could take part in real science by doing bird and bat mortality surveys after the turbines were built. He didn't understand the economics of wind power — of course, we didn't either, at the time — and he didn't understand what was involved in actually surveying for birds killed by turbines. During the course of the meetings, it became obvious that no one involved with the school system, the city, or the energy company had any grasp of how the turbines would affect birds.

It was a useful exercise for us, actually, a first chance to hear the arguments that people with no knowledge of birds would raise on the spur of the moment. We would hear these same weak arguments over and over in the years that followed.

I had a sense of how it would go when one of the councilmen laughed dismissively and shook his head. "I've been to that school a lot and I've never seen a bird there." Yes, of course, most people fail to notice birds. But tens of thousands of bird-watchers come to this area every spring for the migration. Unless they're hallucinating, there must be birds nearby at least part of the time.

The next comment established a theme that would be shockingly consistent: "I don't think the birds are that dumb. I think they'll just fly around these things."

Sure. It would seem logical to think so, wouldn't it? But the reality is different. Look at Altamont Pass in Northern California. The first major wind farm in the United States came online there in the 1980s, taking advantage of big tax credits enacted after energy crises a few years earlier. But by the 1990s researchers found that the turbines at Altamont were killing birds of prey in alarming numbers. Hundreds of kestrels, red-tailed hawks, and others were being knocked down by the spinning blades. Golden eagles were being killed at a rate of 75 to 110 per year, a dangerous level of mortality for a species that was never numerous in the first place. Golden eagles are magnificent fliers, masters of the air, with incredible eyesight; if they couldn't navigate safely around the turbines, what bird could?

Besides, golden eagles fly only in daylight. In our area of Ohio, the migrating songbirds that pass through are mainly nocturnal in their travels.

For many people at the first meeting, the idea of birds migrating at night was a complete novelty: "Flying at night? What? You mean owls?"

We explained the concept of nocturnal migration and the critical element of stopover habitat along the Lake Erie shoreline. Yes, the vast majority of the long-distance migrants make their journeys at night, taking off just after dark, coming down in the dim light just before dawn. During the middle of the night, some of these birds might be high enough to escape the sweep of the wind-turbine blades. But during those all-important times bracketing the night, when migrants were arriving in stopover sites at dawn or departing from them at dusk, concentrated and flying low in bad light conditions, these whirling blades could wreak destruction on large numbers of the most vulnerable birds.

Of course none of our arguments prevailed, and the wind turbines were built at those schools. But now we were involved, and starting to pay more attention to the threat of other wind facilities arriving in the region.

One of the biggest problems we faced, both in early discussions with the schools and in all the later debates, was the assumption that birds already had enough legal protection. "If it's not illegal to build it there, it must be okay." Surely, people said, there must be laws keeping wind farms out of places where they would do harm. Surely this was covered in the regulations. The American public has been hammered with the idea that we're drowning in regulations — or, as they say, "job-killing, growth-stifling regulations." That may be true in some arenas. But the wind industry has been largely free of any binding rules or controls, especially regarding effects on birds.

Around 2006 and 2007, the U.S. Fish and Wildlife Service, the top federal agency in this field, had a good start on developing mandatory guidelines for bird-safe placement of wind-power projects. Early drafts of these guidelines were circulated to a few biologists and wildlife professionals, and they looked promising. But then the industry got wind of the plan, so to speak, and reacted with alarm. Thanks to political pressure from major players in the industry, the Fish and Wildlife Service shelved its original guidelines and formed a new Wind Turbine Guidelines Advisory Committee of more than twenty members.

This new committee included some individuals from federal and state wildlife agencies. It also included representatives from some private conservation groups, including the National Audubon Society and the Nature Conservancy, although some other groups were pointedly excluded. But as you can probably guess, the committee was weighted toward the wind industry and its advocates. Members of this group met and shared correspondence for four years and managed to agree on a set of recommendations for where turbines should be placed and how they should be monitored for effects on nature. The Fish and Wildlife Service compiled and edited these and published them in March 2012.

The new guidelines were better than nothing, but they were merely suggestions. They were not laws or regulations, just *voluntary* guidelines. There was nothing mandatory in the document — no actual rules, no kind of enforcement, nothing to prevent those in the industry from going ahead and doing whatever they pleased.

So we had very limited legal backup to help us along when we got involved in our next fight. And this one, seen from the outside, was almost funny in its irony. *Okay, so you couldn't prevail against the school board and the local city council. But now that you've had your warmup, meet your new adversaries: the United States military forces and the United States Congress.*

Before we got the news, I hadn't really thought much about the Camp Perry Military Reservation. I had driven past it many times; it was on a strip of land about a mile wide, between State Route 2 and the Lake Erie beach, about ten miles east-southeast of the bird observatory on the way to Port Clinton. It was flanked on the east side by a unit of the Ottawa National Wildlife Refuge; private marshes managed by duck clubs occupied much of the area to its immediate northwest. So I knew it was surrounded by prime bird habitat and located in the zone of major bird traffic along the lakeshore.

Even if I didn't know much about Camp Perry, however, most local people did. It's an open base, so anyone can drive in, and a popular hotel and conference center are located on the grounds. It has been an important center for marksmanship training for a century. Camp Perry hosts the national shooting matches every summer, lasting for a month and drawing more than six thousand participants from all over the country, adding a significant bump to the local tourism economy in Port Clinton. The camp is also a training center for several different military divisions. Notably, it's headquarters for the 200th Red Horse Squadron of the Ohio Air National Guard, a highly skilled corps of civil engineers trained to carry out emergency repair and construction work in war zones. As part of their practice and training, teams from the Red Horse Squadron have carried out helpful projects all over northern Ohio, from constructing parking lots and playgrounds to repairing roads and dikes in the wildlife areas. So Camp Perry is well respected in the region and seen as an asset to the community.

A wind-power project at Camp Perry had been proposed back in 2007, but it wasn't the first one suggested for the region. Ideas for wind-power development on the Lake Erie shoreline had been kicked around at least since the early 2000s. By that time the impacts of the Altamont wind farm on birds were already well known, so Ohio's Department of Natural Resources was asked to come up with some guidance on placement of wind turbines. Our friend Mark Shieldcastle was still working for the DNR in the Division of Wildlife during that time, so he was involved and got to see the process firsthand.

One approach by the DNR was to create a map of "avian concern zones" to estimate where the risk to birds would be greatest. The mapped zones of highest concern included areas within three miles of the edge of Lake Erie or Sandusky Bay, the immediate vicinity of major rivers, and within a certain radius of established bald eagle nests. Mark and others also established recommendations for how to monitor a wind-turbine site pre- and post-construction, to predict and then measure the numbers of birds killed. The map and the recommendations were advisory, not mandatory, so they didn't have any teeth for actual enforcement, but they gave wildlife agencies some talking points.

When the wind project at Camp Perry was first proposed, it was with the best of intentions. Our congresswoman, a genuinely decent legislator who takes good care of her district, was looking for innovative ways to bring economic development to the region. Alternative energy seemed a good bet, and Camp Perry seemed the logical spot to try it out, since the government already owned the land. But the site had two strikes against it on the DNR's map of avian concern zones — it was right against the lake and surrounded by several bald eagle nesting sites. So instead of a wind turbine, the camp experimented with renewable energy by installing an array of solar panels.

That was in 2007. But the wind-turbine idea never really went away. It surfaced again in 2011, and this time it appeared that the Air National Guard unit was going to go forward with the project.

Nothing had happened to make the location any safer for birdlife. But our congresswoman was still interested in the potential of wind power, and she had found consultants who were willing to tell her that the risk to birds was within acceptable limits. People at the state and federal wildlife agencies didn't agree, but because of agency politics, they were limited in what they could say. There was always potential risk involved in arguing with an established member of Congress. Any serious pushback would have to come from private citizens.

This was a dilemma for us. We knew our congresswoman and liked her. This isn't a rural district where everyone knows everyone else — nearly a million people live in Representative Marcy Kaptur's district — but she knew that visiting birders have a positive economic impact here. When we had extended an invitation, she had made the effort to come out and meet us, even to go birding with us at Magee Marsh. We liked her positions on many issues. So it was more than a little awkward for us to find ourselves opposed to a project that she supported.

Congresswoman Kaptur meant well, no doubt. And the consultants may have meant well, too, but environmental consultants often walk a fine line. When big corporations or big government grants are paying the bills, there is pressure to tell them what they want to hear. Most consultants manage to operate with integrity, but always there must be the temptation to fudge the data just a little.

In this case, no one with serious knowledge of the area would have tried to deny the huge concentrations of birds in the immediate area of Camp Perry. But the consultants had danced around the subject, minimizing some risks with vague language and simply ignoring others. A well-meaning person without any expertise could have read their report and concluded that there was no danger to birdlife at all.

Clearly that wasn't true. The project was a terrible idea from the viewpoint of bird protection. But who would stop it? The Audubon Society had a strong presence elsewhere in Ohio but not in this part of the state. The Sierra Club had come out strongly in favor of wind power practically everywhere, and its members weren't going to oppose a local project because of wildlife concerns. We couldn't see anyone stepping up to oppose the Camp Perry wind turbine.

At that point Black Swamp Bird Observatory was ill-equipped to take on an activist role. We had a small staff (including Kimberly) with a tiny budget and a dedicated corps of volunteers, but everyone was overworked already with research and education projects. We said that supporting conservation was part of our mission, of course, but we didn't have the resources to take on this kind of challenge. But we moved forward on it anyway, because no one else was going to do it.

Here's the thing about bird conservation work: it doesn't make for a thrilling narrative. It's almost always a long, slow slog of endless boring details, usually operating on a shoestring budget. If you're tackling a widespread or general problem, you have to overcome vast public indifference. If you're opposing a specific local challenge, you're usually up against adversaries with far more resources. It's a slow, thankless drag, and in the end there is a strong possibility that you will lose.

I had seen this firsthand years ago, when I was just out of my teens and hanging around with Arizona birders. There was a project in the planning stage to build a huge dam, Orme Dam, at the confluence of the Salt and Verde Rivers northeast of Phoenix. It was supposed to create a water-storage reservoir, but because of evaporation in the desert sun, it would have led to a net loss of water. It would have destroyed many miles of the last remaining good riverside habitat in central Arizona, driving out two of the few remaining pairs of bald eagles in the Southwest. But politicians and government agencies were gung-ho to pour tax money into the project.

A key character who opposed it was a friend of mine, Bob Witzeman. He would have preferred to spend his spare time birding, but he couldn't ignore the looming destruction of local habitat. So he used his position with the Maricopa Audubon chapter, as president and later as conservation chair, to build a movement. He organized petitions and letter-writing campaigns, wrote press releases, delved into details of law and policy, badgered elected officials, and kept the heat on the dam's proponents. He collaborated with a Yavapai tribe whose land was slated to be flooded out by the dam, collaborated with engineers who were offended by the project's bad design, collaborated with anyone who could bring expertise and influence to the table. And in the end, he succeeded. The plan for Orme Dam was officially withdrawn.

Reduced to a few sentences like that, it sounds dramatic. In actual practice it was incredibly tedious, a slow grind that lasted for years and years, and at the end there was no party or parade, no celebration of triumph, just a dull thud: *Oh. The plan is withdrawn.*

Win a football game and millions of people may praise you as a hero. Save an entire ecosystem and the public response will be a collective yawn. But it's still worth doing.

For us and the Camp Perry wind project, it wasn't about scoring a victory or getting credit. And it wasn't about this one turbine. We were consumed by the certainty that this solitary turbine would be used as a wedge to try to crack open the lakeshore, to bring in wind development on a large scale, permanently degrading the globally important bird habitat of the region.

I had lived here long enough to fall in love with this region, but Kimberly's roots were much deeper. She had lived within sixty miles of here all her life, and she had spent countless hours on Black Swamp Bird Observatory research projects along the lakeshore even before I moved here. For her, the drive to protect the habitat was deeply personal. By this time, in her work at the observatory, she had made the transition from education director to executive director. With approval from the board of directors, she began looking at how to use BSBO as a platform for opposing the Camp Perry project.

This kind of work doesn't make for an exciting story, as I said, so I won't describe every detail. But over the next three years I had a front-row vantage point to watch (and occasionally play a role) as Kimberly, Mark Shieldcastle, and others involved with the observatory stepped up to challenge the powerful forces that were all set to build the first Camp Perry wind turbine.

Most of the early moves were standard and obvious: meeting with county commissioners and other elected officials; getting citizens to sign petitions and write letters. But the biggest focus was on building a coalition of support. This tiny bird observatory didn't have any clout by itself, so we needed lots of backup.

The consulting firm hired by Camp Perry had produced an environmental assessment (EA) of the wind-turbine project, predicting (of course) that the impact on wildlife would be minimal. Biologists from the U.S. Fish and Wildlife Service and from Ohio's Division of Wildlife had examined the EA and submitted official opinions, and these were strongly negative, listing dozens of errors or insufficiencies in the assessment. But those agencies lacked any enforcement role, and the public was almost completely unaware of their findings. BSBO had used freedom-of-information laws to get copies of the assessment and of the agencies' comments, but it would take work to get the word out.

The best vehicle for spreading the word, we decided, would be a detailed, formal letter to the leadership at Camp Perry, spelling out reasons that the wind-turbine project was a bad idea. It was essential to have a solid, complete statement of position, and it was especially critical to nail details of this one project, because of course we supported renewable energy, green energy, in general. Such a letter could be copied to government officials at all levels, from the governor and senators to county commissioners and local mayors, and used as a basis for press releases. The letter would have more clout if it was signed or supported by lots of major organizations.

Drafting this formal letter was a project that occupied months in 2012, but by October we had a concise text, boiling the case down to two pages, concluding with this plea: "We urge you to discontinue any and all plans to install wind turbines at the Camp Perry Air National Guard Station. We urge you to work with local organizations that are willing to provide expertise and knowledge to develop alternative sites. We urge you to help conserve the integrity of the habitat that millions of songbirds and a robust population of bald eagles depend on for their survival. We urge you to recognize the tremendous asset that this habitat represents, annually bringing in tens of thousands of birdwatchers who spend millions of dollars in local businesses. We urge you to support and promote responsible wind energy in highly sensitive lakeshore habitats."

It was a strong letter, and other organizations joined BSBO in signing it, including the Toledo Naturalists' Association, Ohio Ornithological Society, American Birding Association, several Audubon chapters from around the region, and the League of Ohio Sportsmen, a hunters' group that came on board because of Mark's connections. Some major organizations wouldn't sign the letter but took the step of writing their own letters, making the same points and reinforcing BSBO's position. The National Audubon Society was approaching wind-power issues cautiously at that point, but its chief scientist, Gary Langham, wrote a very strong and detailed letter about the importance of these habitats for birdlife. Ducks Unlimited added its substantial clout by sending a letter stressing the numbers of waterfowl relying on this region. The county visitors' bureau wrote to express concern about potential negative impacts on tourism.

Of course we wanted support from as many good organizations as possible, but we were particularly hoping that the American Bird Conservancy would sign on. Founded in 1994, ABC was one of the newer conservation groups, but it had a reputation for being relentless in taking on any issue — as long as there was a position backed up by solid science. Kelly Fuller was the ABC staff person working on wind and other collision issues at the time, and she had already been in communication with Kimberly and Mark about possible approaches on Camp Perry. But for the organization to sign the letter officially, we needed the approval of its president, George Fenwick.

I had known Fenwick for a while. The founder as well as the president of the American Bird Conservancy, he was a man of strong principles and strong opinions, and ABC reflected his fearless attitude and his personal, hands-on approach. A friend suggested I should write to him directly, so I did, laying out the situation and asking for his help, even though he'd undoubtedly heard some of our position from Kelly Fuller already. I wrapped up by writing, "I see this local situation as an opportunity to set a precedent — good or bad. In this site, where the bird migration is so well documented, where visiting birders have such a well-known positive impact on the local economy, we should be able to keep turbines out of the most bird-sensitive habitats. If we can't, it is bad news for the rest of the continent."

George Fenwick's response was prompt and gracious, and it carried a solid commitment. American Bird Conservancy has been right with us, strong and smart, supporting all our efforts to protect stopover habitat in northwestern Ohio ever since.

The arrangement came about partly by accident, but it turned out to be an effective combination. As a larger national and international organization, ABC brought greater resources, experience, and clout. As a regional group, BSBO brought detailed local knowledge and contacts. Together we could cover all angles of the issue.

Our letter to the Camp Perry leadership and the supporting letters from other groups all were delivered in late 2012. Things moved slowly for a while after that, with few developments. Kelly Fuller left her position at ABC and went on to work for an environmental group in California. We continued to send letters to more elected officials and news outlets. Finally, in summer 2013, the Air National Guard responded, briefly, to some of the objections that had been raised by the state and federal wildlife agencies. At the end of the summer, Camp Perry officials released a formal finding of no significant impact, or FONSI, in the acronym-rich world of conservation work, for the wind-turbine project. Brushing aside the concerns of the wildlife professionals, they declared that there would be no significant impact on birds.

The FONSI meant that construction of the turbine project might proceed at any time. Fortunately, in October 2013, Dr. Michael Hutchins joined the ABC staff as the coordinator of its bird-smart wind-energy program. A veteran of high-level wildlife conservation work, he immediately turned some of his focus to the work with BSBO. Michael and Kimberly quickly became a dynamic team. Emails and phone calls flew back and forth as they discussed every aspect of the Camp Perry situation. By now it was becoming apparent that our formal request, even with all the backup from other organizations, had not altered the Air National Guard's decision on the wind-turbine project. We were sure that if the officials actually put up the turbine, getting them to take it down would be infinitely harder, so we had to try something else to stop it.

ABC is not one of those groups that goes around filing lawsuits constantly, but it doesn't hesitate to take legal steps when other options have been used up. And it's represented by first-rate attorneys. Michael Hutchins had provided the legal team with all the information they needed. In early January 2014, after the leadership at both organizations concluded that we had no other choice, attorneys representing ABC and BSBO began the process of taking legal action.

Not with a lawsuit, not at first: the initial step was a notice of intent to sue. It's a formal way of announcing that a lawsuit is imminent, but it opens the door for discussions and possible settlement. A certified letter from the attorneys went out to top officials at the air force, the Ohio Air National Guard, and other agencies, detailing (in more than two hundred pages) our intent to sue "for violations of the Endangered Species Act, Bald and Golden Eagle Protection Act, Migratory Bird Treaty Act, and National Environmental Policy Act" in connection with the Camp Perry project.

It was a big step, especially for our little bird observatory, and we waited nervously to see what would happen — thinking we might be in for a long, protracted legal struggle. The results arrived faster than we expected, and in a more positive way.

Barely three weeks after our lawyers sent their notice of intent, before the end of January 2014, they received a formal reply from an air force colonel identifying himself as the director of installations and mission support. In a straightforward, concise letter, he stated that he had reviewed all the materials and had decided to withdraw the finding of no significant impact. "Since the FONSI has been withdrawn, the project will not go forward at this time."

The pros at the American Bird Conservancy knew exactly what to do with this news. They crafted press releases praising the decision, reiterating the importance of keeping wind development out of this zone, giving lavish credit to Black Swamp Bird Observatory and to other local leaders, and emphasizing that this was a win for northwestern Ohio. We blasted out the news on every channel of social media and invited all our friends to help us celebrate.

Of course it was too early to declare victory. The project was merely halted, not canceled outright. The colonel's letter had gone on to state that his staff would review the environmental assessment and coordinate the work to bring it into compliance with environmental regulations. Clearly there was a chance that the project would come back to life. But in bird conservation work, even a temporary win is more encouraging than a quick and crushing defeat, so you celebrate when you can.

5

Turning Point

Between image and reality there are often major gaps. This is true for many kinds of birds and other animals, but bald eagles represent a special case.

In America, images of bald eagles are everywhere. They are on coins and bills and official seals, T-shirts and billboards and banners, carved atop flagpoles, flaunted in advertising for everything from cars to candles to couches. They are inescapable.

I guess I should be thrilled to see all this attention to a bird. In a way, though, the plethora of images makes it harder for people to perceive the real eagle. As a bird artist, I find it incredibly challenging to portray bald eagles: no matter what I draw or paint, the image either will look hackneyed and stale, or it will clash with the pictures that people carry in their heads. Even if I manage to create a fresh, true portrait of a bald eagle, the public may prefer a caricature.

People see images of bald eagles so often that they cease to notice them at all. Ironically, they seldom notice the eagles themselves. A few decades ago that wouldn't have been too surprising,
because the species was in trouble. Numbers had dropped sharply
during the twentieth century, and by the late 1960s there were
fewer than five hundred nesting pairs left in the contiguous United
States. With the birds so few and scattered, most people weren't
likely to encounter them.

After use of DDT, DDE, and other persistent pesticides was
banned in the 1970s, bald eagles began a very gradual comeback.
Their recovery was painfully slow at first but eventually became
dramatic, with increases from coast to coast, and now there are
well over 10,000 pairs nesting in the Lower 48. Even so, people still
fail to notice them. In our small town of Oak Harbor, I've talked to
individuals who have never knowingly seen an eagle, despite the
fact that eagles undoubtedly fly over the town every single day. Apparently people won't see them if they don't expect to see them, if
they don't ever cast a hopeful glance at the sky.

Northwestern Ohio, with its marshes and lakeshore, has ideal
habitat for bald eagles. But habitat wasn't enough to sustain
them through the years when long-lasting pesticides and other
dangerous chemicals were flooding the environment throughout North America. Weakened by poisons, eagles in many regions
laid thin-shelled eggs that never hatched. By the late 1970s Ohio
was down to just four or five nesting pairs of bald eagles. Some of
those pairs tried year after year without ever succeeding in raising
young. Throughout the 1970s, the total number of young eagles
fledged in Ohio averaged fewer than two per year.

By the end of the decade there was serious concern that the
magnificent raptors might disappear from the skies forever. In the

face of this challenge, the state of Ohio stepped up in a major way. The Ohio Department of Natural Resources, Division of Wildlife, already had been monitoring bald eagles for some time. Its scientists had begun doing surveys by aircraft in 1959, when the number of nests was down to fifteen statewide. That tally dropped to ten nests in 1965 and six by 1970. With only four nests active in 1979, it was clear that if the trend continued, the total would drop to zero. The Division of Wildlife launched an intensive program to halt the slide and bring the eagles back.

Mark Shieldcastle, who had started working for the division in the late 1970s, was involved with the eagle program almost from the start, and by 1985 he was running it for the whole state. The effort had several facets. Education was a major element, especially reaching out to the few landowners — mostly farmers — who had eagles nesting on their property. Monitoring of every nest was stepped up. Wildlife rehabilitators were at the ready to try to save any injured eagles that were found, although only a few ever recovered enough to be returned to the wild.

In the most hands-on approach, Mark and the other biologists at the Division of Wildlife became adept at moving young eagles into and out of nests. If adult eagles were killed or abandoned a nest after eggs hatched, the biologists would take the young in to raise them by hand, or move them into the nest of a pair of eagles that had lost their young. If eggs failed to hatch, the biologists might be able to provide the adults at that nest with young that had hatched elsewhere. The feds were now raising young bald eagles in captivity at the Patuxent Wildlife Research Center in Maryland, and a number of those young were placed in Ohio nests, where their foster parents raised them to successful fledglings.

In placing young eagles for fostering in the wild, the key to success was knowing precisely what was going on at each nest. Mark and other division employees had been monitoring all the nests themselves, but as the number of breeding pairs increased — they were back up to twelve pairs by 1988 — it was becoming harder to keep track of them all. So the division launched a new program: a network of volunteer nest monitors. After intensive training on eagle behavior, these volunteers were assigned to watch nests and keep detailed notes on everything that happened there.

Being an eagle nest monitor was no task for sissies. Adult eagle pairs in Ohio are hanging around the nest site by midwinter and may lay eggs by early February, so the volunteers were often out watching in subfreezing temperatures and windchills below zero. Observing through a spotting scope from hundreds of yards away, each volunteer had to be alert for the next move. For an hour at a time nothing might be happening at all, nothing but the white head of one adult barely visible over the nest rim. Then suddenly the other adult might fly in and, after a brief greeting ceremony, take the first bird's place on the nest. For the monitor looking through the scope, boredom was replaced by intense concentration, watching for any behaviors that might indicate what was going on down in the nest. Were the eggs still being incubated? Were there small young in the nest already? Did both adults look healthy? Any detail might be critically important.

The volunteer monitors played a crucial role in these early years, as the population was expanding ever so gradually, in a time when the survival of each individual bird made a big difference. If eggs in a certain nest failed to hatch by the expected date, for example, the biologists would know the eggs were infertile, and they could supply that pair of adults with a young bird hatched in captivity. If a nest blew down in a storm and a young bird survived unhurt, the biologists — knowing that the parent eagles wouldn't care for it on the ground — could gauge which other pair of adults might be able to adopt a youngster of that exact age. Time after time, it was the detailed, up-to-the-minute information from dedicated volunteer nest monitors that made it possible for the Division of Wildlife to make the right decisions.

With this support, the Ohio population of bald eagles continued to increase: to twenty nesting pairs by 1992, thirty-eight pairs by 1997, over one hundred by 2004, over two hundred by 2009. It was a phenomenal comeback, a level of success beyond what anyone would have dared to hope just a few decades earlier. Nesting pairs are scattered over most of the state, with truly remarkable numbers in northwestern Ohio. If you drive from Magee Marsh east to Port Clinton and then on to Sandusky in early spring, before the trees leaf out and hide their bulky nests, you can see at least thirty eagle nests from the road. Within ten miles of the Camp Perry site on the lakeshore there are no fewer than sixty pairs. There's no concentration of nesting pairs like this anywhere in the lower forty-eight states.

Of course birders appreciate the abundance of these magnificent raptors. But for my friends and me, there's a deeper, more emotional connection. Although I didn't move here until 2005, I can claim that my link to bald eagles in this region goes back much further — at least to the mid-1990s, when a young woman named Kimberly began volunteering as an eagle nest monitor in rural Ohio. Or maybe my connection goes back to 1985, when Mark Shieldcastle took over the eagle recovery program for the state, a few years before he became a key founder of the Black Swamp Bird Observatory.

Kimberly's interest in birds had been sparked by the brilliant gold of summer goldfinches, but watching eagles in the cold turned her interest into a passion for studying and protecting all avian life. This deepening commitment helped lead her to involvement with the bird observatory, becoming an expert bird bander and a keen birder — keen enough to travel all the way to Texas for a birding festival. That was where I met her; our paths never would have crossed otherwise. So eagles played a key role in bringing Kimberly and me together and thus bringing me to live in Ohio.

According to the mavens of Hollywood and the advertising industry, bald eagles don't sound regal enough. When bald eagles appear in movies, TV shows, or commercials, or when they're mentioned in radio spots, the sound dubbed into the background invariably is the harsh, descending scream of the red-tailed hawk.

Admittedly, if you just listen to a bad recording of a bald eagle's voice, it doesn't sound impressive. Played back on a cheap electronic device, it sounds tinny, weak, nothing more than a thin chatter. But context is everything. When you hear it in the wild, it's different.

It was different the way we were hearing it now. We were deep in the swamp, in the waning light of late afternoon at the end of February. Off to the west of us, against the pallid sky, black skeletons of trees blended together into a tangle of obscurity. Somewhere in that shadowy thicket a bald eagle cut loose: a clarion crescendo, ringing with the bold confidence of an apex predator. This was no puny red-tail. It was a primordial sound, ancient, the cackle of a Tyrannosaurus over its fallen prey. This was the sound of a bald eagle in the wild.

"Ah, there's at least one here already," Tom said. "This is early. A few seem to come back to the roost midafternoon some days. Maybe if they've already had enough to eat."

Our friend Tom had brought Kimberly and me to see a secret eagle roost on private land not far from Sandusky Bay. To get here we had traversed a series of locked gates and narrow dirt roads; now there probably wasn't another human within a mile of where we stood, which made it a wilderness by Ohio standards. It truly felt like a wilderness at this moment.

Few people know about this roost. Fewer are likely to stumble across it. The site isn't accessible by water nor by any public road. The eagles that fly here in the evening are converging from a wide area of open farmland, open bay, and empty marshes, and there is no concentrated flight line across any inhabited area, nothing to tip anyone off to its location. The site apparently isn't even used for most of the year. But for a few weeks, at the end of winter and the edge of spring, more than a hundred of the big birds fly here to roost overnight in the deep shelter of the woods.

Evidently the eagles keep returning to the site year after year because it's so undisturbed, and Tom wanted to keep it that way. He had insisted that we wear dark clothing, and now he asked us to keep our voices low and not move around much, even though the woodlot holding the roost site was at least two hundred yards away across the marsh. Of course we complied.

Just to the southeast of us our view was blocked by another large woodlot, but we had a good view to the north and northeast, at least out about a quarter mile to where more lines of trees obscured the horizon. It was a cold afternoon, but the air was mercifully still. Everything was quiet. We could hear the soft tinkling of tree sparrows and the rough chirp of a song sparrow out in the frozen marsh, and occasionally a bald eagle would sound off in the shadowy woods to the west, sending chills up our spines and prodding our anticipation.

We waited almost fifteen minutes before we saw the first eagle approaching, angling in from the northeast. It was a long way off but coming our way, and coming fast.

Bald eagles soaring on a warm day might turn lazy circles in the sky, riding the thermals and barely moving their wings, but bald eagles in direct flight are impressive power fliers. Their broad, long wings — measuring seven feet from wingtip to wingtip — slice through only a shallow arc, and the wingbeats don't look fast, but they propel the eagles forward through the air with surprising speed. The big birds have a purposeful look, implacable, unstoppable, as if they were in grim pursuit of something even when they're not. The eagle crossing in front of us now, a full adult with gleaming white head and tail, continued without hesitation toward the roost site to our west, circled around the north side of the woodlot, and then swooped in to land in one of the taller trees.

It appeared that the procession was starting. Just a minute later two more eagles — both younger birds, mottled brown and white — came in, flying close together and low, just over the trees to the northwest. Then a very dark first-year eagle arrived from the east, passing directly over our heads, while another adult bird approached from the north.

The big birds were coming in to roost. The pace of their arrival was perfect for maximum suspense: one minute would pass, then two, then three, then suddenly another eagle would appear over the trees, startlingly close, flapping in toward us fast and hard. Then another suspenseful gap, and then a sudden arrival of two or three at once, all from different directions. In the waning light we couldn't see anything of the faces of these birds, making them seem more anonymous and formidable. Sometimes one eagle would swoop at another, the second bird turning to face the first, both stalling in midair and then gliding down and away, or circling for a second skirmish—a clash of titans. I found myself involuntarily humming passages from Wagner's "Ride of the Valkyries"—majestic, martial music that seemed entirely fitting for the passage of these lordly birds.

We didn't need background music here. The grand silence of this wild open sky was stirring enough. But thinking about the Valkyries put me in mind of Norse mythology and culture and led me to musing about the fjords and jagged shorelines of northern Scandinavia. In that coastal wilderness, the white-tailed eagle or sea eagle—a close relative of our bald eagle—is the king of birds. Eagles hold at least one place of prominence in Norse mythology. We don't really know what the Vikings thought about eagles, but it's easy to imagine these bold adventurers looking up at the solitary soaring eagle above the wild shore and admiring it for its fierce independence and strength.

I wondered how a Viking would have felt if he could have stood with us this evening, watching the eagles come powering in across the marsh: a dozen, twenty, fifty, eighty huge and magnificent eagles, all converging on the secret woods, carrying an undeniable spirit of wilderness.

The presence of all these bald eagles at a communal roost in late February is especially interesting because it seems many are not local birds. By this late in the winter, adult eagles in the area are already tending nests and may already be incubating eggs, so they are probably sticking to their own territories. At the roost site we're seeing more young birds than adults, but young birds that hatched locally may be far away now, since they tend to wander. Tom had already told us that the roost was mostly abandoned by late March every year, so many of the birds using the site must be migrants, just passing through.

We don't know a lot about where the individual eagles are coming from or where they are going. Some of the adults might be headed for breeding territories much farther north, in Canada, where the nesting cycle starts a little later. Some of the young birds may have hatched in Florida or elsewhere in the Southeast: results from banding studies have shown that young eagles from the South often travel far north in spring, although they generally stay in the South after they reach adulthood. Other young birds may be just wandering widely. So the birds moving through northwest Ohio may be playing out any of several narratives. Regardless, they make for a stirring passage at this season, at the turning point between winter and spring.

Farther south in Ohio the migration isn't apparent. As big and conspicuous as bald eagles are, they are so thinly dispersed across the landscape that they don't draw much notice. But like so many other birds, after moving north on a broad front, the eagles pause when they get to the edge of Lake Erie. There is so much good eagle habitat here, with all the marshes along the lake and around Sandusky Bay, that they're likely to stay a while, especially if ice on the lake hints that waters may be frozen solid farther north. When the eagles do finally move on northward, most don't fly across the lake. Instead they move west-northwest along the shoreline until they can turn the corner and continue north into Michigan. From vantage points near the edge of the lake, on a good day in late February or March, we can expect to see eagles powering past, continuing their mysterious travels.

That is part of the reason that we are so concerned about proposals to build wind-power facilities along the lakeshore, and that the suggested wind turbine at Camp Perry seemed like such a dangerous precedent. People sometimes assume that eagles, with their strong flight and keen eyesight, would be relatively safe from wind turbines. The data, incomplete as they are, say otherwise. Based on what we know, eagles and other large raptors are inordinately likely to be struck by the spinning blades.

In the early development of wind power in North America, golden eagles were being killed more often than bald eagles. Location made the difference: most of the early large wind farms were placed in windy canyons in dry country of the West, prime golden eagle habitat. Some of the known results are shocking: the infamous wind farm at Altamont, California, for example, was killing more than one hundred golden eagles every year. But as more wind development goes up in coastal areas or along major rivers or lakeshores, the bald eagle kill rate will go up also.

Of course, technically the eagles are protected by law. In addition to the Migratory Bird Treaty Act of 1918, there's a more specific Bald and Golden Eagle Protection Act dating back to 1940. Under the terms of the latter, there are severe penalties for anyone who "takes" an eagle — or, more precisely, anyone who might "take, possess, sell, purchase, barter, offer to sell, purchase or barter, transport, export or import, at any time or any manner, any bald eagle . . . [or any golden eagle], alive or dead, or any part, nest, or egg thereof." The very broad term "take" is defined to include "pursue, shoot, shoot at, poison, wound, kill, capture, trap, collect, molest or disturb." Theoretically, a violation of the law can result in a fine of $100,000 for a first offense.

In practice, of course, the feds can't go prosecute an energy company every time an eagle is killed. (Enforcement does happen occasionally—for example, in December 2014 a company operating in Wyoming agreed to pay $2.5 million in fines and mitigation after its wind farms killed thirty-eight golden eagles and hundreds of other birds. But such instances are rare.) It's assumed that some "incidental take" of eagles is inevitable, so it's possible for utility companies to get "eagle take permits" in advance, which gives them a pass on killing a certain number during a designated time frame. These permits used to be issued for five-year periods, but revisions at the end of 2016 extended these to thirty-year permits.

Just about every bird conservationist I know considers it foolhardy to give wind-power companies, or any industry, a thirty-year free pass to kill thousands of eagles. A lot can happen to a wild population in thirty years. It's time enough for a gradual comeback, but it's also time enough for a hard crash, and it's disturbing to know that companies could go on legally killing eagles even if their populations were declining again. But that's how the law reads now. This is part of the reason that we are so determined to keep the wind turbines out of the most sensitive areas along the lakeshore in northwestern Ohio.

All this had been weighing on our minds, but those concerns seemed further away out here, away from manmade things, in the cleansing bite of the cold air. If we ignored the dirt track below our feet and the vehicle behind us and just looked out toward the marsh and the shadowy woods, the scene could have been one from a thousand years ago. Our count of eagles had passed ninety and was headed for a hundred, and we reveled in the abundance of these awe-inspiring creatures.

Tom had told us we wouldn't leave—quietly, with the headlights off—until after the last eagles had settled in for the night. So we waited. The sun undoubtedly was down behind the cloudy western horizon, the sky was getting darker, but still a few eagles were arriving. In the dim light they looked even more formidable, hulking black shapes against the gray sky, faceless, anonymous, ominous. One at a time now, at long intervals, they came beating heavily across the sky, melting into the black woods.

Finally it had been more than ten minutes since the last eagle had arrived. Night was coming on. We were just getting into the car when Kimberly said, "Wait, is this another one?"

I turned, half expecting to see a great horned owl or some other night bird: Kimberly has so much experience watching eagles that there's rarely a question in her voice when she spots one. But it was a bald eagle all right, coming toward us out of the gloom with that typical wingbeat, unhurried but powerful. It cruised on past us, heading for the roost, but we lost it in the darkness of the sky before it reached the trees. Watching it go, I couldn't help thinking that the skies ahead were potentially dark, or at least uncertain, for all of us.

6

Wild March

Everyone knows a duck when they see one. The true waterfowl —the ducks, geese, and swans—are among the birds most readily recognized by the public. Which makes it all the more paradoxical that most people hardly know them at all.

When birders speak of waterfowl, we don't mean just any bird that lives around water. We mean members of the family Anatidae —one of the most widespread of all bird families, with more than 150 species around the globe. A handful of those species have been domesticated for centuries, or even for millennia, and people everywhere are familiar with these domestic versions.

Familiarity with wild waterfowl is harder to come by. Unfortunately, when most people think of ducks and geese, they think of tame barnyard versions or feral populations. Most domesticated ducks are descended from wild mallards—they still sound like their wild brethren, but they look dumpy and misshapen and slow, a far cry from their sleek ancestors. Flocks of escaped domestic ducks live in a semiwild state around park ponds and urban riverfronts all over North America. Wild, migratory mallards join up with these urban flocks, especially in winter, and then some stay to breed with them. As a result, a continuum from wild mallards to pudgy domestics can be seen around many cities, and slightly mongrelized mallards nest in many a backyard. People who know only these feral versions may have no concept of the elegance of wary wild ducks.

Geese have gotten an even worse rap. Fat, waddling barnyard geese are a world away from the elegant graylag goose of Europe, their wild ancestor. But even more recently, our native Canada geese have been degraded by human influence.

It may seem hard to believe, but only a few decades ago a flock of Canada geese was a welcome sight almost anywhere. Canada geese once were symbols of unspoiled wild places. Here in Ohio they passed through briefly during spring and fall, traveling between nesting grounds in the Arctic and scattered wintering areas farther south. The same was true throughout most of the Midwest and the Great Lakes region. The great wilderness advocate Sigurd Olson could write lyrically about them: "The sound of wild geese on the move haunted me and I felt that somehow I must capture some of their mystery, some of their freedom and of the blue distances into which they disappeared." They were wary and elusive, but despite that, by the 1940s their populations were low enough to cause genuine alarm among conservationists.

Efforts to bring back healthy populations of Canada geese succeeded beyond anyone's wildest expectations. Beginning in the early 1950s, the state wildlife agency brought captive Canadas to release at protected areas in western and northwestern Ohio. Similar efforts were under way over large parts of the continent. Most of these birds were sourced from the so-called Giant Canada goose, a population of very large geese native to a region centered on Minnesota. These Giant Canadas were only short-distance migrants, and many of the introduced populations soon became entirely nonmigratory. They quickly lost most of their fear of humans, too, and became a constant presence around cities, parks, lakes — wherever open water was close to open ground.

Within a couple of human generations, the perception of Canada geese shifted from thrilling wilderness symbols to annoying city park pests. Flocks of wild geese from the Arctic still visit northwestern Ohio in fall, but most people see only the big, noisy, semitame birds that poop all over sidewalks and lawns.

Even swans have been compromised. We do still see wild swans here: every year several thousand tundra swans stop through the western Lake Erie marshes in late fall and early spring, on a diagonal migration path that takes them between the central Atlantic Coast and the High Arctic tundra of western Canada and Alaska. In recent years a thousand or more have been staying through the winter.

Tundra swans are magnificent birds, measuring more than four feet from bill to tail and weighing up to fourteen pounds, but they're not the largest swans here. The mute swan, native to Europe, was brought to North America as an ornamental bird in centuries past, and escapees have established feral populations. Mute swans are bigger than tundra swans, five feet long and weighing more than twenty pounds, and they're considered problematic in Ohio marshes where they live.

But even the mute swans are not the biggest swans here. The trumpeter swan — mainly a bird of western North America — averages even larger. Trumpeters may have lived in Ohio long ago; the evidence is sketchy. If it's true, they lived here at a time when vast marshes stretched from horizon to horizon, giving them plenty of room. In a controversial move, Ohio's wildlife agency decided in the 1990s to reintroduce trumpeter swans into the limited habitat that remains. They have thrived. In their native wild range in the West, where they have to watch out for bears and wolves, trumpeter swans are at least somewhat wary; but nothing threatens them in Ohio, so here they are often absurdly tame. We see them standing around on roadsides in farm country, looking even more slow-witted than the golf-course geese or city-park-pond ducks. They're wilderness icons no longer.

So the general public image of waterfowl is tainted by experience with domestic and semiferal birds. Hunters have a clearer view of the magic of wild ducks, but their focus is in late fall, during hunting season. For birders here, peak duck excitement occurs in early spring, when northbound flocks of ducks play a big part in getting the migration rolling.

Admittedly, we have to be quite alert even to notice when duck migration starts, because many stay through the winter. Or through most winters, or parts of them.

As a rule, northern ducks don't migrate as far as the tropics. While various sandpipers, hawks, songbirds, and others may fly off to winter quarters in South America, most ducks don't go any farther than they must to reach open water. This reliance on open water can disrupt their winter plans if unusually harsh weather sets in; ducks attempting to stay over in Ohio or the central states may have to shift farther south in midseason if their marshes or lakes freeze up. Many of the largest flocks wind up on southern reservoirs or along the southern Atlantic and Gulf Coasts — dabbling ducks on the vast marshes, diving ducks on the saltwater bays. But they start moving back north just as early as they can.

The vanguard of the flight arrives earlier than seems possible, somehow finding open water even when I think it's all still frozen. The precise timing varies by the year and seems to be shifting earlier on average, but still it's hard to predict and hard to detect.

I always see the first clues in the sky. Random flocks of mallards may fly around occasionally in midwinter, but when I start to notice a lot of ducks in the air over the open farmland, I know something is happening. Northern pintails in particular are signal birds for me. These are abundant ducks, and tough enough that many go to the High Arctic for the summer, but relatively few stay in northwest Ohio through midwinter. Returning migrant pintails start to show up in February, in some years almost as early as the first silent crows.

My pulse quickens when I spot the first flights of pintails over the wintry landscape. They stand out even at a distance. In flocks arrowing across the sky, each individual is a study in elongated grace: long slim neck, long pointed tail, long tapered wingtips. Even the spacing and arrangement of the flock are beautiful: they're moving too fast to maintain a classic *V* formation, but the pintails are arrayed in chevrons and wavering lines, striking patterns against the clouds. Whether I see them paralleling the edge of ice-choked Lake Erie or passing high over farm fields, they light up the sky with a tantalizing promise of spring.

Eventually I'll find the open water that they have already found and I'll get to admire them at length. Pintails are almost impossibly elegant, trim and sleek, with classic lines. On the water, the male holds his head high, showing off the white stripe that runs up the neck to the rich chocolate brown of his face. The female is a little smaller but just as slim, and colored in a softer cinnamon brown.

Other ducks are moving in as well, and every kind is distinctive and worth celebrating. Green-winged teal are tiny ducks, half the bulk of the pintails, with dark patterns of chestnut and green and gray. They fly in small, tight flocks, twisting and turning in the air. Northern shovelers paddle around in shallow waters, their big spoon-shaped beaks giving them a droopy, dopey expression. Gadwalls look plain and gray at a distance but intricately patterned up close; they arrive here already paired up, and the small flocks flying fast over the marshes are all aggregations of pairs. American wigeons are colorful ducks, the females pink and gray, the males with a white-capped look that gives them the nickname "baldpate." Wigeons dabble for food in the shallows, but they also hang around on deeper waters, stealing food from coots or diving ducks when they come to the surface.

Around the edges of forested swamps, wood ducks arrive in a big way in late February and March, after being mostly absent in midwinter. These are fair-weather ducks anyway, more common in the Lower 48 than in Canada. Adapted for nesting in holes or hollows high in trees, they thread their way gracefully among the branches in rapid flight, their long tails enabling them to maneuver more deftly than most ducks can.

Various diving ducks are moving in also. Thousands of scaups and lesser numbers of redheads and canvasbacks may have spent the winter on Lake Erie if areas of deep water have remained unfrozen, but still there's a big uptick in their numbers by early March, or whenever the breakup of the ice allows. If open water on the lake is limited, they may spend time in the shallow marshes, or even in flooded agricultural fields.

Even though we're surrounded by thousands of acres of wildlife preserves and refuges managed specifically for ducks, some of the best duck habitat in March is out in farm country. With snowmelt and heavy rains, the rich black soil becomes saturated and then floods with sheets of standing water. For a while every spring it appears that the Great Black Swamp, drained and banished more than a century ago, is plotting its return. Out in the farm fields, among the corn stubble and soybean stalks, temporary pools create many square miles of perfect habitat, and the ducks, geese, and swans pile into the fields by the thousands. Often we can barely see them from the roads, but we can see them crossing the sky as they travel among sites.

Much of the excitement of this season is brought by the fact that these early migrants move around the landscape so much. We don't just go to specific marshes and lakes to see them; they're shifting around the whole area and we might see them anywhere. In tight little knots of three or four birds or in flocks of dozens or even hundreds, they crisscross the sky. Looking through binoculars at a distant flight of ducks, I'll see others beyond them, higher and farther away, moving in the opposite direction. The sense of motion and raw energy is irresistible.

As the month goes on and waters thaw, more and more of the ducks move out of the farm fields and into the marshes. Many of them are on land belonging to the private duck-hunting clubs — where there is no hunting at this season, of course, just a vast area of perfect protected habitat. Others are in the state wildlife areas like Magee Marsh and Metzger Marsh, or within the ten square miles of the federal Ottawa National Wildlife Refuge.

An auto tour route winds about seven miles through the heart of the Ottawa Refuge, offering some of the best views of waterfowl habitat anywhere in the region. For most of the year this route is open to the public only one weekend a month. Birders from other parts of Ohio and Michigan keep tabs on the schedule, and they'll make a point of visiting on those weekends to tour Ottawa and then check out other, nearby sites.

There's a big increase in March of people weary of winter and wanting to see the concentrations of migrating waterfowl. We look forward to this time, a chance to see many of our friends from around the region. We'll run into them out on the refuge, or they'll stop by the bird observatory, or we'll wind up at the favorite local diner, Blackberry Corners, all at the same time. The return of the birders is cause for celebration, just like the return of the birds.

Picking a weekend from the calendar is a big gamble in March. The weather can be beautiful or beastly. Sunshine and mild temperatures can prevail, or the region can be locked in a deep freeze, ground covered with snow, ponds covered with ice. Birders who don't check the weather before driving up may find themselves unprepared.

When I look over my weather notes from March of years past, the variations are wild. On March 15 of one year the temperature stayed far below freezing all day, with northwest winds taking the windchill down near zero at times. On March 15 of another year, highs pushed eighty. During the afternoon there were reports of very serious weather to the northwest of us, all over southern Michigan, with multiple funnel clouds touching down, two-inch hail in some spots, heavy rain and flash flooding. A very slow-moving system, it didn't reach our area of northwestern Ohio until after dark. Then it continued to move very slowly through the area for at least the next four hours, with new cells popping up to the west of us and then moving slowly east. Kimberly and I were at Blackberry Corners with friends that evening; by the time we left there a little after nine, to drive to the bird observatory and then down into Oak Harbor, there was almost continuous lightning in all directions and heavy rain falling. Dozens of frogs hopped across the roads in front of us as we headed home. The surreal scene seemed abnormally early, but it's hard to say what is "normal" anymore.

Variable conditions may create uncertainty for visiting birders, but they create life-or-death problems for returning migrant birds. The early migrants that appear in February and March have to be tough, and even more importantly, they have to be adaptable. They have to be ready to shift around the landscape to find food and shelter. And they do. The ducks are not the only birds ranging widely throughout the area during this season.

Gulls seem to be everywhere in March. Of course, gulls have been around all winter — mostly ring-billed gulls and herring gulls, so similar to each other that they seem like the same bird in two sizes, medium and large. Throughout the coldest months they have roamed the lakeshore and open spots on the rivers, stopping by to scavenge scraps at the county landfills. But now their flocks are exploring more widely, and a flock of two or three hundred gulls may suddenly descend on any soggy farm field. They walk about pecking for worms or grubs flooded out of their holes, or gather to feast on carcasses of dead creatures revealed by the melting snow.

Bald eagles come into the same fields as the gulls, to stand around looking slightly awkward or out of place. They're not there to catch and eat the gulls (although that may happen sometimes);

instead, as opportunistic scavengers, they're looking to eat some of the same things the gulls do. These random temporary gatherings of gulls and eagles may form anywhere, even miles from the lake, and they may last for minutes or hours before the gull flocks take to the air and go wheeling away on the wind.

Herring gulls and ring-billed gulls are big, cold-eyed, and raucous, appropriately tough for winter birds. Sometime in March, though, after a spell of warm south winds, flocks of Bonaparte's gulls will show up, and these are smaller, more graceful birds, fitting symbols for spring. The name might conjure up images of an imperial bird, but Bonaparte's gulls were not named for Napoleon; the name honors his biologist nephew Charles, a much gentler man.

A herring gull may weigh two or three pounds, which is a lot for a bird, and its outstretched wings may span five feet from wingtip to wingtip. A Bonaparte's gull usually weighs less than half a pound, and even though its wings are long and slender, they span less than three feet. This is a small, delicate gull, almost dainty in its behavior, shunning the food fights around landfills, typically seeking smaller morsels.

Even at a long distance it's easy to pick out a flight of Bonaparte's gulls by their graceful air and their strikingly pale look. By comparison, any large flock of herring gulls will include some dark brown or patchy brown-and-gray young birds; it takes them four years to reach the clean gray-and-white look of adulthood. But Bonaparte's, even in their first winter, are pale overall, with just a little extra black tracing on their wings and tails. Adults are mostly white, with the pale gray of their wings accented by a long white triangle in the outer feathers. These white triangles flash like signals, even out at the limit of vision.

I have seen Bonaparte's gulls all over this continent, north to the Arctic in summer, south to Mexico in winter, but their sheer numbers in northern Ohio represent one of the best things about living here. Their summer range is mostly in western Canada and Alaska, and in fall many of these birds migrate east-southeast to the Great Lakes. There are times in November when Lake Erie is a blizzard of Bonaparte's gulls, with flocks of thousands all along the lakeshore, probably more than 100,000 present altogether, a major percentage of the world's total population. They don't stay; most are gone by January, especially if the lake starts to freeze, and during February it's hard to find more than a handful.

Given that they arrive here from the northwest in fall, I had always assumed that they continued eastward toward the Atlantic Coast when they left here. But when the Bonaparte's reappear in early spring, many of the flocks seem to be coming straight north, overland across Ohio. Wherever they're coming from, they seem in no hurry to get back to Lake Erie, and they do much of their foraging out in the square miles of farm country.

Seeing a flight of Bonaparte's gulls come into a partially flooded field is like watching a ballet performed on a grand stage. Facing into the wind—and if it's March, the wind is always blowing—they flutter along, white above the dark soil. In long, straggling lines of dozens or hundreds, with shallow, delicate wingbeats, they inch forward, hover, dip down as if to land, then move on. If food is abundant (for example, when large numbers of grubs have been pushed to the surface by flooding), they may land and walk around with light, mincing steps. Hundreds may gather. But before long, for no obvious reason, they take to the air. In a gracefully arranged mass movement they turn and sweep away in the opposite direction, a shower of white crescents pouring away down the wind.

Motion is the theme of March. Not only are migratory birds starting to pass through in increasing numbers, but they move all over the landscape while they're here.

Tree swallows always appear in March, flashing white and steel blue as they sweep by in graceful, continuous flight. It seems a risky move for them to come back so early, because swallows in general feed on insects caught in midair. Tree swallows must be better able to survive cold snaps than the five kinds of swallows that will arrive here in April; they can subsist on old, dried-up berries on freezing days when no insects are flying. Later in the season the tree swallows will be widely dispersed, placing their nests in holes in trees or in bluebird nest boxes, but now they move around in flocks, gathering at the edges of ponds or rivers. If the weather turns really harsh they may disappear for a few days at a time, only to show up again at the same spots; do they fly back south during those times, or just go into hiding? No one knows.

Right now, in March, flocks of blackbirds are among the most conspicuous elements of birdlife. They stream across the sky in wavering, shifting rivers of birds. They cross the bare fields in a continuous rolling motion, with birds from the back of the flock constantly picking up and flying up to the front. They crowd the branches of leafless trees in the isolated woodlots, their voices blending into a creaky, discordant chorus.

To be clear, "blackbirds" is a generic term encompassing several species, most of them related. In this region it includes the red-winged blackbird, common grackle, and brown-headed cowbird, all very abundant, and the rusty blackbird, a swampland bird with declining populations. The European starling, introduced on this continent, totally unrelated but also mostly black in plumage, often associates with our native blackbirds, so it may get lumped into the category. All of these species have different habitats and habits during the nesting season, when they mostly split up into pairs. But for the rest of the year—from late summer to early spring—they gather in large flocks.

Redwings, grackles, and cowbirds all stay through the winter in northern Ohio. But that doesn't mean we see them regularly. Several thousand may be in the local area (as opposed to the tens of thousands here in summer), but they are concentrated in a few large, tight flocks. Their winter flocks shift their foraging sites from day to day; at a given place we might go days or weeks without seeing any at all and then suddenly see a flock of thousands. Starlings can be somewhat more scattered, but even they tend to be concentrated in localized flocks.

The only places where blackbirds are seen consistently in winter are at their nightly roosts. Twenty thousand may spend the night in a limited patch of marsh or swamp, either near Lake Erie or along one of the major rivers. Visiting these roosts or the surrounding area, we can see blackbirds every evening or morning as they arrive or depart. Elsewhere they may escape our notice altogether.

The flocks that stay through the winter are mostly quiet, focused on mere survival. In January we may see them overhead in the cold dawn, heading out in a determined search for whatever food they can find in the short hours of daylight. Late in the afternoon we might see them headed the other way, going back to their communal roost, where they will pack in close together and endure the long night. No time for anything but eating, sleeping, and staying alive. In winter they are all business.

At the approach of spring, a gradual transformation comes over the flocks. For one thing, their numbers begin to increase. The arrival of migrants is hard to detect: most blackbirds apparently migrate in the daytime, but flocks of blackbirds might be seen flying in any direction even in midwinter, so a northbound flock in early spring might or might not be migrating. But by late February we start to see the roving flocks more and more often, and by March it becomes obvious that huge numbers of blackbirds are pumping into the region from farther south.

Their behavior starts to change, too. Midwinter blackbird flocks may be relatively subdued, but by March they crackle with extraordinary energy. When they pour into a woodlot, their voices can be heard from three quarters of a mile away, all the separate notes blended into a rough murmur. As we approach, the sound increases to a cacophony. Thousands of red-wings, grackles, cowbirds, and starlings jam together on every twig of the trees, like black leaves filling the branches. They all face the same direction, into the wind, and they all seem to be singing and calling at once, for no obvious reason. Many of their notes are surprisingly low-pitched, and this gives the whole chorus a deep, throaty tone. If the flock abruptly snaps into an eerie silence — like an alarm call in reverse — or switches to high, piercing whistles, it may mean they've spotted a hawk or other predator. The moment of silence may be followed by the roar of ten thousand wings as the flock takes to the air. When they settle again, in treetops of another woods, the chorus begins again. It's as if the whole flock were a single living thing, a gigantic organism with thousands of parts, breathing and moving as one. We can't pick out individual voices, just a deep, rich music, as wild in its own way as the songs of wolves or whales.

By late March these flocks include many rusty blackbirds, which are just passing through: none are here in summer and very few in winter. Their presence is of extreme interest to conservationists.

Given the striking abundance of red-winged blackbirds, grackles, and cowbirds, people find it surprising that any blackbird could be rare or possibly endangered. But rusty blackbirds are surprising creatures. In spring, when most birds are at their most colorful, rusty blackbirds wear a flat dull black; they take on bright rusty-brown feather edges only in fall. They spend the winter mostly in southeastern swamps, which was a good strategy centuries ago, before most of those swamps were drained. They spend their summers in the vast boreal forest that stretches across Canada and Alaska, north of any other blackbirds. Until the last couple of decades no one thought about them very much, and certainly no one worried.

Now we're starting to worry. We don't know their actual status, because rusty blackbirds are hard to count. Their roving winter flocks are patchy in distribution and easy to miss, and easy to confuse with those of other blackbirds, so Christmas Bird Count results for this species aren't reliable. Their summer range is largely in a trackless wilderness, mostly beyond the reach of the continent-wide Breeding Bird Survey. But as sketchy as the available numbers are, every attempt to analyze them suggests that the population is dropping drastically. Some scientists think that the total population has dropped by more than 90 percent since the 1960s.

This prevailing view is intriguing to us in northwestern Ohio. In this region, no major decline in numbers has been detected. Rusty blackbirds are fairly common migrants in late fall and early spring, and it's still possible here to find hundreds in a day at the right season. Looking at the last century, the only period for which we have good records, we don't have strong evidence that these birds were ever much more numerous here than they are now.

Does this mean that concerns raised elsewhere are unfounded? Not necessarily. Instead, maybe, as populations shrink, this region has become one of the last refuges for big numbers in migration. It's easy to imagine that this would have been a tremendously important stopover site in centuries past: migrating rusty blackbirds may have swarmed throughout the vast Great Black Swamp and western Lake Erie marshes, perfect habitats for these wetland blackbirds. If tradition still brings them here, their diminished numbers still can swarm in the tiny remnants of that former wilderness. But that doesn't necessarily mean they're doing well anywhere else. It could just mean that our remaining fragments of habitat are more vital than ever for survival of the species.

In fact, in recent telemetry studies, researchers from Ohio State found that individual rusty blackbirds were staying in the western Lake Erie marsh region for a month or more in both late fall and early spring. What's more, they weren't just dropping into one swamp and staying put. Many of these rusties were moving around the landscape, from the Ottawa Refuge and Magee Marsh over to Sandusky Bay and back. The whole region, it seems, is their stopover site.

That study sheds a whole new light on what we see of rusty blackbirds here in northwestern Ohio. Yes, they move through the region for all of March and much of April, but we're not seeing wave after wave passing through; instead we're seeing the same flocks as they shift around the local area. We see them out in the muddy farm fields, and landing in the small woodlots, and streaming into swampy woods at Magee, and they're all the same birds. Their temporary abundance here is at least partly an illusion.

The challenges of bird conservation come into sharper focus with this view. Those precious patches of protected wetlands — federal, state, and private — are crucial, but they're not enough. In early spring the various ducks, swallows, Bonaparte's gulls, rusty blackbirds, and many more species are moving all over the Lake Erie plain, still dependent on the faint outlines of what had been swamps and marshes in centuries past. To protect these birds we'll have to think outside the bounds of the refuges and sanctuaries, think about effects on the entire landscape.

7

Creatures of Light

Calendars that label a date in March as the "first day of spring" rather than the vernal equinox don't do us any favors. It might seem an easier concept, but it's a false one, and it distracts us from the reality of the season. People might look out the window and see daffodils blooming before that date, or snow falling after that date, and conclude that this "first day of spring" was a meaningless human invention, like Groundhog Day. But the equinox is real and it carries immense importance.

Ever since the winter solstice in late December — the shortest day and longest night here in the north — the days have been gradually getting longer. As Earth orbits the sun on its permanent tilt, the equinox marks the day when the plane of the equator points directly at the center of the sun. On the equinox, at most places on Earth, day and night are of approximately equal length, with sunrise and sunset about twelve hours apart. Beyond this day the

Northern Hemisphere will be angled more and more toward the sun. Daylight hours will grow longer, the sun will climb higher in our sky. Although the change in temperature tends to lag behind, warmer weather gradually will be on the way.

Most wild creatures are exceptionally attuned to daylight. In the temperate zones, the gradual increase in the length of the day — earlier sunrise, later sunset — provides the most important clue to drive changes in their hormone levels in springtime. Migratory species become restless and begin preparing for their journeys, resident species assert their claims to territory or start seeking mates, all based on the slight increase in the length of the day. Dawn and twilight, angle of the sun, quality of light — these are all crucial markers for creatures that live outdoors.

I believe that humans can be equally attuned to the quality of light. That isn't always evident when we spend so much time indoors, under artificial light, but the potential is there. Even if we walk a few city blocks outdoors, we notice the light subconsciously and recognize when it changes. When a heavy storm rolls in at midday, for example, the darkness that falls has a different quality from the darkness near sunset; it looks alien, menacing. Even though we can't see the sun, we still sense the angle of light through the clouds, and sense that this darkness is not right. The instinct for light is always there. Landscape painters struggle mightily to convey its effects; no matter how perfectly they portray the shapes of the trees, rivers, or hills, their landscapes will look flat and dead if they can't capture some sense of the quality of light.

When I moved to Ohio I was disoriented by the light, out of touch with the seasons. The light was so different from what I had known in the southwestern deserts. It took three or four years before I was in tune with seasonal shifts in light in my new home. But getting to that stage didn't take a conscious effort; it came about naturally, from walking outside and looking at the sky day after day, and I wasn't aware of it until afterward. It was an adaptation in some internal calendar. Although I don't know if this has been studied, I believe that humans have an instinct to sense and learn the annual regime of light in the place where they live.

Now, after more than a decade in northern Ohio, I'm more in tune with seasons here. It's the latter part of March, just past the vernal equinox. The landscape still has a wintry look, with bare trees, bare fields, and lingering patches of snow. The weather has been bitterly cold on some days in the last week. But the light is different now from what it was in midwinter, and that makes all the difference.

The birds are different now as well. Killdeers have been back for more than three weeks, and now pairs of them are everywhere, crying plaintively in the sky above the soggy fields. More gulls are landing in those fields, but there are fewer ducks there than last week; most of the ducks have probably moved into the marshes as they open up, but others may have gone on north.

When I say "the birds are different now," I mean it in more ways than one. It's not just a turnover in the kinds of birds that are present. Even those that have been here all along are different now, different in their behavior.

In the coldest weeks of midwinter, when days were short and nights were long, dawn merely signaled the resumption of the birds' intense search for food, trying to build up enough fuel to keep them going. Diminishing light toward dusk meant it was time for them to seek shelter and try to survive another night. But now things are changing. The day grows longer, the night grows shorter. As sunrise and sunset move further apart, they are no longer merely the end points of the day. Now dawn and dusk take on a significance all their own. They come into focus as some of the most important times in the daily cycle for many birds.

There's a shift in the soundscape of dawn. It can be a chillingly quiet time in midwinter, when silent night gives way to the cold gray light of morning, with hardly a bird's voice to break the stillness. But sometime in late winter or early spring, the dawn chorus begins. It's tentative at first, just a few cardinals or song sparrows tuning up at first light, nothing like the exuberant choir that will greet the sunrise later in the season. But as the month of March goes on, the songs at dawn grow stronger and more confident.

A bird that sings is not just trying to fill the world with music —at least, we think not. Birdsong is charged with more practical functions. Most of the singing is done by males on their breeding territories, and they broadcast their tunes mostly to warn other males to stay away or to invite a female to stay and mate. Especially in the early part of the breeding season in spring and early summer, they sing most intensely and most constantly at dawn, the time of day when new arrivals are most likely to intrude on the territory. If new migrants have come in overnight, moving about in the dim light before sunrise, they must hear the song and know that this patch of turf is already taken.

By late March the song sparrows are singing every morning, at least if the weather is decent. The tune is pleasant enough, a brisk, varied series of short notes, trills, and buzzes, each male having his own slightly different repertoire. Resident males perch up on bare twigs above thickets to belt out their songs, and we can see and hear them in the same spots every day.

They're not the only ones of their kind around right now, however. In addition to the permanent resident population, large numbers of other song sparrows pass through in spring and fall: wintering to the south of here, breeding somewhere to the north. Some of these transient song sparrows also sing while they're here, although not as consistently or forcefully; we may just hear fragments of their songs from out in the thickets or along the weedy ditches. Why are they singing at all, when they won't be holding territories anywhere near here? It may be that they're simply practicing, or that their hormones are firing up and filling them with the urge to sing even before they reach the nesting grounds.

That last point—the fact that migrants also may sing—is especially relevant at this season. Given its name, we might imagine the song sparrow to be the best singer in its family (even its scientific name, *Melospiza melodia,* translates roughly to "singing singing finch"). But there are other sparrows with genuinely beautiful voices, and they just weren't so conspicuous to the pioneer biologists who named these birds two centuries ago.

The American tree sparrow, for example, has a bright, sweet song of whistles and trills, but its nesting grounds are mostly on tundra north of the Arctic Circle. We see big flocks of these small birds here in Ohio in winter, and a few of them begin to sing a little at the early edge of spring, just before they depart for the north.

Their larger cousins the fox sparrows are the virtuosos of the family. Fox sparrows, named for the foxy red tones of their plumage, are never really common anywhere. The eastern population spends the winter in dense woods throughout the southeastern states and retires to spruce forests of northern Canada for the summer. In most places a birder is lucky to see more than two or three in a day during migration seasons. But here in northern Ohio, migrating fox sparrows seem to concentrate in woodlots along the shore of Lake Erie in early spring. Sometimes at the end of March, a loop of the boardwalk at Magee Marsh may produce two or three dozen. They're not easy to see as they lurk in the undergrowth, but if we listen we'll hear rustling as these big sparrows scratch for food in the leaf litter, vigorously kicking with both feet at once.

And if we're out in those woods at dawn or dusk, we may hear something else: rich, sweet whistles, the notes swooping and soaring, falling and rising, a birdsong of uncommon beauty. It has a slow and contemplative sound, and there is a long silence before the song comes again. This is the voice of the fox sparrow . . . tuning up now, practicing the song that it will deliver from the deep shadows of spruce trees in northern Canada a few weeks from now. It's one of the secret sounds of the season in Ohio, to be heard only by those alert enough to go out and listen at these moments between winter and spring and between day and night.

There are other secret sounds of this cusp of the season, like the clicking rattle of chorus frogs in shallow roadside marshes and migrant rusty blackbirds gurgling and creaking in swampy woods. But there's one moment of singular importance when the first robin shows up outside our door, usually sometime in March, to pour out its song at the first hint of light. That's the harbinger, that's the undeniable sign of spring.

The songs of robins are essential sounds of dawn over large parts of this continent in spring and summer. They're also a deep part of my personal connection to daybreak. When I was ten or eleven years old, family friends insisted that I go along to an Easter sunrise church service at an amphitheater in a local park. I don't remember a thing that was spoken during the service, but I vividly recall the lusty, full-throated caroling of the robins, far and near, all over the park, a glorious chorus to raise the sun above the horizon. He is risen, indeed. Ever since then I've considered robin songs to be sacred music of the highest order.

In terms of popularity, the American robin suffers from the fact that it's so common. (In reality the bird isn't suffering, because of course it doesn't care whether or not it's popular with humans.) People with any awareness, if they spend any time outdoors at all, become so accustomed to the sight and sound of robins that they blend into the background. Birders look right past robins, or right through them, as we watch for something "good."

But if we took the time to look and listen, we'd have to agree that robins are stunning birds. Robins are so *intentional*. Even when they run a few steps and then pause, they pause in a forceful way. They are quick in every movement, especially at this season, dashing across lawns, flashing across roads. As males start to stake out their breeding territories, they stage battles at the boundaries, with strident cries, long chases, and actual knock-down pecking-and-clawing fights. Their songs are loud and rich and their colors are bold, from the deep yellow of the beak to the bright rufous orange of the chest. If the American robin were a rare bird, we would climb mountains or walk through fire to catch a glimpse of it. Why should we appreciate it any less just because it's around us every day?

It's about this time of year, any time from March through April, that people start posting on listserves or social media that their "first robin of spring" has just returned. Invariably, as soon as that happens, some seasoned birder will jump in to squash their enthusiasm. *No, you're wrong, it's not the first one of spring. Robins don't leave in winter. Flocks are around all through the cold months, and you just haven't been seeing them.*

Technically the curmudgeons are right, but it's still a fact that robins go missing from tens of thousands of backyards and farm-yards and parks throughout the winter. There are flocks at this latitude, it's true, often ranging through swamps overgrown with poison ivy and wild grape or stationed in cemeteries with major plantings of fruiting trees. But there are vast areas that won't see a robin between November and March. When the actual first robin of spring suddenly appears in every yard, it signals a significant change in the season and a new chapter for the robins themselves. And it brings a stirring change to the sounds of sunrise.

If the American robin is the bird of dawn, the bird of dusk is the American woodcock. It takes more of an effort to catch its performance, but it's well worth it. This is one of the most remarkable birds on the continent.

Even the name is improbable. Like so many other weird bird names, it originated with the British; there is a related bird in Europe. The woodcock is actually a member of the sandpiper family, but it doesn't look like one. Its body is almost as round as a grapefruit, topped with a small head and no neck. Its big eyes are up near the top of its head, enabling it to watch out for danger above and behind itself even when its long beak is plunged into the mud. Short legs, short tail, and a dead-leaf camo pattern complete the look. Technically it belongs to the shorebird group, but it never goes to the open tidal flats frequented by most of its kin. Instead it lives deep in the woods, on the forest floor, coming out to boggy fields at night.

Scientists consider the woodcock to be one of the most numerous of the shorebird clan, with a population in the low millions, outnumbering the familiar killdeers of the open fields by more than three to one. This estimate is based partly on the fact that hunters shoot a few hundred thousand woodcocks every fall and winter without making a noticeable dent in the total population. Hunters find the birds with keen-nosed dogs, or with dogged determination in solo searches, plowing through every likely patch of dense cover. But bird-watchers might walk through the same woods all day without seeing a trace of these birds. Woodcocks are legendary for their ability to go unnoticed.

Woodcocks melt away and disappear from northern Ohio in late fall, and we're confident that none stay in the area through midwinter. Sometime in February they begin to sneak back into the swamps and flooded fields of the counties along Lake Erie. I have heard their distinctive callnotes on unseasonably warm nights as early as the third week of February. Then when cold weather returns in force, these odd, elusive birds go unseen and unheard for days or weeks at a time.

But now it's almost the end of March, peak season. Kimberly and I walk out on the trail behind the Black Swamp Bird Observatory just before sunset. Out beyond the stream it still looks like winter — the low dogwood and willow scrub still leafless, last year's dead grass still damp from snowmelt — but the sounds are different now. Robins and red-winged blackbirds are flying around in the failing light, making sharp alarm calls and tentative songs; they know the needle has shifted off winter, starting that slide into spring. And after a few minutes we hear the sound we're waiting for. It's distant but unmistakable: a sharp, buzzy, piercing, unbirdlike note, *pzzeent!*

It's the call of a male American woodcock, just now starting his warmup for his ritual. Thirty seconds later we hear it again: *pzzeent!* Another long pause, then another call. But this time there's an answer from down the path behind us. The woodcocks are starting to tune up.

Quietly we move along the trail, trying to find a bird in an open spot. There's a ventriloquial quality to the sound, and the voices seem to shift around, but the calls are becoming more frequent; we zero in on one bird that is calling *pzzeent* at a rapid but irregular rate, maybe one call every three to ten seconds. Cautiously we approach, and the sound gets louder, more penetrating. We are close enough now that we can hear the funny, froglike hiccup tossed in randomly between the *pzzeent* notes. Kimberly taps me on the arm: she has spotted the woodcock on the ground.

He is only a few yards away, in a grassy opening among spindly saplings. To the naked eye he is only a darker shadow, but the light-gathering qualities of binoculars resolve the shadow into a woodcock's shape. Sitting as upright as he can, head reared up, long bill pointed down, he seems to rock back a little before calling: *pzzeent!* A pause, that funny hiccup, then another call: *pzzeent!*, strikingly loud at close range. Now he makes a quarter turn, as if remembering to share his voice with a neglected quadrant of the audience, and calls again. In silhouette he looks puffed up with self-importance, the emperor of this little patch of ground. But the amazing part of his performance is still to come.

We know what to expect, but still we jump with surprise as he abruptly springs up from the ground with an explosive flutter of wings. Twisting up past the saplings behind him, he begins a steep climb. Clearing the tops of the scrub and beginning his ascent, black against the darkening sky, he looks so heavy-bodied and short-winged that it seems implausible that he should be airborne at all. Wings beating in a furious blur, body rising slowly, it seems that at any moment he will sputter to a stall in midair and fall back to earth. But he doesn't. He continues his slow, steep climb in a broad, sweeping spiral, and now his wings are making a loud twittering sound that follows him higher and higher into the sky. Somewhere up there — a hundred feet up, two hundred, it's hard to say — he levels off.

Now the pattern of his wingbeat changes, and so does the sound. On the wings of a male woodcock, the outermost three feathers are oddly narrowed, and the flow of air around these feathers creates the funny twittering sound of the bird in flight. Apparently he can control this to some extent, because in this phase of the display flight, the sound begins to vary. The wing-twitter seems to fade in and out, and on top of it the bird throws in a choppy chirping: *cheep-churp-chup-cheep-churp-chup*, odd, loud, repeated. We're still following the woodcock through binoculars, a darker shape against the dimming sky. He zigzags a few times, swoops, descends, circles back around, getting lower. Finally he goes silent and drops like a rock, braking at the last moment and then landing in the same precise spot from which he had taken off.

Of all birds in North America, this pudgy, stubby-winged, long-nosed oddity might seem the least likely to perform spectacular aerial displays high above the ground. But birds are full of surprises.

As one more example of such surprises, we are coming up on the time of year when legions of songbirds, creatures of sunlight, will rise up in the dark to fly across the night sky.

Back at the beginning of the season, at the first stirrings of migration in February, almost all the movement happened during daylight hours. The first straggling strings of crows, the first hawks, the first small flocks of horned larks that chose to move north, all flew in the daytime over a wintry landscape. The water-fowl and cranes, when they began to move, were also mostly traveling by day. But as the season went on, the composition of the flight began to change.

By May the overwhelming majority of the migrants will be songbirds that travel at night — especially the long-distance migrants coming from the tropics, such as the orioles, tanagers, vireos, and the popular and varied little warblers. Right now, in late March, the changeover is just beginning. The fox sparrows and song sparrows passing through, the tree sparrows picking up and leaving — these are all nocturnal migrants, and they will be followed by many more.

It might seem odd and contradictory that as the days grow longer and the nights become shorter, more of the migratory birds will be traveling at night. But that's the reality. More and more of these small birds will be taking off just after nightfall, flying through the night, and then descending and landing in the darkness just before first daylight.

The cycle of the day is divided into darkness and light, but it's the time in between — the dim, shadowy moments around dusk and dawn — when the majority of migratory birds make their most dangerous moves, when they are at the greatest risk. That's when they take to the sky or come in to land. In a region of major stopover habitat, such as the shoreline of Lake Erie, vast numbers of long-distance migrant birds will be flying low in the murky half-light, navigating the space above the treetops but within a few hundred feet of the ground.

That was why we were so alarmed to find out, in the spring of 2015, that the Camp Perry wind project was being pushed forward again. Of course it wasn't a total surprise; when the project was halted in January 2014, we knew it might be only a temporary victory. The official letter from the air force had stated that the project was "suspended indefinitely," not canceled outright. But we had not expected it to come back so soon, only a little more than a year later.

A tall tower with spinning blades, planted in the heart of one of the best stopover habitats on the continent, could only spell disaster. These migratory birds were so well adapted for nocturnal flights in the original wilderness, with innate drives honed by thousands of generations. They knew instinctively to wait until the edge of darkness before leaping up from their hiding places, slanting up through the gloaming to begin their night's travel. But nothing in their evolutionary background would have prepared them for this new danger: this rushing sound added to the wind, these racing shadows, these long blades springing out of nowhere to sweep great circles of death in the darkening sky.

8

Sifting the Mysterious Sky

It's like the shadow of a nervous mouse. Almost invisible, it moves through the undergrowth, dark and darting and furtive. A tiny brown wren with a stubby tail, it seems more rodent than bird until it makes an abrupt, low flight across a clearing in the woods.

Officially this bird is called a winter wren, but here it's a sign of early spring. Winter wrens spend the summer in eastern Canada and the northern states and scatter throughout the Southeast during the colder months. Here in northern Ohio, few linger past November. Their spring trek through the area begins in late March, but they are devilishly hard to see, passing unnoticed by anyone not tuned in to their squeaky callnotes. This winter wren was in southern Ohio yesterday. Beating north on tiny wings through the night sky, it arrived here on the Lake Erie shoreline just before dawn. No human eyes were watching as it flitted low over the marsh, lurked along the edge of the woods, scurried into the densest twiggy tangle of the leafless thickets. Winter wrens have been doing this, on instinct, for thousands of generations, so it's nothing new.

But something new and extraordinary is about to happen. As the wren flies across a gap in the bushes in the dim dawn light, it senses the faintest hint of an obstacle, like a wisp of black gossamer silk. In an instant the tiny bird has hit a soft, flexible web, bounced off it, and fallen a few inches into a fold in the netting.

Now the thinnest of fine black threads, gentle but unyielding, hold the bird immobilized, dangling a few feet above the ground.

Humans couldn't follow the wren through the undergrowth, but we'll soon catch up to it another way.

Bundled up in sweatshirts against the early April chill, three of us are walking silently along a trail through the woods. The narrow path skirts the trunks of huge cottonwood and hackberry trees, arrows through dense thickets of dogwood and honeysuckle, detours around fallen logs. Years of footsteps have worn the trail deep into the soil, and low spots are bridged by boards; this is a heavily used trail, even though the surrounding forest looks untouched.

Ashli, in the lead, turns left where a narrower trail juts off into a rectangular lane cut through the thickets. A few yards in we pass a thin aluminum pole, eight feet tall. Another just like it stands at the other end of the cut, forty feet away. In between them floats a shadow, like a vague black mist. Its presence is noticeable mainly because two small birds are suspended in it, hanging in midair.

"Ah, here's a winter wren," says Ashli. "I'll get this. Sparrow down there. Maybe a swamper. Can you get that one, Dan?"

Up close we can see the mist net in detail. A precise mesh of incredibly thin nylon threads, forming squares about an inch across, the net is separated into several horizontal sections by a thicker string at the bottom of each. When a bird hits the soft, yielding mesh, that part of the net sags past the horizontal string, creating a pocket and trapping the bird firmly.

Wrens sometimes get themselves thoroughly snarled up in the nets by bouncing around and grabbing at the mesh with their feet, but this individual isn't too badly tangled. Ashli reaches in, with a confidence built on handling thousands of birds, and deftly disengages the net from the wren's feet, wings, and head, sliding back one thread at a time. The wren squawks and fusses, but Ashli soon has it loose, pops it into a small cloth bag, and hands it to me. I loop the bag's drawstring through a carabiner, the type of metal clip popular with climbers, mark it with a crimson ribbon, and suspend it from a sturdy plastic coat hanger. Dan comes back with the swamp sparrow he has plucked from the other end of the net, its bag goes onto the hanger also, and we carry it as we continue toward the next net.

It's another morning at the Black Swamp Bird Observatory's main bird-banding station on the edge of Lake Erie. Every day in spring and fall, except in the worst weather, experienced banders are out here walking the trails, checking the nets, continuing the long-term monitoring of songbird migration.

The next net is empty, and the next. Then a lineup of three nets reveals a junco, small and gray, and a red-winged blackbird. "Hey, the redwing is a recap," says Ashli. A recapture—a bird that already wears a band on one leg. We pause to write the band number in a pocket notebook before popping the blackbird into a bag.

After a dozen more nets we head back, carrying seven birds, a good haul for a single net run. The people who had gone to check nets on the north side meet us at the banding shack—a sturdy plywood shed with a clear plastic roof for good lighting—bringing five birds. We step up onto the wooden floor of the shack and the banders sit down at the table to start processing the birds.

Ashli Gorbet is now in charge of running the banding operation for the bird observatory. Mark Shieldcastle, who started the whole thing, is now the observatory's research director, and he doesn't come into the banding station most days. He's here today, since the weather forecast had looked good for this to be a big flight day. They sit down at opposite ends of the table. Ashli will band the smaller birds and Mark will do the large ones, separating them out by the color-coded ribbons on the bags.

Now Ashli reaches into the first bag and pulls out the winter wren.

If time could stand still, we could get lost in just gazing at this one bird. It's a tiny miracle, this wren, a scrap of precious life measuring barely four inches from the tip of its bill to the end of its absurdly short tail. At a glance, its feathers look all brown. But look more closely. There are a hundred shades of brown, from soft and subtle to deep and rich, the browns of hot chocolate, warm earth, tawny terra-cotta altars in ancient temples, chestnut stallions running through red-rock canyons—a wilderness of browns. Some feathers are smooth blends of browns and buff; others are adorned with stripes, bars, spots, or speckles of black or tan or cream. But if it had no color or decoration, this wren still would hold our gaze through its sheer intensity. Even as it sits motionless in Ashli's hand, the bird conveys a sense of being vividly alive in this moment, its deep dark eyes staring right through us.

Such stunning close-up views are among the perks of banding, but they have to be very brief. We won't examine the wren for more than an instant; it's imperative to release each bird as quickly as possible. "Zero-A," says Ashli, pulling up a string of minuscule 0-A bands while Barb, across the table, puts the sheet for that band size on top of the clipboard. Ashli reads off the number of the next band on the string, and Barb confirms it should be the next one in sequence. Holding the wren gently but firmly in one hand, Ashli uses a special set of pliers to open the band, remove it from the string, and then close it on the wren's right leg. The tiny aluminum ring fits perfectly, loose enough to avoid cutting off circulation, snug enough that nothing will get caught under it. The unique number embossed on the aluminum band will identify this bird if it's ever encountered by humans again.

Turning the wren over, Ashli reels off more information for Barb to write down. "Winter wren. Age . . . aah . . ." — gently spreading one wing to look at feather details — "better call it AHY." Meaning "after hatch year," which would apply to all birds here at the moment, since no birds hatched in this calendar year would be flying around yet. This wren showed a pattern of abrasion on certain feathers suggesting it might be SY, or second-year, which would be more precise, but it won't be written down that way unless the banders can be absolutely certain. "Sex: unknown. Wing chord: umm . . . forty-six point two." The length of the folded wing in millimeters. Ashli blows at the bird's belly feathers to part them and look at the skin underneath. "Fat: one." The amount of body fat carried by a bird reflects how well it has been eating and how much fuel it has for migrating. A score of just one, on a scale from zero to four, isn't surprising for birds just arriving here after migratory flights.

This has all taken place in less time than it takes to describe it, and now it's time to weigh the bird. Randy, manning the digital scale at the end of the table, holds out a paper cone, and Ashli slips the wren in headfirst. After the wren holds still and the scale stabilizes, Randy reads it off: "Eight point six two." The weight in grams. "Got it," says Barb. Randy takes the paper cone off the scale and shakes it out gently. The winter wren flies a few yards to a low twig by the path, pauses to look back at us, gives a couple of sharp callnotes, and then zips away into the thickets.

Just down the table, Mark is going through the same process with the larger songbirds — a cardinal (in a bag marked with a dark blue ribbon for "biter"), a couple of grackles, and the already banded red-winged blackbird. On the recaptured bird he confirms the band number, checks for body fat, and has the bird weighed before it's released. "Probably one of our birds from a past year," he says, but he'll have to check the number to be sure. Mark has amazing recall for details, but it doesn't extend to memorizing thousands of band numbers every year.

This sequence — inspecting, measuring, reciting, recording — has been repeated at this table half a million times. Skilled workers from Black Swamp Bird Observatory have staffed this banding station, weather permitting, seven days a week during spring and fall migration since the early 1990s.

When Mark Shieldcastle started some occasional banding of migratory songbirds near Lake Erie, he set up nets in the woods at Magee Marsh. It was 1978, a decade before the Magee boardwalk would be built, and visiting birders still wandered everywhere through the woodlot. After interruptions became too frequent, Mark looked around for another site. The Navarre Unit of Ottawa National Wildlife Refuge was just five miles farther east along the lake, so he got permission to cut a few net lanes in the woods there starting in 1981. After 1983 he stopped trying to band in the crowded woods at Magee Marsh, shifting over completely to Navarre.

It turned out to be an inspired choice. Navarre holds the largest remaining patch of beach ridge forest in northwestern Ohio, and the most diverse, with the full range of trees that grew there historically. Better yet, access is restricted, because the tract lies behind the Davis-Besse nuclear power plant. No one comes in without passing through security; no random outsiders would wander through.

After several years of frequent banding sessions at Navarre, Mark concluded that once or twice a week wasn't enough. Numbers of migrant birds varied radically from one day to the next. Days chosen at random wouldn't reflect the season accurately. The only way to monitor the migration was to run the banding station every day. Mark had a full-time job with the state's Division of Wildlife and was doing the songbird banding on his own time, so he couldn't do it seven days a week. But a team could. Seven experienced bird banders from northern Ohio and southern Michigan got together and started a new organization to do just that, and the Black Swamp Bird Observatory was born.

Because the safety of the birds is all-important, all banding activities are tightly regulated. Only a couple of thousand Americans have master banding permits, with a few thousand more holding subpermits under them. The Bird Banding Lab of the U.S. Geological Survey requires that all projects have some specific research goal; people are discouraged from simply banding birds out of curiosity. Even with these requirements, more than a million birds per year are banded in the United States.

At the beginning a major goal of banding in America was to learn more about the migratory routes of birds. If a bird was banded at one site and then encountered again elsewhere, it would reveal something about that individual's travels. Indeed, this worked out well for migratory waterfowl. In the 1920s, Canadian and American game departments focused on banding as many ducks and geese as they could, and then hunters were asked to turn in the bands from any waterfowl they shot. Significant numbers of returns soon built up. Analysis of the travels of these waterfowl suggested that they were following four main flyways north and south across the continent. The idea was simple enough to be grasped easily, and it soon gained traction and popularity. For decades many people assumed that this flyway concept applied to all birds, not just waterfowl.

As subjects for banding, songbirds are very different from ducks. It's harder to capture large numbers at once, and few are ever recovered away from where they were banded. Out of the thousands of small birds banded by BSBO at Navarre every year, a handful will be recovered elsewhere: a yellow warbler captured at a banding station in Ontario, for example, or a hermit thrush picked up after flying into a window in Arkansas. And every year the station at Navarre will recapture a few birds already banded elsewhere: perhaps a catbird banded in Michigan or a Lincoln's sparrow banded in Texas. Such "foreign" recoveries give us some hints about where the birds have traveled.

If the whole point were to get band recoveries elsewhere, it wouldn't be worth the effort to run the BSBO station. But the value of the project at Navarre doesn't rest on such distant recaptures. Instead the consistent daily sampling gives us a reliable index of what is happening right here.

Birders can go out and count birds we see and hear, of course, but it's hard to do that in a way that's truly consistent and comparable from day to day. The mist nets at Navarre are totally consistent: they stand there passively collecting data in the same spots every day, every year, catching even those elusive skulking birds like winter wrens that birders might miss. The nets don't tell us the total numbers of birds present — no method can do that for a large, complex habitat like Navarre — but they tell us relative numbers, and more.

When birds are passing through a stopover site like Navarre, they're often captured more than once, days apart. They almost always have higher weights and higher fat levels when recaptured, proving that these small travelers are benefiting from the stopover habitat here, putting on more fuel for their next flight.

For a given species of migrant, the numbers captured will vary from year to year, because weather patterns over the whole continent have such an impact on where individuals will stop over. But in the long term, trends emerge. Numbers of golden-winged warblers have dropped during the last two decades. On the other hand, numbers of black-throated blue warblers have held steady here, even while studies have shown that they're declining farther east.

When a blocking weather system settles over the region, the daily banding totals will show fewer new birds and more recaptures. When the weather clears, suddenly we get a flood of new birds and few recaptures, as the migrants move out. All of these changes can be correlated with highly detailed weather records kept by the Davis-Besse power plant next door.

For many species, the age and sex of the individual can be determined much more reliably in the hand than in the field. These data are recorded for every bird captured. If adult male bay-breasted warblers are passing through earlier, on average, than second-year males or adult females, the data will show that. If the timing changes, the data will show that, too. If the overall timing of migration shifts to earlier dates, as many scientists think it might, that will show up clearly in the data from Navarre.

Occasionally there are exciting finds: Capturing a Wilson's warbler that was banded in Mexico. Recapturing a yellow warbler that's more than eleven years old, setting a new longevity record for the species. Capturing a dusky flycatcher, a cryptic bird from the West, the first one ever identified in Ohio. For birders, these are highlights. But the real value of the BSBO banding operation at Navarre is the accumulating set of data—tens of thousands of points of information every year, a mountain of data that can be analyzed in myriad ways, answering questions we haven't yet thought to ask. It may not be sexy, but it's the stuff of science.

The first bird bander in North America was John James Audubon. In 1804, fresh off the boat from France, the teenaged Audubon spent weeks observing a pair of eastern phoebes in Pennsylvania. The phoebes had built a nest above a small cave near a stream. As the young man sat nearby to watch them day after day, the slim gray birds grew accustomed to his presence. When the young phoebes in the nest were almost old enough to fly, Audubon marked each one by tying a silver thread securely around one leg.

The following spring, exploring up and down streams in the area, Audubon found two of his marked phoebes, attending their own nests. It was the first definite proof that young songbirds, after migrating away, were likely to return to the place where they had hatched. The point has been confirmed countless times by later generations of bird banders.

Through simple observation, Audubon pioneered other ideas. At a time when the very concept of migration was still a novelty, he was among the first to assert that many small birds migrate at night. In his *Ornithological Biography,* published during the 1830s, he wrote this about his first sighting of the phoebes: "I concluded also that these birds must have reached this haven, either during the night, or at the very dawn of that morn. Hundreds of observations have since proved to me that this species always migrates by night." Describing the passage of the yellow warbler near the Gulf Coast, he wrote: "Its migration, in as far as I have been able to ascertain, is principally performed during the night. I have observed many in the course of one day in a place, which, next day, if the weather had become warm, scarcely contained a single individual."

It's one thing to deduce that songbirds must migrate at night. It's quite another thing to observe them in the act. Decades after Audubon, people started figuring out ways to do that.

On a clear night with southerly winds during spring migration, if you aim a telescope at the moon high overhead, eventually you will see a bird fly across the moon's face. If you keep watching, you'll see more. If you keep a count and note the bearing of each, you can extrapolate from your visible sliver to the whole sky and calculate the overall rate and direction of nocturnal migration.

This method was put to good use by George Lowery, a Louisiana ornithologist, during an epic argument in the 1940s. Lowery was a leading proponent of trans-Gulf migration: the idea that vast numbers of songbirds flew north across the Gulf of Mexico, from the Yucatán Peninsula to Louisiana and other Gulf Coast areas, every spring. A Texas ornithologist, George Williams, argued that most migrants went *around* the Gulf in spring — in other words, north through Texas. State pride was at stake. Finally, in 1946, Lowery published a definitive defense of the trans-Gulf theory. One of his lines of evidence: he had perched on a ship anchored on the north coast of Yucatán and aimed his telescope at the moon on nights in May. All the birds that crossed his line of sight were headed straight north, across the Gulf.

It was a good method for the time, but this approach was about to be supplanted by something much more high-tech: the use of radar.

Radar—short for "radio detecting and ranging"—is a system that "listens" for echoes, using radio waves instead of sound waves. The radar unit shoots out pulses of radio waves and then captures any signal that bounces back. The timing and strength of the returned signal help determine how far away an object is, and how large.

The first major practical use of radar was for detecting aircraft. During the 1930s several nations pushed to develop radar technology for military use in the buildup to war. Scientists in Britain, trying to perfect their systems for detecting enemy planes, were plagued by mysterious images showing up on their screens. One night in March 1941, for example, the Royal Air Force went on red alert when radar showed numerous blips moving across the Channel from France toward the southern coast of England. German bombing raids were ongoing that spring, and this appeared to be a big one; but as the echoes approached the coast, they broke up and faded. A similar invasion of phantom echoes appeared the next night, and again later in the season. RAF fighters were even sent out to intercept these shadows, but they found nothing. Military leaders worried that the Germans had systems to fool the radar, jamming it with false signals, to cover a real invasion. The pattern of northbound echoes at night continued for weeks and finally ended, still unexplained, at the approach of summer.

With the improvement and spread of radar systems after the war, similar echoes—now dubbed "angels"—were seen all over the world. In some circles they were still considered unsolved mysteries. Ornithologists had suspected the truth almost from the beginning, but it took years before military leaders would admit that those sinister echoes moving north across the English Channel in spring had been caused by something as small as migratory song-birds.

By that time radar ornithology was about to gain recognition as a genuine science.

The first thorough network of weather radar stations in the United States, the WSR-57 system (weather surveillance radar, de-signed in 1957), was deployed beginning in the late 1950s. In Lou-isiana, WSR-57 units were established at New Orleans and Lake Charles. George Lowery, who had championed the study of trans-Gulf flights, was still a professor at Louisiana State University; one of his grad students, Sidney Gauthreaux, became fascinated with the potential for radar studies. With Lowery's enthusiastic sup-port, Gauthreaux spent his spring seasons learning how to analyze the echoes of migrating birds on radar. Birds were taking off from Yucatán just after dark, but most of them took more than twelve hours to cross the Gulf, so they were arriving over Louisiana in daylight the next day. With binoculars and telescope aimed at the sky, Gauthreaux was able to see the birds coming in overhead and work out the conversion between the observed "traffic rate" and the density of echoes on the radar screen. His published results helped establish the foundation for all future studies.

Gauthreaux went on to teach at Clemson University in South Carolina. He continued to study migration by radar, but his in-terest went through the roof in the early 1990s when he got his first look at the brand-new weather radar system: the WSR-88D, or Nexrad. Short for "next generation radar," Nexrad was radically better than the previous system, far more powerful and far more sensitive in its resolution. And it used Doppler technology—not only could it find things in the atmosphere, it could determine which direction they were moving in and how fast. The new system was better for tracking details of weather, and as Gauthreaux pointed out, it was also vastly better for tracking birds. Data produced by Nexrad have kept the Radar Ornithology Lab at Clemson hopping with activity ever since.

Today the output from the whole Nexrad network—more than 160 radar units, evenly spaced across the United States—can be accessed in real time via websites and smartphone apps. Ornithologists are applying more and more sophisticated analyses to these radar data, but now thousands of birders watch them as well.

For many of us it has become a nightly ritual in spring to go online and look. If it's a big night for migration, birds will take off just after dark, eventually rising far enough to register on radar. The circular sweep of the beam from each radar unit picks them up as a broad ring of confetti in pale blue. We can see blotches of green and yellow and orange elsewhere on the map, indicating major storms, but those wide blue circles tell us that birds are on the move.

On our computer screens or on our phones, we watch the echoes of nocturnal migration as it happens. Any birder today can get a comprehensive, real-time view that ornithologists of the past never would have imagined.

But even as we watch the night flights develop and pass overhead, we're left with questions. Yes, we can see birds moving en masse. We can figure out what directions they're moving in and how fast, and we can deduce at least a rough index of their total numbers. But how can we possibly tell what kinds of birds are moving on a particular night?

•   •   •

When songbirds migrate at night, they are not silent. They give occasional callnotes as they fly. The reasons for this are not obvious, and the callnotes themselves are similarly obscure: usually very short, one-syllable sounds, and often different from the common callnotes that the same birds give in daylight. If you stand outdoors on a quiet night, away from city noises, you can hear the soft voices of these travelers overhead in the dark.

As long ago as 1896, an ornithologist named Olin Libby sat on a hilltop near Madison, Wisconsin, on a September night, counting the flight calls of migrants. In the space of about five hours, lasting until three in the morning, he counted 3,800 callnotes, giving a hint of the enormous numbers of birds passing overhead.

Libby couldn't name most of the birds he heard beyond broad categories, such as "the harsh squawk of a water bird" or "the fine shrill notes of the smaller Sparrows or Warblers." But within a few years people were actively working on trying to pin down identifications for these mysterious nocturnal calls. By 1916, Winsor Tyler was writing about certain distinctive calls he'd heard at night in Massachusetts, tying them to particular birds by their peak dates or by tracking them down at dusk when the birds were taking off. By the late 1940s, Stanley Ball had figured out the nocturnal flight calls of four species of brown thrushes and was using those calls to document timing of migration of those birds in eastern Quebec. But after that there was little progress for several decades.

In the 1980s an independent researcher named Bill Evans started working seriously on identifying more of the night flight calls. He produced a cassette tape of thrush calls in 1990, attracting the attention of ace birder Michael O'Brien, who was studying the same subject on his own. Evans and O'Brien teamed up to continue the detective work, pooling their knowledge and their hundreds of recordings of birds calling in flight. Many of the light, thin little calls, seemingly identical at first, became more distinctive if analyzed spectrographically, printed out as visual representations.

By matching up "mystery calls" with known timing and routes of migration, and by occasionally finding the birds giving the same calls in the daytime, Evans and O'Brien gradually were able to assign notes to more and more species. When they released the results of their research in 2002, on a CD-ROM that included sound recordings, text, and visual spectrograms, it was a watershed moment for active birders. We all bought the CD-ROM and spent hours studying the various seeps and chirps, working to recognize more of the nighttime sounds.

But Bill Evans wanted to go beyond merely helping birders to identify more birds. He envisioned using nocturnal flight calls to actually monitor migrations in a standardized way. He developed a microphone setup specifically designed for aiming at the sky to pick up these night sounds. While the mic itself was a high-tech device, the rest of the setup was an ingenious combination of cheap, simple items like a dinner plate, a flowerpot, plastic wrap, and duct tape. It furnished an affordable way to automatically record a whole night's worth of flight calls.

At the same time, other scientists were working on software to analyze these recordings. Eventually it became possible for anyone, with a little effort, to record an entire night's worth of sounds from the sky, then run the recording through software that would count the flight calls and identify many of them. This opened the door for automated stations that could be run every night, all season, monitoring the birds passing overhead in a new way.

• • •

Monitoring of night flight calls, like radar studies and long-term bird-banding stations, can give insight into the passage of migrants through a specific area. But what if we could come at the subject from the opposite direction, by following an individual bird in its travels?

Actually we've been doing that for decades, at least with a few larger species. In the early 1980s scientists at Johns Hopkins University worked to develop tracking transmitters small enough to be placed on birds. The transmitters would send signals to satellites, using the same general technology that the satellites used to receive signals from buoys and weather balloons. These early devices were marvels of miniaturization, but they still weighed about six ounces, twice as much as a robin or starling, so they weren't appropriate for use on anything but the largest birds. In 1984 these experimental transmitters were attached to a bald eagle in Maryland and a few swans in Alaska. The researchers successfully used satellite data to track a couple of the swans for several weeks and the eagle for nine months, proving the concept.

In following years satellite tracking was used for albatrosses and other seabirds, ospreys, and other large birds. By 2005 continued improvements in the transmitters had them down to about a third of an ounce, light enough to be used on some of the largest sandpipers. Years of data had produced some amazing stories: An albatross that flew more than three thousand miles in a single foraging trip away from the nesting colony. A sandpiper called a whimbrel that literally flew through a hurricane in the Caribbean while migrating from Canada to South America. Another sandpiper, a bar-tailed godwit, traveling nonstop from Alaska to New Zealand, a trip that took eight days of continuous flying.

Reading about these studies, we were excited about each new

revelation. But the satellite transmitters were still too heavy and bulky to be attached to most songbirds, so we were still in the dark about the movements of the most abundant migrants.

The case was finally cracked open by a completely different technology: light-level geolocators. These ingenious devices were designed to measure the level of ambient light at intervals (as often as once every minute) and then store that information along with a time stamp. Because they don't have to transmit the information, they can be very small and lightweight and they use very little power. The downside is that the geolocators have to be recovered before the information can be retrieved from them. But for migratory birds returning annually to the same breeding territory or the same wintering territory, unlike those captured during migratory stopovers, there's a fair chance that the same individual can be recaptured a year later.

Why record the level of light? It's the simplest measurement that can give a key to location. The shift from darkness to light and from light to dark provides the time of local sunrise and sunset; the time halfway between, or local noon, gives a good reading of longitude. The length of the daylight hours, combined with the date, provides a rough idea of latitude. These measurements aren't precise, but they can usually fix a location within a hundred miles or so, good enough for detecting general patterns of movement.

Scientists with the British Antarctic Survey originally had used light-level geolocators to track elephant seals and albatrosses, but by 2007 the smallest such devices had been brought down to about one twentieth of an ounce. Dr. Bridget Stutchbury was the first to try them out on songbirds. Working in western Pennsylvania, she and her team attached geolocators to fourteen wood thrushes and twenty purple martins in the summer of 2007. These birds all migrated to the tropics that fall, of course, as they always do. But the following spring five of the thrushes and two of the martins returned to the study area, and Stutchbury was able to recapture them and retrieve the geolocators.

The data downloaded from these devices revealed the whole story of each bird's travel. Look: this wood thrush spent a couple of weeks on the central Atlantic Coast and a couple more in the southeastern states before flying across the Gulf of Mexico, winding up in Nicaragua in the first week of November. This purple martin wandered around the Amazon Basin in Brazil until almost the middle of April and then moved north rapidly, reaching Pennsylvania in less than two weeks. Never before had we had such a glimpse into the individual journeys of these small creatures.

That was just the beginning. Stutchbury and her team followed up with many more studies. Wood thrushes are faithful to individual winter territories in the tropics, so the researchers were able to tag and recapture individuals wintering in Belize and Costa Rica. They were able to compare the migrations of the same individuals in different years, confirming that these wood thrushes were consistent in their timing but more variable in the routes they took. As further refinements made geolocators even smaller and more efficient, it became possible to use them on songbirds as small as warblers. Studies are still expanding and producing new insights.

Although we are a long way from understanding the mysterious, endless parade of bird migration, we are constantly picking up new kinds of clues. A light-level geolocator can give us a whole year's worth of data on a single bird, if we can catch the bird again to retrieve it. For larger species, a satellite tag can track the individual all year in real time. Radar studies can tell us a lot about the magnitude and direction of a movement of birds over a local region. Recordings of nocturnal flight calls can tell us something about which birds are moving overhead on a given night. And a long-term banding study in a stopover site, like the one carried on by BSBO at the Navarre Marsh, can provide a detailed baseline on the migrants passing through one spot.

When a bird is given a unique numbered band at a site like Navarre, it serves mainly to identify that individual while it stays at that site and is captured again, allowing researchers to learn about its stopover behavior. Occasionally, though, such a marked bird will be recaptured somewhere else, revealing things about the route and timing of its travels. Such "foreign recoveries," as they're called, are not common, but they do happen.

On May 18, 2015, volunteers at Navarre reached into a mist net and pulled out a gray-cheeked thrush. It was the peak of migration for these slim, shy, gray-brown birds, and many were lurking in the thickets around the banding station that day. But this one was special: it already wore a band. When the volunteers took a closer look, they realized this bird was a foreign recovery in every way—the band wasn't from the United States or Canada. Mark Shieldcastle followed up and discovered that the thrush had been banded the previous spring in Colombia, South America.

The Santa Marta Mountains in northern Colombia, at the northwestern rim of South America, represent a major stopover area for migrating thrushes. Every spring big numbers of gray-cheeked thrushes, moving north from wintering territories in the Amazon Basin, pause in the Santa Martas to feed and fatten up. They need their strength for the long haul north across the Caribbean and into North America, headed for breeding grounds across Canada, Alaska, and eastern Siberia. Over the course of six springs, researchers from the Colombian organization SELVA had banded more than two thousand migrating gray-cheeked thrushes there. Out of all these, the bird recaptured at Navarre was the first one ever to be found in North America.

It wouldn't be the last. By the end of spring 2016, the number of gray-cheeks from the Santa Martas detected in North America had jumped from zero to forty-four.

Why the abrupt change? It wasn't luck or coincidence, and it didn't reflect a sudden deployment of large numbers of mist nets in the north. It was the result of a new technology and a new approach, the Motus system.

"Motus" sounds like an acronym but actually comes from the Latin word for movement. The system is based on very small radio transmitters that send out an identifying signal at regular intervals. Of course, variations on that approach have been used for decades. Larger versions of such devices form the basis of satellite tagging, but radios powerful enough to send a signal to a satellite are still too large and heavy to be carried by most songbirds. Tiny transmitters have been used to track birds as small as warblers on a local level, but these studies are labor-intensive, since a researcher must go out with a directional antenna to find the creature and usually must get within a couple of miles to pick up its signal at all.

However, the Motus system doesn't involve sending out grad students with antennas and battery packs. Instead it relies on a network of stationary receivers that scan for signals twenty-four hours a day year-round. Mounted on short towers, these receivers can detect any Motus-tagged creature that passes within about nine miles. The tiny Motus transmitters, or nanotags—some of which weigh less than one one-hundredth of an ounce—all transmit on the same frequency, and each has a unique digital signature so it can be identified individually. Every researcher involved registers his or her nanotags with Motus to avoid any overlap in tag IDs.

Results have been spectacular. The first experimental trials began in 2012. Within its first five years the system had been used to track more than nine thousand individual birds (as well as nine species of bats, and even large insects like dragonflies). More than 550 receiving towers had been deployed from Canada to northern South America, and these towers had detected tagged individuals a staggering 250 million times. With several radio pulses per minute, of course, most of those detections happened near where the birds were originally tagged; but in some projects, more than 80 percent of the individuals were later detected away from the original site. Every study so far has turned up surprising new things about the movements of small creatures.

One of those studies focused on migratory gray-cheeked thrushes, coming north from wintering grounds deep in the interior of South America, pausing in spring in the Santa Marta Mountains of Colombia. Scientists from SELVA already had several seasons' worth of experience with thrushes there, so they added Motus technology to their work. During the spring seasons of 2015 and 2016, they attached nanotags to 133 gray-cheeked thrushes and then kept tabs on their local movements by way of two Motus receiving towers near the study area.

Most of the thrushes stayed in the area for several days, feeding and fattening up for their next flight. When the signals from a particular nanotag faded and then blinked out shortly after sunset, the researchers could surmise that that bird was on its way north.

Astonishingly, in those two springs, fully one third of the tagged birds were detected again by Motus towers in North America. Signals from 43 of the 133 tags were picked up either along the

Gulf Coast or in the general region of the Great Lakes. For a number of these birds, the timing suggested that they had flown non-stop from South America.

On May 8, 2016, one such tagged thrush departed from the study site in South America, the last detection coming a couple of minutes after nine in the evening. Just forty-six hours later, its unmistakable signal was picked up by a Motus tower in southern Ontario. This champion thrush evidently had flown without a pause across the Caribbean and across the eastern half of the United States, going from Colombia to Canada at an average speed of about forty-seven miles per hour. Even assuming it had good tailwinds to help it along, the feat was remarkable. And prior to the Motus project, no one would have guessed that this modestly colored little bird would make such a trip as a nonstop flight.

At the end of this long chapter about bird migration, I have to admit that it's really all about humans. We observed this, we developed this theory, we tried this, we ran these experiments, we captured these birds and tasked them with carrying these devices for our own education.

I love science and I hate it. I love pushing the frontiers of knowledge, learning every new thing, finding every little piece of the puzzle that will tell us more. Humans have an unquenchable drive to explore and discover and learn. It's part of what defines us as a species. Science is in our DNA; science is the reason we even know we *have* DNA. Just as a tiger has the instinct to stalk its prey through the jungle, a human has the instinct to pursue knowledge. But migratory birds are different from us.

Even though our knowledge about them is all recent, they have been migrating for many thousands of years. They would be migrating whether or not we paid any attention to them. The birds are living their lives, and they have no reason to care about us.

From a practical viewpoint, from a bird conservation viewpoint, it's important for us to know as much as possible so that we can work for the survival of their species. That's how we justify all this research, all the times when we may have inconvenienced the birds, possibly even risked harming them, by capturing them repeatedly and fitting them out with markers or electronic devices. The idea is that we will learn enough to help the species as a whole. If I stop and think about it, I firmly believe that's true and believe the research is worth it.

In a way, we know more about their travels than they do. I have mixed feelings about that. I'm stuck with human instincts, so I can't help being addicted to knowledge. I follow all the research, eagerly reading every new published study, hoping to glean a little more understanding.

But at some level I rebel against the science, too. At some level I would trade it all for the chance to become one of these migrants for just one night. I would give away all the knowledge in exchange for the feeling—to be a bird, flinging myself into the night sky with nothing but the simple faith of instinct, flying wildly into the unknown.

9

Threading the Needle

On my way to the bird observatory one April morning I stopped by the Boss Unit. This small area, managed by Ottawa National Wildlife Refuge, is on a separate tract south of Route 2. It was farm ground until a few years ago, but it was farm ground that flooded every spring, so the refuge was able to buy it and turn it into wildlife habitat. Now every spring, before the marsh grass grows up too high, it serves as a stopover site for migrating shorebirds.

I parked in the gravel lot at the corner of the unit and started scanning west and south. A few ducks were swimming in open water toward the far side of the tract, but I was looking for less obvious birds. Studying the patchwork of water, soggy mudflats, and beaten-down marsh, I soon began to pick out the expected shorebirds. Several lesser yellowlegs waded in the shallows, slim and elegant, their eponymous yellow legs half submerged. At the water's edge a few Wilson's snipes skulked quietly, probing the mud, blending in against the dead reeds with their pattern of bars and stripes. About two dozen pectoral sandpipers, equally well camouflaged in streaky brown, hunched along in short grass and bare soil toward the south side of the area. I scanned in vain for the flock of golden plovers that had stopped there a few days before.

The term "shorebird," as used by American birders, is confusing to nonbirders. It might seem logical to apply it to any bird on a shore, but in fact we use it only for certain taxonomic groups: the sandpipers, plovers, and their relatives. (Gulls, herons, pelicans, and most others are excluded.) And shorebirds often spend time in surroundings most people wouldn't label as "shore." In spring some of the largest flights of these migrants go through the Great Plains, east of the Rocky Mountains and west of the Mississippi River, about as far from the coast as you can get. There are places in Kansas and Oklahoma that host more shorebirds than we'll ever see here in Ohio. But for a location halfway between the coast and the Great Plains, the Lake Erie region in northern Ohio offers good shorebird-watching, and we take advantage of it every spring and fall.

The name "sandpiper" is misleading, too, because most don't seem to appreciate sand. Go out to a beach along the coast and you may see flocks of little sanderlings chasing the waves, pattering along on short legs like wind-up toys, and perhaps a few others. But most sandpipers won't be there, because they're more like mudpipers or grasspipers, really. During their migrations most will stop over on muddy tidal flats, edges of rivers or lakes, flooded farm fields, or even the impoundments at sewage treatment plants. Birders who seek them are often in places that most people wouldn't go.

For shorebirds as a group, long migrations are standard. More than three dozen kinds of shorebirds occur regularly here in Ohio, and all are migratory. One, the killdeer, a noisy plover of open fields, can be found year-round in southern Ohio, though it vacates the northern part of the state in winter. Another three species stay through summer to nest here in small numbers. The other thirty-plus are simply transients, passing through in spring and/or in fall. At least two thirds of those transients go very far north for the summer, to northern Canada or Alaska, even to tundra far north of the Arctic Circle. Most turn around and go very far south in fall, and more than a dozen species fly all the way to southern South America. These birds are strong and graceful fliers because they have to be, because their journeys span the entire length of the Americas. When they stop to visit us on their way through, I can't help but regard them with awe.

Despite their herculean journeys, migrating shorebirds often go unnoticed, especially inland. Along the coast, on some large muddy estuaries or bays, the sheer numbers of small waders spread across the flats at low tide may be obvious, even to a casual observer. Inland, though, their good stopover sites are less predictable. We observe that every year in northwestern Ohio: tens of thousands of shorebirds come through here, but it takes a serious effort to see even a fraction of them.

Shorebirds undoubtedly have been using this region as a stopover for millennia. Historically, when the western Lake Erie marshes and the Great Black Swamp occupied vast tracts, there always would have been prime spots: those ephemeral boundaries where the shallowest water meets the edge of the wettest soil. The sites would have shifted from day to day, or even hour to hour, as water levels changed, but in the wide-open territory the birds would have had no trouble shifting and adapting.

Now humans have broken the land into artificial sections. The

farm country is divided up by roads. The protected wildlife sanctuaries are divided up by dikes, canals, and other water-control
structures. On the national wildlife refuge and state wildlife areas,
managers may try to create ideal shallow waters and mudflats for
the birds, but they have to deal with malfunctioning pumps, broken floodgates, sudden deluges that flood the impoundments, and
the ever-present need to control invasive nonnative plants. It's
no wonder that some of the best temporary sites for shorebirds
spring up by accident on flooded farm fields. Migrating plovers
and sandpipers, winging over the region a thousand feet up, spot
these prime sites and drop in to take advantage. Birders, driving
random roads through hundreds of square miles of farmland, can
only hope to find these concentrations while they last.

Spring shorebird migration through northwestern Ohio begins
by late February and lasts into the second week of June. This spot,
the Boss Unit, ceases to be ideal for them by sometime in May, as
grass grows up too tall to leave any open flats. But I will stop here
dozens of times up to that point, since it's such an easy place for a
quick spot-check.

On this April morning I had completed my scan and was turning to leave when a sharp, high whistle spun me around. A lone
bird was arrowing in from the west with quick, flicking wingbeats,
circling once and then alighting in the shallow water. Even as I
raised my binoculars, I knew what it was: a solitary sandpiper, the
first I'd seen this year. It was slim and delicate like the lesser yellowlegs but even smaller, barely the size of a robin. Darker brown
than most sandpipers, it had a bold white ring around each eye,
making it look hyperalert or surprised. It stood still for a moment,
bobbing its head back and forth nervously, looking around.

Right on time, I said to myself. Every year, predictably, the first solitary sandpipers arrive here in early April. By the time they show up, killdeers have been around for almost two months, and greater yellowlegs and lesser yellowlegs have been passing through for at least a few weeks. But the solitary sandpipers aren't late to the shorebird party — they usually get here ahead of the least sandpipers and short-billed dowitchers, and weeks before the first ruddy turnstones reach Ohio.

That's one of the fascinating things about migration. Despite a few odd individuals that show up out of order, the general sequence of arrivals is remarkably consistent from year to year.

One pleasure of watching spring migration in a single place is becoming familiar with the timing of things. Small variations from year to year are interesting, but the larger lesson is that the overall patterns stay the same. Different groups and different species of birds arrive, depart, or pass through in peak numbers in a predictable sequence. After a few springs of birding in one spot, we can forecast which migrants will be next to appear. It's like listening to a favorite piece of music: after hearing it many times, we know exactly what's coming next, and we anticipate our favorite passages and savor them while they last. Familiarity doesn't breed contempt; it breeds love of the reassuring, predictable wholeness of the season.

After a decade in northwestern Ohio I had memorized the whole symphony of the spring bird migration, from the tentative opening notes in February until the last chords faded away in June. One thing had become apparent: big shifts in the weather of a season won't change the overall pattern of bird movement. Yes, big flights take place on days or nights with the most favorable winds, but weather in general doesn't have much effect on changing broad patterns. For example, snow buntings, visiting from the

High Arctic, may swirl over fields by the hundreds during January, but their flocks are already pulling out by the first of March. Even if it's an exceptionally cold spring, they won't linger into May. Red-eyed vireos, drab but persistent singers of the treetops, start to show up at the end of April and reach peak numbers in the latter part of May. Even if record heat strikes earlier in spring, they won't bump up their schedules for an earlier arrival.

Scientists sometimes divide migratory birds into a couple of categories, "obligate" migrants and "facultative" migrants. Saying "hard-wired" and "flexible" would work just as well. Most birds fall somewhere on the spectrum between these ideals, but the majority are closer to the first type: the timing, direction, and distance of their movements are dictated by instinct and not subject to much variation. A few are more flexible. They still operate on a rough schedule, but their timing may vary by a couple of weeks or even more, depending on weather conditions.

These more flexible migrants tend to be from species that travel only short distances, which makes sense. In fall, some types of waterfowl in the interior of the continent may linger at northerly latitudes until waters freeze up and force them to move out. They may fly only as far as necessary to get to open water. In late winter or early spring, a few kinds of birds wintering in the southeastern states may begin to move early if the season is mild. They can make short hops northward, gauging the weather each step of the way, pausing if they run into bad conditions. A few birds like this may arrive well ahead of schedule in a warm spring. But they are the exceptions.

Most of the consistent patterns of spring timing make sense if we think about them a little. Here in Ohio, crows and blackbirds are among the earliest migrants. These are tough and adaptable omnivores, able to find food even under harsh conditions, so they can survive the weather swings on the edge between winter and spring. By comparison, the flycatchers, as a group, are the latest spring migrants here. These birds feed mostly on insects captured in midair, and of course it's hard to find insects flying in cold weather; in northern Ohio, peak flycatcher migration is in late May. At a casual glance, it all seems perfectly logical.

Questions start to crop up when we take a closer look and start to study variations within groups. Some of my favorite mysteries along these lines involve shorebirds. Differences in timing among certain shorebird species are not easily explained.

During my stop at the Boss Unit on this April morning, I wasn't surprised to see pectoral sandpipers. After all, the first flock had shown up a month earlier, and I'd been seeing them regularly since. I knew that these chunky, streaky sandpipers were more impressive than they looked: they had already come six thousand miles from their wintering grounds in southern South America, and some of them might go equally far beyond here, passing through Alaska and continuing far west into Siberia. They weren't flaunting their exploits, though. Today they were all business, foraging quietly in the short grass.

That quiet demeanor was going to change, I knew, when they got to the breeding grounds. On the windswept tundra near Point Barrow, the northernmost tip of land in Alaska, I have watched in amazement as male pectoral sandpipers perform their courtship displays. Standing atop a high hummock, a male makes growling, squawking, coughing sounds, then puffs out his body to a ridiculous degree by inflating special air sacs under the feathers of his throat and chest. Launching into the air, he flies with slow, deep, exaggerated wingbeats, looking like a blobby brown balloon, making a series of low, throbbing hoots: *doob doob doob* . . . The whole thing is bizarre and more than a little comical. So graceful and strong in normal flight, the pectoral sandpiper transforms himself into a dorky showoff in courtship. (Just as with males everywhere, making fools of ourselves for love.) It's weird, but it's unforgettable.

Pectoral sandpipers are not the only shorebirds near Point Barrow. On multiple trips there, brief visits in June or July of several years, I usually saw at least fifteen shorebird species. They made up a major feature of that strangely beautiful landscape, and I came to think of them as "tundrabirds" at that season. Most of the shorebirds there belonged to species that pass through Ohio on migration, and several had winter ranges overlapping with that of the pectoral sandpipers in southern South America. Of that lot, the most interesting to me were trim, long-winged birds with the inelegant name of white-rumped sandpiper.

White-rumped sandpipers are often overlooked, even by birders (the trademark white patch on the rump feathers is usually hidden by the wingtips except during flight). Their courtship displays aren't nearly as crazy as those of the pectorals. But white-rumps are extreme in other ways. They nest very far north, up to the islands of the Canadian High Arctic. They winter as far south as they possibly can, down to the southernmost tip of South America and on the Falkland Islands, and they have been known to cross the Drake Passage and wind up on the Antarctic continent.

Over most of their range in summer and winter, though, white-rumped sandpipers overlap completely with pectoral sandpipers. Both species migrate through my region of Ohio in good numbers in spring. Both come here from South America. But they don't arrive together. Pectorals show up in March, or even at the end of February. White-rumps rarely appear before the end of April, and more typically the first sightings are in May.

We still don't know much about the northward movements of shorebirds through South America. It's a big continent with many regions that are difficult to survey, and until recently there weren't many resident birders or ornithologists. Winter ranges have been mapped out fairly well—after all, the birds are present there for months—but migrants passing through are easy to miss. Even so, we have enough data for some general comparisons. Pectoral sandpipers don't seem to have major stopover areas in South America; they move north on a broad front, and early, with major flocks reaching North America by the beginning of March. White-rumped sandpipers start north much later, with hundreds still present in southern Argentina in May. Many apparently stop over in northern South America, on seasonally flooded grasslands or on shallow flats along the coast. Surveys on the wide-open llanos of Venezuela found the first white-rumps in late April, with peak numbers in mid-May. A little farther east, on the coast of Suriname, some passed through as late as mid-June.

So these two related types of sandpipers, sharing much of the same summering range and wintering range, are strikingly different in the timing and strategy of their spring migration. Pectorals arrive early in North America and may spend weeks in the lower forty-eight states and southern Canada, feeding and building up their stores of essential body fat before making the final push to the Arctic. White-rumps reach North America much later and pass through the temperate latitudes in a much shorter period of time.

But why? What dictates the timing of a bird's travels?

Most migratory birds don't make conscious choices about what time of year to migrate or where to go. For most it's a hard-wired instinct, one that has evolved over thousands of generations. If they could consider their options and make decisions, they'd be trying to balance certain demands. Timing of actual arrival on the breeding grounds is critical: Males need to be there early enough to claim the best territories. Females need to arrive while males holding good territories are still unmated. So there's pressure to move in as early as possible. But if they arrive too early, before winter has loosened its grip, then harsh weather and lack of available food may be fatal.

For a bird to hit the perfect date at its destination is like threading a needle, except that the needle is moving, because no two springs are exactly the same. If it's an unusually warm season, birds with an instinct to arrive earlier than the norm may have an advantage. If the season is exceptionally cold, the early birds may die, and those with an instinct to arrive slightly later may be the most successful ones.

Timing of final arrival is only half the story. The migratory flight may be like a marathon, but unlike a human runner, a bird can't burn up all its energy to cross the finish line and then collapse in triumph and exhaustion. Instead it must arrive poised for action. In addition to the usual pressures of having to find food and evade predators just to survive, the bird must defend a territory, find a mate, and succeed at the challenging task of raising young.

So in addition to arriving at the right time, ideally the bird must arrive in good physical shape. This is where its migration strategy comes in. If its journey is a long one, it must have stopovers where it can rest, feed, and build up its strength and its fat reserves, so that it reaches the breeding grounds in peak condition.

Some key stopover sites have been studied in detail. Along the shores of Delaware Bay on our Mid-Atlantic coast, hundreds of thousands of shorebirds of several species converge in May. That's the season when horseshoe crabs, ancient arthropods from the deep, crawl up on the beach to lay their eggs. Each female crab lays tens of thousands of eggs. For a time, on some beaches, their millions of small, round, greenish eggs seem to outnumber the grains of sand. Migrating shorebirds — red knots, semipalmated sandpipers, ruddy turnstones, and others — arrive from wintering grounds in South America and gorge on horseshoe crab eggs, fattening up for their final long flight to the Arctic tundra. In recent decades bird conservationists on the Eastern Seaboard have fought to stop overfishing of the crabs, to keep this whole migration system from collapsing.

The Delaware Bay phenomenon may be the best-known shorebird stopover site, but there are other large concentration points on all our coastlines and on the Great Plains, and several moderately large ones, including the wetlands of northwestern Ohio. All of these sites are vulnerable. If habitats are destroyed — or if a changing climate makes the areas too wet or too dry, too hot or too cold, when the birds arrive — the systems of migration can break down, leaving the shorebirds ill-prepared for the final stages of their journeys.

Of course changes are already under way. The shifts in climate will have some effect on practically all migratory birds. Since most are more or less locked into instinct, unable to make big alterations in the timing or routes of their journeys, won't they be doomed as conditions change?

Not necessarily. The individual birds may not be able to change their timing by much, but the species can. Over the last few decades, at several points in the Northern Hemisphere researchers have found migrants posting earlier average returns in spring, including some arriving as much as two weeks earlier. It seems they've already responded to the advancing warmth of the season.

The seeds of change are always present. In any population of migrants, some individuals will travel earlier or later than the average. If spring heats up earlier than in the past, that will benefit the birds that arrive early. If they raise more young successfully than migrants that came later, the genes for early migration may be passed along to more of the next generation. Over time, if warm springs become standard, the local population will evolve toward earlier arrival dates.

That's an oversimplification, of course. As detailed studies come in from all points of the birds' annual cycles, we're learning how much more complicated the reality can be.

One long-term study looked at a small songbird, a warbler called the American redstart, wintering on the Caribbean island of Jamaica. The redstarts had been marked with unique combinations of colored bands so researchers could recognize individuals and follow their behavior each winter. In seasons of extreme drought—leading to a scarcity of the insects that the redstarts ate—the birds would depart later in the spring, by as much as five days, as if it had taken them longer to build up their strength for traveling. Another study of redstarts, on breeding grounds in far northern Michigan, found that the birds arrived earlier than average in warmer springs. A likely explanation was that they had encountered favorable warm conditions all along their route, allowing them to fatten up quickly at their stopover sites and make faster progress northward.

Of course, these are individual responses to conditions of the moment. They won't be passed along genetically to their offspring. But some other factors may come into play, as suggested by many years of study of a shorebird in Iceland, a big sandpiper called the black-tailed godwit.

The Icelandic breeding population of godwits migrates to western Europe for the winter, returning to Iceland between mid-April and mid-May. Observations of color-banded birds have shown that they are very consistent in their return dates. As individuals they are not coming back any earlier or later, regardless of the season's weather. However, weather can affect the timing of their breeding activities and the date when they lay their first eggs. In a warm spring they may start almost right away; in a cold spring they may wait. Incubation takes a little over three weeks, so the godwits' eggs may hatch any time between early June and July.

This is where it gets strange. Researchers followed the fortunes of nesting pairs, color-banding the young in the nest so they knew the histories of those individuals. What they learned was startling: young birds that hatched earlier in the season would also return to Iceland earlier the next spring, establishing the pattern they would follow thereafter. In other words, the timing of their migration was not inherited directly from their parents; instead it somehow resulted from the timing of their hatching. No one is quite sure how this works, but it has resulted in a shift in the overall timing of migration, as more and more of the young godwits (hatched early in warm seasons) come back earlier in the spring.

So one way or another the birds will adapt, it seems, or at least some of them will, as the climate changes. The shorebirds, if they survive, will have to continue to migrate. No conceivable amount of warming would make it possible for them to thrive on the Arctic tundra year-round. No matter what we do to the atmosphere, Point Barrow will still have nine weeks of continuous darkness centered on the winter solstice, and the pectoral sandpipers will have to go elsewhere. They, like so many other shorebirds, will have to take to the air for thousands of miles, and probably some will continue to vault all the way to the opposite end of the Western Hemisphere.

From our vantage point in northwestern Ohio, it will be hard to track any changes in shorebird migration. Big changes in annual numbers of shorebirds here, and some differences in timing, are mostly caused by temporary local conditions: briefly flooded farm fields, briefly perfect shallow units in the wildlife areas. We take advantage of the good concentrations while they last and try to discern what we can about the larger picture.

Right now, in April, we're still ahead of the peak passage. Right now we're in the stage when shorebirds linger here, building their strength and biding their time before pushing on northward. They will pick up the pace later, as numbers and variety pick up also.

In this region it will be hard to focus on peak shorebird migration in May, because that also will be the peak for a dazzling variety of colorful songbirds — warblers, tanagers, orioles, grosbeaks, vireos, thrushes, and others — arriving from the tropics. Those are the migrants for which northwestern Ohio is famous. Still, at the same time that birders are staring in rapt attention at warblers in the trees along Lake Erie, flocks of shorebirds will be circling over the marshes and mudflats behind them.

May is the time when northwestern Ohio sees a special category of shorebirds: those that are scarce all over the interior of the

East except in the immediate area of the Great Lakes. Sanderlings, ruddy turnstones, dunlins, and black-bellied plovers are examples of this group. They may be arriving via nonstop flights from the Gulf Coast, about eight hundred miles to the south of us, or they may be angling northwest from points on the Atlantic Coast, on their way to the High Arctic of western Canada or Alaska. Either way, when they pause in the counties close to Lake Erie, they convey a sense of urgency and restlessness.

The dunlins in particular add to the background sense of excitement. A few are around earlier in the spring, but their numbers will pick up considerably around the second week of May. They'll be coming into full breeding plumage then, bright reddish brown on their upper parts (they used to be called red-backed sandpipers) and whitish below, with contrasting black belly patches. Flocks of them will gather anyplace they can find very shallow waters right next to open flats. Moving about nervously, probing in the mud with their long bills, they will forage for a few minutes and then pick up to fly around.

Even more than most sandpipers, dunlins are masters of synchronized flying. They're fast — their normal cruising flight has been clocked at fifty miles per hour — and they'll fly in dense flocks of dozens or even hundreds of birds, only inches apart. Twisting and turning in unison, the flock will flash bright white as they turn away, exposing the pale undersides of their wings and bodies, and then practically vanish when they flip in the other direction, turning their dark topsides in our direction. On a big migration day the flocks of dunlins moving along the lakeshore will convey the full rush of the season, the unstoppable drive that will take them on to the Arctic.

Right now, however, the yellowlegs and the solitary sandpipers and the pectorals are feeding in the chilly marsh here in Ohio, and they're not in any hurry to push the season. Right now the May rush is still a month away. As if we were listening to a favorite symphony, we will have to wait awhile for that part, and other movements will come first.

All photos by the author unless otherwise noted.

For a few weeks every year, during the peak of spring migration, the boardwalk at Magee Marsh Wildlife Area, Ohio, becomes one of the most popular birding spots in the world. (Photograph by Kimberly Kaufman)

Hundreds of thousands of waterfowl pass through the western Lake Erie marshes every year, including spectacular flocks of tundra swans in early spring.

Flocks of American tree sparrows flit through fields near the Great Lakes and elsewhere in the northern states, but only in winter. They depart in early spring for the High Arctic tundra of northern Canada.

Before the end of February, massive flocks of red-winged blackbirds are migrating north across the northern states and southern Canada. At the same time, individual males start to stake out nesting territories in the frozen marshes.

Contrary to popular belief, many robins stay through the winter as far north as southern Canada. A true sign of spring is the point when their winter flocks break up and male robins start singing to announce their territorial claims in millions of backyards.

Seriously endangered in the 1970s, the bald eagle has made a strong comeback all across North America. Northwestern Ohio now holds one of the greatest concentrations of nesting eagles in the lower 48 states.

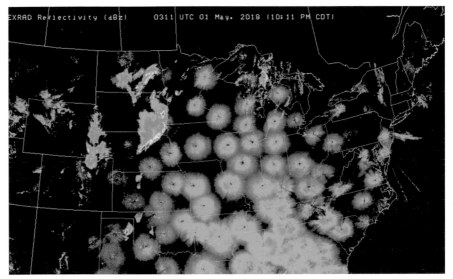

A composite Nexrad weather radar picture for about 11:11 p.m. Eastern Time on April 30, 2018. Blue and green circles show where radar is detecting large numbers of nocturnal migrant birds; gaps between circles show a lack of radar coverage, not a lack of birds. The image shows very few birds moving over the northeastern states. Yellow and green slashes over Nebraska and the Dakotas indicate rain, not birds. Farther west, it's just getting dark and the migration hasn't ramped up yet. (Image courtesy of UW–Madison AOS Department)

As one of the activists working to keep wind turbines out of sensitive habitats for migratory birds around the Great Lakes, the author designed and paid for this billboard along Ohio's State Route 2 near the Lake Erie shoreline.

For many birders in eastern North America, spring's highlight is the migration of warblers: more than three dozen species of small, active, colorful songbirds. Ohio's Magee Marsh region, an exceptionally good place to see them, is sometimes called the "warbler capital of the world."

Blackburnian Warbler

Bay-breasted Warbler

Black-throated Green Warbler

Yellow-rumped Warbler

Cape May Warbler

Cerulean Warbler

Belying their modest appearance, gray-cheeked thrushes are champion migrants. In spring they fly from southern Brazil north and west through North America, with some crossing the Bering Strait into Siberia. Recent cutting-edge research shows that some individuals can fly nonstop from Colombia to Canada in less than forty-eight hours.

Migration allows eastern kingbirds to live in two worlds. In winter, flocks wander in South America, feeding on small fruits in the tops of rainforest trees. In summer, they're scattered across the eastern two-thirds of North America, feeding on flying insects in open country.

The adult male blackpoll warbler in spring (left) has a snappy pattern, including the black cap responsible for the name. But it performs a more impressive migration while wearing its drab autumn plumage, flying long distances over the open sea en route to South America.

A flight of dunlins (a type of sandpiper) sweeps over a Lake Erie marsh in May. Thousands of dunlins, coming from coastal wintering sites, stop through on their way to breeding grounds in the High Arctic.

Alder flycatchers, after wintering in South America, arrive in the Great Lakes region in late May. Most go on to the boreal forests of Canada and Alaska. Like many such long-distance travelers, they migrate north through the eastern half of the lower 48 states, spreading westward as they approach Canada.

The Magee Marsh boardwalk experience is a unique combination of serious birding and warm, welcoming social occasion. As people bond over close views of migratory birds, lasting friendships are formed and rekindled every year. (Photograph by Kimberly Kaufman)

10

This Slice of Sky

During my years of obsession with bird migration, I have often brought up the subject in conversations with total strangers. I've found that most people, even if they claim no knowledge of birds at all, seem to have some ideas about how migration works. When I talk to someone about the big concentrations of migrants along the Lake Erie shoreline in northwestern Ohio, I can predict that eventually their face will light up with recognition: "Oh, you must be on a flyway!"

The whole idea of bird migration flyways seems to have seeped into the public consciousness to a surprising degree. And it's all the more remarkable because flyways are mostly imaginary. A few kinds of birds do follow routes that fit the concept well, but for the majority of migratory birds, the very idea of flyways is irrelevant, even misleading.

To be fair, the concept had its origins in good scientific research. Frederick C. Lincoln was in charge of all bird banding in the United States from 1920 to 1946, and he built up the banding program into a serious tool for studying migration. One early focus was on the banding of migratory waterfowl, especially ducks. In order to conserve their populations and set appropriate bag limits for hunters in different regions, wildlife agencies had to know where the ducks were going. Lincoln and his Canadian counterparts organized a serious effort to band more ducks, and with band returns sent in by hunters, they soon knew more about the migrations of ducks than of any other birds.

Lincoln was interested in all birds, but for analysis he had to use the best data at hand. Compiling the points where ducks had been banded and recovered, he saw clear patterns emerging. In 1935 he published these patterns in a book, *Waterfowl Flyways of North America*. This landmark work set the stage for an approach to waterfowl management that has been used ever since.

Migrating ducks don't necessarily move straight north or straight south, of course, but most of them move in at least a general north–south direction. And since they need to stop over regularly at water, they mostly avoid the deserts and the high mountains. Frederick Lincoln was thus able to ignore some sections of the country and to focus on corridors that would carry a lot of duck traffic. He called them the Atlantic, Mississippi, Central, and Pacific Flyways.

These divisions are still used as administrative units by government agencies that deal with waterfowl. In that context they work well. In each of the four named flyways, a Flyway Council of representatives from state wildlife agencies meets regularly to share information, review research, and make recommendations to the U.S. Fish and Wildlife Service. The people engaged in this work know what they're doing; they understand that many birds angle across multiple flyways. Still, the framework provided by the four flyway groups provides a good structure for dealing with waterfowl conservation, and there's no reason to change it.

For most birds, though, the concept doesn't apply nearly as well.

It's understandable that people would gravitate to the idea of birds following invisible "highways in the sky." After all, humans almost always travel by established routes. If you're going to drive from Nashville to Baltimore, for example, you're very unlikely to leave the pavement and go cross-country in the straightest line. (And if you try, you won't get far, unless you're driving a tank.) Instead you'll probably hop on Interstate 40 going east, picking up Interstate 81 near Knoxville and angling northeast, along with tens of thousands of other drivers going in the same direction on the same narrow freeway. If you're traveling by train, of course the train will follow established tracks. If you're traveling by air, most jet traffic runs on standard routes between major hub airports, with regional flights fanning out from there. Even ships at sea mostly travel in major shipping lanes. The idea of established routes is so ingrained in human culture — going back to the ancient highways of the Roman and Inca Empires, among others — that we may not even think about other possibilities.

But for migrating birds, one piece of sky is much like another. In general, they don't form concentrated lines of travel unless they're forced into it by geography. They don't concentrate in limited areas unless they're forced to by availability of food or habitat when they stop. Most of the time it's more beneficial for them to spread out, and they do.

One problem with the idea of distinct corridors of travel is that it implies gaps between the corridors. And to some extent, for ducks those gaps actually exist. When Frederick Lincoln was drawing his maps, he could ignore some of the high elevations and arid country of the West. He could draw his flyways thick or thin, he could have branches angling off and crossing other flyways, and his resulting maps actually did give a good idea of where the ducks were going.

For most birds, however, migration doesn't work that way. The majority of species advance on a broad front, spread out, moving in the same general directions but not following particular routes.

Let's look at our migratory songbirds. Most kinds — sparrows, warblers, vireos, orioles, tanagers, most thrushes, most flycatchers, and so on — migrate at night. If we could look down at North America from out in space on a night in May and see where the migrants were flying, we would not see rivers of birds flowing northward. Instead the birds would look like a bumpy blanket stretched all the way across the continent, being pulled toward the north. Or, actually, like several such blankets overlying each other, with some sliding north, some northeast, some northwest. The blankets would be thicker in the East, where the volume of the migration is greater, and more threadbare in parts of the West. But we wouldn't see any distinct gaps separating areas of travel. Nothing in the pattern would make us think about dividing the flow into corridors or flyways.

Like the nocturnal migrants, most birds that travel by day move all across the landscape, not in concentrated pathways. In daylight, though, there's a little more tendency for the birds to follow leading lines such as rivers or mountain ridges. (Winds striking high ridges can create updrafts that make for easier flying, but even without any wind, some birds seem to latch onto the long ridgelines as visual clues.) And daytime concentrations are especially likely where land meets water, as along the seacoast or the shores of major lakes. Diurnal migrants traveling over land often turn and follow shorelines instead of striking out over the water, so in certain conditions big numbers can build up.

The Lake Erie shoreline is a classic place to observe this during the season when migrants are moving north. It begins with the very first stirrings of spring, in February. American crows are among the first birds to start the northbound trek, and they are easy to overlook as they flap silently over the frozen farm fields. When they reach the lake edge, however, they don't continue straight north over the ice-choked water; instead they turn and follow the shoreline. In our area of Ohio they move west along the shore, following as it angles toward the northwest and toward the westernmost point of Lake Erie, on the outskirts of Toledo. Then they turn northward, spreading out and dispersing as they move overland into Michigan.

The crows are just the vanguard of the daytime migrants that will follow the same route. Many of these are small birds that travel in flocks. On days in March with winds from the southwest, we can go out to the lakeshore and see small groups of horned larks, or larger flocks of grackles or red-winged blackbirds, paralleling the shoreline as they move toward Michigan. On a calm day they might be spread out across the landscape, but southwest winds push them to the edge of the lake and concentrate them enough that their passage becomes noticeable.

As the season goes on, other birds take their places in the parade. Later in the spring most species are moving at night, and we know from radar studies that they'll go straight on across Lake

Erie if they arrive here during the hours of darkness. Daytime travelers such as swallows and goldfinches are more likely to follow the leading line of the lakeshore. But the most notable birds on this route are the birds of prey.

Most diurnal birds of prey — hawks, eagles, vultures, kites, and falcons — avoid crossing long stretches of open water when they migrate. As they detour around large bodies of water to stay over land, big concentrations may build up. Huge numbers stream down the coastal plain of Veracruz, in eastern Mexico, pressed into a thin lane between the mountains and the Gulf of Mexico. Vast flights funnel through a few narrow points in the Middle East as they travel between Asia and Africa. Numbers can run into the hundreds of thousands in a single day. Nothing of this magnitude occurs in the United States or Canada, but we sometimes see impressive concentrations of raptors as they skirt around the margins of the Great Lakes in spring and fall.

In northern Ohio, bald eagles and a few other raptors may be shifting north in February, and more of a movement develops by March. At first we see mostly the hardy, short-distance migrants. Red-tailed hawks and Cooper's hawks can be found in our area all year, but some pass through in spring, going farther north. Red-shouldered hawk, more of a forest bird than its relative the red-tail, is absent from the immediate area of Magee Marsh for most of the year, but dozens pass through in March. They're making short journeys, coming from no farther away than the southern United States. Broad-winged hawks spend the winter in the tropics, and they don't arrive here until April. Turkey vultures have a long, drawn-out passage through our region, from late February to early May, with some arriving from the southern states and others possibly coming all the way from South America.

Throughout March and April local birders watch the extended weather forecasts, hoping for conditions that will produce a big hawk movement. The ideal setup occurs when several days of cold northerly winds are followed by a warmer day with winds from the southwest. Winds from any southerly quarter might motivate birds to move, but if they're from the southwest, we know the raptors will concentrate along the lake. When conditions look right, we head to some lakeshore vantage point to watch the flight.

The top of the sledding hill near the beach at Maumee Bay State Park is a favorite spot. It's not a huge hill, maybe a hundred feet high, but it commands a good view of the woods and fields of the park as well as the shoreline and Lake Erie. Standing atop the hill, bundled up against the wind, we scan toward the east and southeast for approaching raptors.

Even if it's a good day, there won't be a steady flow of birds. We may have to wait a while, keyed up, constantly scanning, for the first definite migrants to appear.

In March — when the trees are still bare, when the tawny yellow fields still hold patches of snow, when even southerly winds carry a chill — it might seem improbable that spring migrants would come out of that eastern horizon. But they do. Far out along the shoreline, past the park lodge, we pick up a speck in the air, moving this way. Turning and gliding, coming steadily closer, it resolves into a red-tailed hawk. It could be a local resident, but it doesn't act like it. A master of the air, the hawk hardly flaps its wings as it sweeps in wide loops, angling across the wind, steadily circling westward past our hilltop perch. We watch as the red-tail continues along the shoreline and disappears to the west-northwest, heading toward Michigan and points north.

The pattern has been set, and other birds follow it. A few minutes later a red-shouldered hawk comes right over the hill, flapping fast and then going into long glides, heading off to the west. Then a long, straggling line of turkey vultures appears off to the southeast of our vantage point—ten birds, twenty, thirty, widely spaced but all gliding slowly and ponderously across the wind. The big birds soar with their wings angled up in a shallow V, rocking sideways on wind gusts but continuing past us toward the western horizon. Then a Cooper's hawk, more of a power flier, comes beating past us at eye level.

And so it continues: only a few birds at a time, but they add up, a procession of determined migrants pushing back the edge of winter and announcing spring.

If we get ideal conditions a month later, in April, numbers may be lower for vultures but higher for hawks, especially if we've hit the right timing for a big movement of broad-winged hawks. These small soaring raptors are coming from the deep tropics, and many are heading far north into Canada, so hundreds may pass our lookout on the right day. By April the sky may be filled with other kinds of birds as well, with flocks of swallows, distant gulls, and so many more. Our eyes pick up a search image for hawks, locking onto their shapes and distinctive movements when they are almost too far away to see. There's a broad-winged hawk off to the east, there are two more circling overhead, there's a little knot of eight or ten slipping past on our southern flank. We have to watch in all directions at once if we hope to spot them all.

Other raptors are on the move also. Sharp-shinned hawks, those intense little bird-hunters of the woods, come zipping along, some moving at treetop level, some down along the lakeshore and barely above the water. A few ospreys are moving, big pale fish hawks almost the size of eagles, passing high overhead. Occasionally a merlin will flash past; these dashing little falcons always seem to be in a hurry, on their way to cause trouble somewhere. Every merlin comes as a surprise, rocketing past on angular wings as it heads for the horizon.

This disjointed parade is a stirring thing to watch. The Lake Erie shoreline in northwestern Ohio is famous for its migratory birds, of course, but mainly as a stopover site: the transients arrive and depart under the cover of night, and we see them as they go about their daytime activities of feeding and resting up for the next flight. But these raptors are actively passing through at the moment we see them. That knowledge gives a sense of immediacy to every sighting. This broad-winged hawk circling over the hill right now, for example, has just this moment arrived from the south. It won't pause here; when it disappears to the northwest it will be gone for good. It won't pass this way again until next year, if ever. We have to be out here right now, paying attention, to see this bird at all.

Are we on a flyway? At this moment the raptors are telling us we are, even if we don't know what to call it. We're almost exactly halfway between the Atlantic Coast and the Mississippi River, so are we in the Atlantic Flyway or the Mississippi Flyway? Do we care? The birds don't. They are filling the air here because we're at the edge of the lake, and their line of travel shifts and detours to go around the lake instead of across it. There may not be any "highways in the sky" that go clear across the continent, but there are small stretches that carry heavy avian traffic. At the moment this narrow slice of sky above the Lake Erie shoreline is incredibly important for the survival of these birds.

For many years people working in bird conservation defined habitat only in terms of what was on the ground: this forest, this marsh, this prairie. But now there's a growing realization that the sky overhead—the air column, as it's called—is essential habitat also. Certain corridors of the air, regardless of what lies on the ground below, are filled with migrating birds at critical times of year. Measuring the conservation value of the air column will require new ways of thinking, and protecting that space is sure to be a challenge.

11

Second Wind

Reggie Luzader was as hard as the rocks that peppered the soil of his central Ohio farm. He was tough on himself and hard on his children, with an abrasive love that wouldn't abide sissies. It was okay for the kids to shoot at each other with BB guns while they zoomed around on dirt bikes in the dark, but he'd better not catch them doing anything as frivolous as reading a book, at least not until after the chores were done.

Reggie had never lived in a world that valued book learning, so he applied his good mind to other things, like becoming a master mechanic. Any trucks or motorbikes or all-terrain vehicles on the Luzader farm might look like shit, but they would run clean and fast. If a boy from a more prosperous farm came over on a shiny new ATV, looking for a race, he was sure to be humiliated as any one of the Luzader boys or girls left him in the dust. But after Reggie had tuned up a junker a few times, the next breakdown was on the kid: *Here are the tools. Here's what you need to fix. Now go figure it out.* He was hard and rough but he taught responsibility, if only by example. When the blizzard of '78 shut down the whole county, Reggie went out and crisscrossed the landscape on his snowmobile, checking on shut-ins, taking food to the stranded. It was just the thing to do.

By the time I met him he was near the end of his life, exhausted from fighting early-onset Alzheimer's. So I never saw Reggie in his prime. But I still catch glimpses of him all the time, because I married his daughter.

Fortunately for me, Kimberly inherited her generous, kind, loving disposition mostly from her mother, Darlene. But she has her father's strength, too. When push comes to shove, when there's something worth fighting for, when there are impossible odds to be overcome, Kimberly is Reggie's daughter all the way, a beautiful and formidable force of nature.

When we got the news that the Camp Perry wind project was back on the table, we were all irritated and concerned. Kimberly may have taken it harder than anyone else, but it seemed to make her more determined to prevail, to protect this vital habitat.

By now the Black Swamp Bird Observatory, with Kimberly as executive director, had stepped up its conservation efforts in general. Mark Shieldcastle was still officially the research director, but now he was devoting much of his time and energy and expertise to conservation issues, including questions of wind power. We had received donations that allowed us to hire a good attorney to advise on legal aspects. Michael Hutchins at the American Bird Conservancy was now in regular contact with BSBO about wind issues in the region.

Early on we had hoped it would be possible to have honest debates about the effects of wind-energy development on wildlife. Of course that was naive thinking; our little nonprofit conservation groups like BSBO and ABC were up against entities of immense power, and honest debate was not in their best interests. The companies standing to profit directly from the Camp Perry project were not particularly large, but the major players in wind energy included huge international corporations with big sums of money riding on the success of the industry in general. In this field, as in so many others, it's money that rules.

We see the corrosive effect of money at all levels in the debate. The very framework of electric-energy production favors the largest companies. It would be possible to distribute power generation more widely, to have arrays of solar panels on individual homes or small wind turbines around individual farms, but companies can make bigger profits if power generation is kept centralized.

Huge three-bladed wind turbines are standard everywhere today, and we know they can be deadly for birds and bats. Other designs might be safer for wildlife, but the major corporations are all totally committed to the current design, having invested vast sums in their production, so there's very little interest in or funding for any effort to develop more bird-friendly wind turbines.

At the bottom of the economic ladder related to wind are biologists who work as paid consultants. Biologists never get rich; no one goes into this field for the money. But those who work as consultants for the wind industry, advising on placement and doing pre- and post-construction surveys, are under extreme pressure to tell companies what they want to hear. Some of these consultants are people of impeccable integrity who never stray from solid fact, regardless of what their clients might want. Others, I'm afraid, find it all too easy to fudge the findings and slant their reports.

This fudging occurs in a variety of clever ways. I studied one environmental assessment of a project that suggested that very few waterfowl would use wetlands closest to the site—but this was based on one survey in early October, much earlier in fall than the main waterfowl migration through that region. That same EA's estimate of bald eagle movements through the area was based on limited surveys in midwinter, before the season of peak eagle activity. In studies of bird mortality at turbines elsewhere, consultants have suggested that when large numbers are killed in one night, those figures are "anomalous" or "atypical" and shouldn't be counted into the averages. And such mortality surveys are often set up to lowball the actual kill, to minimize the numbers in the results. People without knowledge of birds, even if they make a sincere effort to understand what's going on, have a hard time finding information that isn't slanted to paint a rosy picture.

The companies, too, have ingenious ways of presenting onesided views and getting around regulations. In our state, new developments have to be cleared with the Ohio Power Siting Board. If the projects are above a certain size, they must get approval from the Division of Wildlife. So if a company wants to put up five wind turbines, for example, it will designate them as two separate projects—one with three turbines, one with two—each of them just under the size that would trigger the wildlife review. The five structures may stand close together as an obvious unit, but the company has evaded any assessment of whether they will have an impact on wildlife.

Environmental groups are all over the map regarding their positions on wind energy. At one extreme are antiwind groups that are supported by the fossil-fuel industry or by people who deny that climate change is happening at all. It was immediately obvious to us that we had to avoid those toxic connections: we know climate change is a genuine threat, and we're not going to take money from those who deny it, even if that money would help us keep wind power out of sensitive bird habitats.

Toward the opposite extreme, some groups have concluded that climate change overwhelmingly outweighs every other threat, so they support wind development almost everywhere, regardl⟨ ⟩s of potential damage to wildlife. Sierra Club is close to that pos⟨ its representatives will say that wildlife factors have to be considered, but they always seem to come down on the side of the wind industry. Many other organizations seem to be somewhere in the middle. Often they seem reluctant to speak out against any particular wind project, for fear they might be tarred as being "against green energy." It takes a fearless organization like American Bird Conservancy to brush those worries aside and go full speed ahead on protecting bird habitat.

In debates among conservationists about the pros and cons of wind power, a frequent argument is that other things out there kill so many more birds than wind turbines do. People will trot out graphics showing tremendous numbers of birds killed by things like prowling house cats, vehicles on roads, power-line collisions, window collisions, etc., and then a tiny number killed by wind turbines. They'll present these as if they represented the final argument to win the debate.

But if we think about them carefully, these figures actually convey the opposite message. They tell us that these birds already face enormous hazards and that we should be extremely cautious about doing anything that adds to the cumulative effect.

Yes, those other threats are real (and some groups like American Bird Conservancy are working on all of them). But different factors affect different kinds of birds. Catastrophic numbers of birds are killed by house cats that should never be allowed outdoors, but many of those are common birds that live near houses. Huge numbers of birds are killed by vehicles, but they tend to be common birds that live along roads. In contrast, wind turbines placed in the middle of essential stopover habitat are likely to kill disproportionate numbers of long-distance migrants, birds that are already pushing the limits of survival.

It's a fact that large numbers of wild birds are killed by human activities, directly or indirectly. As a part of conservation work we have to recognize this and put it in perspective. Wind turbines placed anywhere are likely to knock down at least a few birds, and realistically we have to accept this as one of the costs of renewable energy. No reasonable person is going to demand zero mortality. But it's critically important to know what *kinds* of birds are being affected. If humans cause the deaths of a hundred robins, that is terribly sad, but it won't threaten the continued survival of this abundant species. If we cause the deaths of a hundred eagles, that's a serious concern, because eagles are far less numerous and they reproduce much more slowly.

So it's not a matter of sheer numbers of generic birds; we have to make distinctions. The locations of these wind facilities can make all the difference. But people who should know better continue to push the narrative of comparing numbers, as if it somehow gives a free pass to putting up wind towers everywhere.

Location, location, location. I don't know why the concept is so hard to understand. We made the point over and over: we're not opposed to wind power in general; we just want to keep wind developments out of the places where they will do the most damage to wildlife.

In debates people would counter with a question: All right, if not here, then where? If you don't want wind turbines right on the Lake Erie shoreline, where would you recommend that we put them?

At some level I resented the question. It was as if I tried to stop someone from jabbing me in the eye with a sharp needle and he asked, *Okay, where would you like to be jabbed?* Honestly I'd rather not be jabbed at all, but I'm going to fight hardest to keep him from sticking that needle in my eyes, or my face or hands, or sensitive private areas. It won't do as much damage if he jams the needle into my arm or leg, maybe, or somewhere in my back. But it's hard to relax and help him pick a different spot while my eye is being threatened, or while the most vulnerable bird habitat is under attack.

Still, there was logic to the question. Based on everything we knew about bird behavior, we calculated that wind turbines in the area of Camp Perry would be disastrous for migratory species and for dense local concentrations of eagles and waterfowl. But it would be helpful for discussion if we had baselines for comparison, if we could point to reduced bird mortality rates at wind developments that were far from the most sensitive areas. So we started looking around for examples of wind farms in places that ought to be comparatively bird-safe.

Far out in farm country of western Ohio, along the Indiana state line, the Blue Creek wind farm began operations in 2012. It featured 152 wind turbines, each one a giant two-megawatt machine with the sweep of the blades reaching almost five hundred feet above the ground, spread across farm country in Paulding and Van Wert Counties. The area was far from Lake Erie, far from any known major stopover area. If anyplace in Ohio could be considered a bird-safe location for a commercial-scale wind farm, we figured this would be the place.

At that time wind-power facilities in the state were required to report any data on bird kills to the Division of Wildlife, and through a cooperative agreement the information was also shared with the U.S. Fish and Wildlife Service. Going through official channels, BSBO contacted both agencies, state and federal, to ask for copies of the bird mortality data from Blue Creek.

To our surprise, we didn't receive them. The agencies told us that the company owning and operating Blue Creek, the international energy giant Iberdrola, didn't want the data released to the public because they contained trade secrets.

At first we wondered if that was a joke. Trade secrets? What about this data could possibly be a secret to be kept away from competitors? If unexpected numbers of birds were being killed at Blue Creek, we could see why Iberdrola might not want the public to know, but nothing about that information would give away proprietary advantages to competing companies.

BSBO's attorney pushed back and continued to ask for the data. After considerable wrangling back and forth, representatives from Iberdrola agreed to meet with the bird observatory to discuss the issue. Kimberly, Mark Shieldcastle, and BSBO's attorney drove down to Paulding County for the meeting.

I was up against a book deadline at the time so I couldn't go, but the meeting was well attended. Iberdrola was represented by seven or eight people, including managers of the local facility, attorneys, at least one public-relations specialist, and a biological consultant who conference-called in. Three people from Ohio's Department of Natural Resources were there, including the chief of the Division of Wildlife. Apparently the questions raised by our little bird observatory were being treated as a big deal.

The meeting took place in a nicely furnished conference room in a big industrial building out in the country near the wind farm. At the outset Kimberly laid out our position: "We're not going to sign any nondisclosure agreements, because we won't agree to keep secrets from our members. So don't tell us anything and then say that it's confidential."

After a whispered discussion around their end of the table, the company reps agreed.

They proceeded to show a presentation on a screen in the conference room, with slides of information, narrated by the biologist on the phone. They started by describing the surveys they'd done after construction, walking transects under the turbines, looking for dead birds and bats. The description of the methodology was brief and superficial, as if they hoped to satisfy BSBO by giving us the bare minimum amount of information. Mark, who knows a lot about methodology and study design, just rolled his eyes and took notes. After some extraneous points, they finally showed a couple of slides listing the species of birds found dead under the turbines in two different years.

Not the numbers of individuals, just the species. Kimberly and Mark leaned forward in surprise. We had expected the turbines would take down birds of open farm country, like horned larks and blackbirds. But more than forty species made the list each year, including scarce migratory songbirds like golden-winged warblers and black-throated blue warblers. Out in a zone that we would have considered the middle of nowhere for these long-distance migrants, far from any stopover habitat, the Blue Creek wind farm was knocking them out of the sky.

At the conclusion of the meeting, the reps from Iberdrola expressed the hope that the limited information they'd provided would be enough to satisfy BSBO's questions. But in discussing it afterward, we concluded that it clearly wasn't enough. Merely having seen a list of species without any indication of numbers couldn't tell us the whole story of what was happening at Blue Creek. It was more than a little disturbing that those turbines in farm country, far from prime habitats, would take out scarce species like golden-winged warblers. Were those isolated flukes, or were they knocking down multiples? What did their total numbers look like?

So after more discussion, including consultation with Michael Hutchins and others at ABC, we told the Division of Wildlife that we still wanted the total mortality figures for Blue Creek. The division gave Iberdrola thirty days to comment or respond. Before the thirty days had passed, Iberdrola had brought its own lawsuit against the Division of Wildlife, the Ohio Department of Natural Resources, and the Ohio Power Siting Board: suing to stop them from releasing the bird-kill data to anyone.

Clearly the company felt it had something to hide — so much so that it would go to court to keep the information from getting out to the public.

The information offered up in the meeting with Iberdrola had included nothing about bats found killed under the turbines, so Kimberly had asked about that. The question had led to more whispered discussion around the far end of the table, and then a brief statement: "Bats were more prevalent than birds" in the mortality surveys.

There was also a sense of surprise that "the bird people" would be asking about flying mammals. But we are interested in the conservation of all species, partly because everything in nature is connected. Bats are essential members of ecosystems around the world. With more than forty species of bats in North America north of the Mexico border and at least ten found regularly in Ohio, they represent part of our heritage of biodiversity.

Besides, some of those bats are strongly migratory, like some birds. In woodlots near Lake Erie in spring we'll sometimes spot an eastern red bat, one of our common migrants, roosting high among the foliage, sleeping the day away. These bats wear pinkish brown to orange-red tones, and if we happen to see them flying by day, they shine like gold in the sunlight. Eastern red bats are beautiful animals, and entirely beneficial to humans, feeding on insects like gypsy moths and tent caterpillar moths. Of course we care about protecting their populations.

"Bats were more prevalent" among the victims at Blue Creek. This has become a common refrain in many places, as we learn that wind facilities are taking out shocking numbers of these animals, running into the thousands at some sites. As bizarre as it seems, there are even hints that bats actually may be attracted to wind turbines. And they don't have to be struck by the blades to be killed: unlike birds, they are very vulnerable to barotrauma, damage done by the abrupt drop in air pressure as the blade sweeps past. As many as half the dead bats found under turbines may show no signs of impact; instead their lungs or other internal organs have exploded in the sudden air-pressure drop.

To make matters worse, we may be severely underestimating

bat mortality. In Britain, studies using dogs to sniff out carcasses showed that human searchers were missing many dead bats: the dogs found more than three times as many. So the situation may be even worse than we thought, and if the kills continue at their current rate, some bat species may be threatened with extinction.

It doesn't have to be inevitable. Studies have found that a high percentage of bat kills at turbines occur at slower wind speeds. Apparently the bats are far less likely to fly as high as the sweep of the turbine blades if the wind is blowing more than about fifteen miles per hour. If wind-farm operators keep the blades stopped at wind speeds slower than that, at least on nights in summer and fall when bats are most likely to be flying, their mortality can be sharply reduced.

Unfortunately, in most cases the cut-in speed — the wind velocity at which the turbines start operating and delivering power to the grid — is substantially slower, about eight or nine miles per hour. Some guidelines have been proposed to keep the turbines still at those wind speeds, and some wind-farm operators are willing to follow these voluntary guidelines, but others say they can't afford to lose those hours for generating power. It's still very uncertain whether the wind industry as a whole will be willing to take the steps necessary to avoid the extinction of some bat species.

We never did get the bird mortality data, let alone any bat data, from the Blue Creek wind farm. Iberdrola was firm in its refusal, having sued to keep the information private, and we didn't have the resources to fight that.

Besides, our main focus had to be on the crucial stopover habitat in our own area, along the Lake Erie shoreline in northwestern Ohio. Kimberly was still working closely with Michael Hutchins at the American Bird Conservancy, and we were all watching to see what would happen with the proposed wind turbine at Camp Perry.

Back in 2014 our notice of intent to sue had been enough to have the project halted, but now it was back. The Air National Guard and its consultants had not been able to address the concerns we had raised about a series of environmental laws, from the Migratory Bird Treaty Act to the Bald and Golden Eagle Protection Act, but they had come up with a brand-new workaround. Now they were referring to the single wind turbine not as a source of electricity but as an experiment. *Let's put up one big turbine here and treat it as "experimental." Let's just put it up and see if it kills a lot of birds. We can even turn it off during periods of highest risk. Nothing wrong with an experiment, right? Let's just try it.*

To us, the subtext was something else altogether: *Let's put this up to start the process of getting the public to accept these things. We can always downplay the bird mortality. Put up this one and maybe it will open the door for hundreds more, all over the lakeshore.*

Kimberly and Mark and the rest of the BSBO conservation team were disgusted by the new spin on the project. Michael Hutchins and the ABC attorneys were nonplussed by the flawed reasoning. If it was an "experiment," if there was no intention of generating significant amounts of electricity, then there was even less justification for the turbine; its only possible purpose was to see if it would kill birds and bats. The legal team had filed another notice of intent to sue in the fall of 2016, and when we received no formal answer, we went ahead with the lawsuit.

I keep writing about this as if I were deeply involved, but the truth is that I played only peripheral roles most of the time. Although I discussed the latest developments with Kimberly several times a week, I wasn't one of the individuals in there doing the actual work.

I did have a chance to provide one bit of support in terms of public relations. I had inquired about billboard space along Route 2 close to Camp Perry and discovered that the cost of renting a billboard for a few months was within my reach, especially if I did all the graphic work for it myself. I had designed many full-page magazine ads for my nature books in earlier years, so I tried my hand at billboard design — simple graphics, large words, short text that people could read at fifty-five miles per hour. Accompanied by images of turbine silhouettes and a flying eagle, my final billboard message was:

KEEP WIND TURBINES *OFF* OUR LAKE SHORE

PROTECT

— BALD EAGLES

— WATERFOWL

— BIRD WATCHING

— TOURISM

— THE LOCAL ECONOMY

LOCATION MATTERS!

I don't know how much impact the message had, but during the time it stood by the highway it would have been seen over and over by a few thousand local people who wouldn't have seen our press releases or heard any of our programs. Images of this billboard continued to crop up in news stories and on social media for a couple of years afterward, so perhaps it had some effect in framing the issue for some segment of the population.

But if my role was only peripheral or advisory most of the time, Kimberly's role in the whole wind-power debate was central. For me it was intriguing and inspiring to watch the giant strides she took during those few years, educating herself about so many aspects of climate change, renewable energy, environmental laws and policies, and the politics of activism. She drew in people with all kinds of knowledge and skills, building coalitions that could do highly effective work. Even though she constantly gave the credit to everyone else, her leadership skills were paramount in making a difference.

Some might have said that nothing in her background had prepared her for this, but I think the fact that she was Reggie Luzader's daughter played a part in her success. He was a genius in figuring out how to make things work, and he was as hard and strong as he needed to be. Kimberly knew how to moderate her approach, to debate things calmly and rationally, and she was too diplomatic to ever go Full Reggie on any of her adversaries. But if her dad had been watching, I know he would have been proud of the way she refused to back down, ever, from doing what was right.

12

Waiting for Warblers

Imagine we had the power to create new kinds of birds. Imagine we decided to invent the ideal group of birds for avid birders, perfect for firing up the most dedicated watchers.

Ideal: with dozens of different kinds, because birders, even more than most people, love variety. Ideal: just the right balance of challenge and reward. We'd make them tiny, active birds, adept at dodging behind leaves, hard to see, but painted with bright colors and patterns, so they'd be worth the effort. Some would be easy to recognize at a glance; some would be much more difficult. Some would flit through treetops; others would lurk in thickets, to keep birders looking everywhere. All these birds would be strongly migratory, passing through in a rush at certain seasons, so that no one would ever, ever have time to get tired of them. Each migration season would end all too soon, leaving the fans eager for the next visit of their perfect birds.

In other words, if we were trying to create the ideal birds to keep the birders endlessly enthralled, we would invent the American warblers.

The name "warbler," in itself, is not a precise term. It has been applied to almost three hundred species of birds on six continents. Almost none of those birds ever makes a genuine *warbling* sound, and many species bearing the name are utterly unrelated. The name was first given to a handful of European birds long ago, and during the age of exploration it was slapped onto anything that fit the general profile: very small, active birds, hunting tiny insects among foliage. Apparently this niche is a fruitful one, and different groups of songbirds have evolved to fill it, over and over, in different parts of the world. As a result, birds called warblers today could belong to any one of thirteen distinct families — unrelated, but with convergent lifestyles.

Nothing in the job description requires these small insectivores to be colorful. Indeed, most are not. Almost all the things-called-warblers in Europe, Asia, and Australia wear drab tones of olive, gray, or brown. So do most of the things-called-warblers in Africa. But America is oddly blessed. For no obvious reason, most American warblers, members of the family Parulidae, have bright colors or striking patterns or both. Aside from a few dull exceptions, most American warblers — especially adult males in spring — are decked out in bright yellow, green, blue, orange, or chestnut, with patches or stripes of black or white. With more than fifty species north of the Mexican border, the diversity of color patterns is phenomenal. Their bright hues and sheer variety make the American warblers perennial favorites for those in the know.

No other birds draw such a stark separation between birders and nonbirders. The average nonbirder is unaware that warblers exist. They're so small, so filled with nonstop flitting energy, so good at hiding, that it takes an effort to see them at all. Most of the time they're high in treetops or deep in brushy tangles. They seldom come to bird feeders. In winter, when they would be easier to see in leafless trees, they're gone: all our northern warblers migrate south in fall, most going deep into the tropics. So the typical nonbirder has never seen warblers and has no reason to think about them.

Birders, on the other hand, think about warblers a lot. We obsess over them. The elusive nature that makes warblers invisible to the typical person only makes them more alluring for us. We want to track them down and see them all, and then see them again.

In my own birding history, I came to warblers late. Birds captured my imagination when I was six years old, so by the time I was eight or nine I certainly knew about warblers. I had read all about them, but I'd never seen one. No warblers nested in our suburban Indiana neighborhood. Undoubtedly a few came through in migration, but my eyes weren't attuned to noticing creatures so quick and small. I had no binoculars yet, so even if I had spotted a warbler, it likely would have been just a puzzling little bird that got away.

Then when I was eleven, after my family had moved to Wichita, Kansas, I connected with adults of the local Audubon chapter and began to join their field trips. I vividly recall the May day when a handful of the Audubon adults stood looking at a nearby grove of trees, casually mentioning birds they were seeing: a Nashville warbler, a blackpoll warbler, an orange-crowned warbler. I was staring at the same trees and seeing nothing but a wall of green leaves. I wondered, wildly, if these people were making things up to make fun of me. Finally a bird flitted out onto an open twig where I could find it in my cheap department-store binoculars: a tiny bird, brilliant yellow, with red stripes down its chest. Yellow warbler! It twitched this way and that on its twig, an intense flame of nervous energy, before zipping back into the foliage. After that I had only vague glimpses through the leaves. But that quick, clear view moved warblers from abstract idea to reality in my mind. The fact that I had waited so long to see them fueled a fascination that would never fade.

As a boy in Kansas, and later as a teenager bumming around North America, I sought out the warblers and managed to see all the different species at least once. But then I moved to Arizona. The Southwest had a few special western warblers but not the sheer variety of the eastern states. So I still didn't feel that I knew the warblers well. For that I would have to go east. The vast, colorful, northward parade of warblers is the peak experience of spring, but only in the East.

At most localities in the eastern states, a few dozen kinds of warblers can be found — but not for long. They pass through in a rush during brief periods in spring and fall. A few stay through winter in the southern states, but most go on to the tropics then. A few can be found through summer in most areas, but many go on to boreal forests of the far north to breed and raise their young before turning around and heading south again. For birders at mid-latitudes in the eastern United States, narrow windows of time in spring and fall offer the only chances to see most warblers.

Especially springtime. In the East, that's when warblers are celebrated. A serious birder looks for them in fall, too, of course, but they take more work at that season. They move south before the leaves begin to fall, when foliage is thickest and such birds are hardest to see. Many wear fall plumages that are muted and confusing. No, spring is the season when warblers shine. They wear their brightest colors then, the males are singing, the birds are buzzing with energy. They are not among the first migrants to arrive in spring, but when they do finally show up, we can be sure winter has been banished. For birders fatigued by a long, cold winter, the longing for spring warbler season can become a sharp physical pang, to be relieved only by scores of rainbow-hued treetop sprites.

Timing of warbler migration varies with latitude. In the southernmost states, where a few kinds stay for the winter, a big influx of warblers begins in March. Numbers and variety peak there in April, and only stragglers remain after mid-May. In the northern states, things don't really get going until sometime in April, and the peak is in May. Everywhere, though, the main passage is relatively brief. For birders with normal lives, obligated to things like work, family, and school, it's a challenge to connect with the spring warbler migration.

It's an addictive game to experience spring warblers. If you're making the attempt, you pray for the best migrant waves to hit on weekends, or you dash out on mornings or evenings if you can. You go over and over to that park or cemetery or nature center where local birders report good warbler luck, prowling the trails, hoping to find a little mixed flock. When you find the flock, you follow as long as you can, willingly suffering "warbler-neck" as you gaze into treetops. Every trip is a grab bag of treats. You never know which ones you'll pull out. On any given day you see only a few of the dozens of possible warblers, and you revel in what you see while still wanting more. You exult in the brightly patterned, obvious ones and puzzle over others: that bird hiding among the leaves, is it a pine warbler or a female blackpoll warbler? And as the season winds down in late May, thinking about warblers you found and ones you didn't, you're already looking ahead to the next spring.

That's how spring warbler season plays out in most places. Here in northwestern Ohio the season has a different flavor, because the warblers concentrate here in such numbers. At Magee Marsh and other "migrant traps" along the Lake Erie shore, where the trees are relatively short, the birds can be surprisingly easy to see. On a good day in May it's not unusual to see several hundred warblers here, representing twenty-five or more different species. On a good day in May visitors are likely to agree with the tag line we invented for this region: "the warbler capital of the world." The warblers are the brightest stars of the amazing local festival, appropriately named the Biggest Week in American Birding.

But that's in May. That's when most birders visit. If you live here, April is the month of anticipation, even frustration, waiting impatiently for the warblers to arrive.

The anticipation is sharper in the Internet age than in the past, because now we read every day about birds people are seeing farther south. A decent handful of warblers remain through winter at the subtropical edge of the United States, especially in southern Florida and Texas, and by late March those regions see influxes of fresh arrivals from the tropics. By April wave after migratory wave is arriving along the Gulf Coast. Friends in Louisiana and Texas start posting photos of warblers in glorious spring plumage, and we peruse them enviously.

Even in parts of Ohio things pick up early. A few "southern" warblers—those that breed mainly in the eastern United States, not in Canada—arrive in the southern tier of Ohio counties in the last days of March, and we read about yellow-throated warblers, pine warblers, and others singing on territory there. Meanwhile, up on the northern edge of the state, on the Lake Erie plain, we go out day after day, vainly looking for the first warblers in the leafless trees. Other migrants are around, including foxy-brown fox sparrows rustling in the thickets and flocks of blackbirds rolling across the fields. But when we see small birds flitting in the branches, they turn out to be kinglets or chickadees: tiny, drab, cute, but not *warblers*.

Sometime around the beginning of April, though, warblers do arrive in northern Ohio — at least, one kind does. The yellow-rumped warbler, also called the myrtle warbler, is one of the most abundant members of the family. In some ways it's also one of the least typical. Moving north earlier than any of the others, it makes up the vanguard of the warbler migration.

In terms of looks, the yellow-rump isn't too different from the average warbler. About five inches long from the tip of its bill to the end of its tail, it weighs about half an ounce. Adult males in spring are beautifully patterned in blue-gray, black, and white, with accents of yellow. Females and fall birds are duller, as is often the case with warblers. The breeding range of the eastern/northern "myrtle" type stretches across boreal forests of Canada and Alaska and south into the edge of the northeastern states, a pattern of summer distribution shared by several other members of the family.

Its winter range, however, marks a sharp departure from the warbler norm. Most warblers fly south into the tropics for the season. By contrast, most yellow-rumped warblers spend the winter within the southern United States. While other warblers feed mainly on insects at all seasons, yellow-rumps can survive on berries and small fruits. There are times when thickets of bayberry and wax myrtle shrubs along the Atlantic Coast swarm with thousands of yellow-rumped warblers in winter. This choice of winter distribution can be a death trap on rare occasions when storms coat the thickets with ice for days at a time, locking the abundant berries away from the warblers. Usually, though, it's a good strategy, sparing the yellow-rumped warblers the dangers of a longer overwater migration.

Although bayberry and wax myrtle are at the top of the menu along the coast, yellow-rumped warblers elsewhere may feast on berries of red cedar, dogwood, and other plants throughout the South. Even as far north as Lake Erie, a few yellow-rumps stay through the winter deep in the woods, feeding on berries of poison ivy. So when warblers start to move north in spring, the yellow-rumps are closest to us, scattered all over the southern and central states, and they arrive here first.

At this season the birders' attention is focused more and more on wooded areas close to the lake. Earlier in spring the waterfowl, blackbirds, and other migrants were more spread out over the landscape, and we ranged widely to look for them. But the warblers and other long-distance migratory songbirds will be most concentrated in trees near the lake's edge. Members of the extended local birding community, people from much of Ohio and southern Michigan, start making regular visits to this immediate area and checking favored sites along the Lake Erie shoreline, especially the boardwalk through the woods at Magee Marsh.

Magee starts to come into its own when the first yellow-rumped warblers return. As we walk in through the boardwalk's west entrance, we're scanning everywhere with anticipation. All the twigs are still leafless, everything is brown and gray, and the place may not look different from the way it did in February, but it *feels* different. We can see far away through the bare branches, and the first few birds that we see turn out to be the hyperactive little fuzzballs of golden-crowned kinglets and ruby-crowned kinglets. But then there's another bird — also small, but with a bolder and more alert look. In binoculars we pick up the snappy color pattern: white throat, black-striped chest, yellow patches at the shoulders, blue-gray on the back. The bird flies, flashing a yellow patch above its tail, and joins a second yellow-rumped warbler in the next tree. There's a small, loosely formed flock here, half a dozen birds moving through the woods together. As we get closer we can hear their callnotes, a sharp *tchek,* the sound of early spring. Warbler season has arrived.

From this point on, I'm tempted to go out every day. I'll check other lakeshore sites — the woodlot at Metzger Marsh, the larger tracts of trees at Maumee Bay and East Harbor state parks — but I always come back to Magee, the center of the experience. Numbers of yellow-rumped warblers there vary by the day. Sometimes in early April there are few or none, sometimes there are a dozen or more, and later in the month it's often possible to see forty or fifty in a trek through the whole loop of the boardwalk.

Every wild bird is perfect in its own way, but warblers may be more perfect than most. They're so small — smaller than the average sparrow, less than one fifth the bulk of a robin — but still big enough to pack the necessary energy for migrating thousands of miles. As I watch these yellow-rumped warblers now, their movements are precise, fast but not frenzied. The bird hops along a twig, pauses to look around, flutters up a few yards to another twig. Pauses again, opens its bill, and gives a rambling little song. Hops along the twig and picks at a couple of tiny items. Flies over to the next tree. Constantly moving, constantly posing, a compact little bundle of confidence. This warbler carries an aura of unconscious elegance in every moment, and its beautiful color pattern is just the icing on the cake.

By the third week of April a few other warblers start showing up. Palm warblers consistently appear early. Many palm warblers spend the winter in Florida (although not in palm trees: like several other warblers, this one is poorly named), and they move north almost as early as the yellow-rumps. They're often low around the edges of the woods, rather dull-colored but with a patch of yellow under the tail, drawing attention by constantly bobbing their tails up and down. Late April always brings a few Nashville warblers (which have nothing to do with Nashville) and some pine warblers (which, bucking the trend, actually do favor pine trees). If we sift through the roving flocks of yellow-rumps, we might find a black-and-white warbler, with its heavy stripes, or a black-throated green warbler, singing a hazy, buzzy song.

But over and over, as we search, we'll spot another warbler-sized bird, look at it eagerly, and then say, *Nah, just another yellow-rump.*

It's human nature. Only a few weeks earlier we'd been so eager for the yellow-rumped warblers to arrive, so happy when the first ones showed up. And we still appreciate them, of course, but we can't help but think about the waves of migrants still to come. Sometime before the last day of April, the first really big wave is bound to hit, abruptly pumping up the numbers and variety of migrant warblers and other birds along the lakeshore. We know it's coming, and we're impatient for it to arrive.

We know it's coming. We should be savoring this early stage, but we're so distracted by looking ahead. It's like when we were kids and we couldn't wait to be eighteen, couldn't wait to be twenty-one. Much later in life we look back on those younger years as a golden time and we might wish those days could have lasted, or that we could get them back; but at the time we were just impatient for time to go faster and that landmark birthday to arrive. That's how it feels now as we impatiently scan all the yellow-rumped warblers, hoping to find something different, hoping for the next chapter of spring.

One afternoon in late April I went out to the Magee Marsh boardwalk and stayed into the evening, following the yellow-rumped warblers around, thinking about other warblers that were still to come. It must have left me feeling restless, because I was fitful that night. Sometime after midnight I realized I wasn't going to fall asleep, so I got out of bed, threw on my winter parka, and went outdoors.

The sky was clear, and in our rural darkness, away from the lights of town, I could see a million stars overhead. Scanning around for familiar patterns, I saw Scorpio above the southern horizon. I'd always thought of this as a summer constellation, because it's so prominent just after sunset in July and August. But of course the position of Earth shifts with the seasons, so Scorpio was a predawn constellation at this point in spring.

Wide awake now in the chilly air, I spent a while locating and naming all the constellations I could remember. It occurred to me that any migrating warblers up in the night sky would be looking at the stars just as intently as I was, or more so, since their lives might depend on it.

One more element in the endless magic of these small birds is the fact that they can navigate by the stars. Scientists have proven this by raising baby migrant birds in a planetarium, where the appearance of the night sky can be controlled. In fall, when the young birds became restless at night, their movements were oriented toward the south. But when the scientists shifted the projection of the night sky, rotating it one way or the other, the birds changed their orientation, aiming for what would have been south under the new fake sky. Even when the scientists invented their own bogus constellations and raised birds under those, the migrants could still recognize "north" as the point in the sky around which all the star patterns appeared to rotate. So those birds were hatched not with a star map in their heads but with the ability to learn what they saw.

While I was thinking about this and gazing at the sky, I listened for the nocturnal flight calls of migrants, but heard none. A cold wind was blowing out of the north, and probably few migrants would attempt to travel against the headwind.

In a couple of nights, though, things were likely to change. The weather maps showed the change coming. A couple of nights from now, a powerful current of wind would flow from the south. A couple of nights from now, the persistent heavy rains to the south of us would clear out, releasing vast numbers of migrants that had been pinned down by the storms. The dam would break, the birds would flood north, a wave of migratory warblers and other birds would wash over northern Ohio.

Thinking about it, I was excited, yes, but feeling resentful as well, because of the timing of something else. Any time now the feds might respond to our lawsuit regarding the Camp Perry wind turbine — and when that happened, the clock would immediately start ticking down the brief time that we would have to rally support for our position, to try to meet with lawmakers, to try to get the project stopped by other means.

Of course our involvement was our own doing. We had made

the conscious decision to step into this controversy. But it seemed ironic and unfair that in this brief springtime, in this brief life, we should be trapped indoors, arguing about politics and regulations and money and power.

We would do it because we cared about migratory birds. But that put us at a disadvantage, because we'd be up against opponents who did *not* care. The people who might eventually construct the turbine were just part of a chain of command, without much input to the decision. Those behind the scenes who were pushing the project, those who stood to profit from this carnage, wouldn't understand what motivates us. They wouldn't see the miracle of these tiny sparks of life, these myriads of tiny messengers of hope, carrying spring on their wings as they streamed northward across continents, driven by ancient rhythms, guided by the light of distant stars.

13

Boardwalk People

Underneath an ornate wooden arch, the wide, smooth boardwalk leads back into the green shadows of the woods. The entryway beckons with promise and mystery; in the soft light of sunrise it looks as if it could be the entrance to a magic kingdom. In a way, it is. Every spring this woodlot at Ohio's Magee Marsh Wildlife Area does become a place of magic.

Among dedicated birders, this is the most celebrated boardwalk in North America. Some others have heavier human traffic; for example, many more people visit the boardwalk at Anhinga Trail in Everglades National Park. Florida specialty birds like anhingas and purple gallinules are among the attractions there, but most people visit for the alligators and the overall swamp experience. At Magee Marsh almost all the visitors have come for the birds, and they have come from everywhere. For a few weeks in spring, this storied spot on the edge of Lake Erie hosts a genuine community of birders.

It's fitting that it should. The history isn't widely known, but birding in a modern sense really began on the Lake Erie plain, only a couple of counties east of Magee Marsh.

That was all the way back in the 1890s. Serious ornithologists of that era still insisted that to identify a bird with certainty, you had to hold it in your hand and study fine details, so a shotgun was considered essential birding equipment. But some enthusiasts had started using the poor-quality binoculars of the day to try to see those same fine details on free-flying birds, to recognize more of them in the wild.

A couple of guys in Lorain County, Ohio, were pushing the limits of this approach. Lynds Jones, about thirty years old, an instructor at Oberlin College, and William Leon Dawson, a student in his twenties, were both rabidly intense birders. They became obsessed with seeing how many kinds of birds they could find within the limits of Lorain County. Cooperating and competing, they prodded each other to do more. Finally, on May 17, 1898, they made an all-out one-day run. Starting well before dawn, they walked the woods and fields around Oberlin, then took the trolley up to the lakeshore (this was just before the era of mass-produced automobiles) and hiked some more, hitting every good habitat they could reach. By nightfall they had counted 102 species. It was the first time that anyone, anywhere in the world, had identified more than 100 bird species in a single day.

Jones and Dawson were sharp and energetic, but another factor in their success was location. By taking in the Lake Erie shoreline, they tapped into the enormous concentrations of migratory birds that build up there every spring.

Others followed in their footsteps during the twentieth century, all around the edge of Lake Erie. On the north side of the
lake, at Point Pelee, Ontario, observers discovered that major
numbers of migrants would build up under certain weather conditions in both spring and fall. Spring concentrations could be truly
phenomenal if birds were moving north on southerly winds and
ran into rainstorms directly over the Canadian shore; in that situation, birds would drop out at the nearest land, the long, narrow
peninsula of Point Pelee itself. By the 1960s scores of birders from
around Canada and the United States would head to Pelee in May,
hoping for such a migrant bonanza.

Across the lake on the Ohio side, naturalists from Toledo
found that spring migrants would collect along the shoreline even
without bad weather to put them down. Little Cedar Point was just
a few miles east of the city, a convenient place to seek these birds,
but access became more difficult after it was turned into a federal
wildlife refuge in 1964. But there were other wooded patches farther east. One of the best was at Magee Marsh, administered as a
wildlife area by the state of Ohio.

Local game warden and naturalist Laurel Van Camp had noticed
remarkable gatherings of migratory songbirds at Magee as early as
the 1960s, especially in the woodlot right next to the lakeshore.
Van Camp marked out a footpath through the woods in 1970. Birders soon began using it. This trail worked well at first, but as the
handful of visiting birders grew to dozens at a time in the 1980s,
the trail gradually widened and side trails began to crisscross the
woods in all directions.

By this time our friend Mark Shieldcastle was working for the
Division of Wildlife out of the Magee office. Every time he went
back to those woods he saw more trails and more trampling. With

a huge parking lot along the edge (because the adjacent beach was then a state park, popular for summer swimming), there was hardly any limit to the number of birders who might venture into the site in spring. The birders loved that woodlot, but it appeared they might soon love it to death, degrading the habitat that migratory birds so desperately needed for their stopovers. Mark had a suggestion: run a boardwalk through the woods and restrict foot traffic to that one path.

As with any government agency, it took some political maneuvering to push this through the Division of Wildlife. Higher-ups had to be persuaded that it had been their idea in the first place. Paying for the construction was a potential political minefield also: much of the division's funding comes from the sales of hunting and fishing licenses, and it would have been dicey to pay for a birding boardwalk with dollars from that source — or with taxpayer dollars pulled from the state budget. But Ohio had just instituted a voluntary one-dollar checkoff on the tax forms for people who wanted to support wildlife projects, and the Magee boardwalk became the first big project covered by those funds. Mark laid out a suggested route through the woods, following Laurel Van Camp's original trail, and the boardwalk was completed in 1989.

Sturdy and solid, eight feet wide, with flat guardrails at a comfortable height for leaning elbows, the boardwalk loops for almost a mile through the interior of the boggy woods. It's accessible to wheelchairs and electric carts. Even for the most able-bodied walkers, though, it provides an easy stroll through places that otherwise would be a swampy slog. And although its original intent was to protect habitat for birds, it has become an incredible boon to bird-watchers.

Incredible. That's the right word. Even the most seasoned and well-traveled birders who come here agree that the close-up views of small migratory songbirds often possible here, all along the Magee boardwalk in spring, would be hard to imagine in most places.

Maybe it's something about the structure of the woods, with so many short willows, box elders, dogwoods, and other shrubby trees close to the boardwalk's path, under the canopy of tall cottonwoods. Maybe it's something about the sheer numbers of birds making stopovers in this habitat, so that at any given moment, by the law of averages, a few will be nearby. Maybe the birds quickly adapt to the fact that humans will not stray from the boardwalk or parking lot, so we pose no threat—just as wild birds will forage within yards of a busy highway, sensing that the motor vehicles will not leave their paved pathway. Whatever the reason, the Magee boardwalk is an exceptionally good place to get very good looks at warblers and other small migratory birds.

For birders with experience elsewhere, the phrase "good looks at warblers" may sound like an oxymoron. Warblers are famously hard to observe. Seeing them at all is often a neck-straining exercise of staring at treetops. Even at Magee, of course, some warblers go to the highest foliage of the tallest cottonwoods, especially on warm days. But almost always some are down at eye level or below, and within mere feet of the parking lot's edge or the boardwalk's handrails. These close views are good for experienced birders, but they're absolute dynamite for newcomers. If you're taking someone out for her first birding experience, you don't want to try to get her focused on a distant hiding scrap of feathers. You want to show her a brilliant jewel of a warbler cavorting at arm's length in front of her face, so close that binoculars would be extraneous. That kind of look can captivate anyone, can make her fall in love with these little creatures.

As a result, the Magee boardwalk has played a major role as a recruiter of new bird-watchers. Many a person, drawn there by idle curiosity or dragged there by friends, has become totally enchanted by these avian treasures. Many a newbie on the boards has gone on to acquire binoculars and bird guides, to start a life list, to seek out new species all over the landscape. But such people will come back whenever they can to this magical spot where it all started. People who have experienced the wonderful views of warblers and other songbirds here find it hard to stay away.

Visitation to the Magee boardwalk has been gradually increasing for years. I moved to this area in 2005, and during the next few spring seasons I noted a few times in May when the parking lot was completely filled, with more cars out in the overflow grassy area to the east. (To give an idea of numbers involved, I counted/ estimated that the lot would hold at least seven hundred vehicles.) That was most likely to happen on the Saturday before Mother's Day, also designated as International Migratory Bird Day. That holiday, IMBD, is still celebrated at sites all over the Western Hemisphere, but locally it has been overshadowed by a longer event, the Biggest Week in American Birding. Now there isn't as much of a spike in visitors on IMBD, but overall visitation throughout the end of April and the first three weeks of May has continued to increase, on weekdays as well as weekends and at all hours of the day.

The social scene on the boardwalk is hard to comprehend until you experience it. People who haven't been there, seeing photos of birders clustered on the boardwalk, sometimes react with shudders: "Too crowded! I couldn't stand it!" But when you're actually there, it doesn't seem crowded, at least not most of the time.

There's usually a logjam right at the west entrance, because people start walking in and almost immediately pause to look at the closest birds. But beyond that, crowds form only where particularly notable birds have been spotted. If there's a sighting of Kirtland's warbler, the rarest member of that family, a mob scene may result; fortunately, Kirtland's favor open woods or edge situations, so they seldom linger in the deep cover along the boardwalk itself. A lesser local rarity like a worm-eating warbler or cerulean warbler can cause a traffic jam of a hundred people at once. But if you're not pausing to look at that bird, you can almost always make your way past and go on to an empty stretch of the boardwalk.

Some people who have never been there and who claim they wouldn't be caught dead in such a mob are perfectly accustomed to birding in crowds in other situations. For example, if you go to the hawk-watch platform at Cape May, New Jersey, or to the lookouts at Hawk Mountain, Pennsylvania, on a big flight day in fall, you might be standing shoulder to shoulder with scores of other birders, watching the raptors come past. If you go on a popular seabirding trip off either coast, you might be in the middle of a crowd at the ship's rail, scanning the ocean for rarities. If you go to the Illinois Ornithological Society's "gull frolic" on the edge of Lake Michigan, you might be jammed in with 150 other avid birders studying the fine details of Iceland gulls.

Hardly anyone objects to crowding in those situations. In fact, the social connection is a big part of the fun. I look forward to these chances to catch up with friends, to hear all the latest. And the scene on the Magee boardwalk is the same. We're shoulder to shoulder at the rail sometimes, but instead of hawks or seabirds a quarter mile away, we're looking at warblers ten feet away. The sense of fellowship is just as strong, the discussions are the same, and conversations can go on, with a revolving cast of participants, for days at a time.

If I visit in March I'm likely to see only a few birders from the local area, or none at all, on the boardwalk itself, although usually some people are watching the bald eagle nest high above the edge of the parking lot. Visitation swells during April, although it's still mostly local birders, plus some coming in from as far away as Columbus, Indianapolis, or Detroit, especially on weekends. By the end of April many of the visitors are from out of state, and a week into May many are from other countries, as the community of boardwalk people becomes international in scope.

Toward the peak of migration, anytime I walk the boardwalk I'll see dozens of people I've never seen before and dozens of familiar faces. I greet many of these people warmly, as old friends, and I genuinely mean it, but I don't necessarily remember their names. Maybe I never knew their names at all and I just remember the faces. Frequently I admit up front that I'm terrible at names and make some joke about how I should write a field guide to humans. It doesn't matter; bird people are generous enough to just laugh about it and tell me their names.

A wonderful thing for me about the boardwalk in spring is the chance to reconnect with old friends. At any moment I may run into someone I haven't seen in years. An even better thing is seeing all the new people, and seeing how the overall profile of the visitors is becoming more diverse all the time.

Ohio has a thriving Amish community in the east-central part of the state. An Amish friend of ours, Robert Hershberger, runs a store called Time & Optics near Millersburg, about a hundred miles southeast of Magee Marsh. Robert is an expert birder and he's also Ohio's most respected dealer of binoculars and telescopes for nature study, and partly owing to his influence, birding is hugely popular in that area. Many of the Amish birders are legendary for their skills. Most of them follow beliefs that prevent them from driving motor vehicles, but that doesn't stop them from hiring drivers to take them places, so vanloads will show up at Magee on most days in spring. We see whole Amish families out on the boardwalk together, even the youngest children spotting and identifying birds. I treasure my conversations with people from this wonderful community.

Indeed, the boardwalk serves as a meeting place for people from diverse backgrounds. It's inspiring to see the patriarch of an Amish family deep in discussion about hawk migration with a trio of biologists from Mexico. It's inspiring to see a group of teenaged birders from Michigan trading stories about rare birds with a retired couple from Alaska. Shared interest and a safe, welcoming place are the only ingredients needed to make these connections.

A big part of the attraction for birders here is the chance to see birds low and close. As you might guess, this is a powerful draw for photographers as well. I actually had my first inkling of that years ago, in the 1990s, more than a decade before I even considered moving to Ohio. At a small gathering of friends in California, one guy brought a whole carousel of 35mm slides to show us, and we all gasped in astonishment as he put up one beautiful point-blank image after another of eastern songbirds, especially warblers. "Warblers! How on earth did you get photos like these?"

"It's this *place*," Ed told us. "Magee Marsh in Ohio. The boardwalk there. It's just incredible for bird photography, and hardly anyone knows about it."

In the quarter century since that conversation, things have changed. Magee is still incredible for bird photography, but now absolutely everyone knows about it. The sheer numbers of cameras there in spring are mind-boggling. I believe that during the month of May, more warbler photos are taken in northwestern Ohio than in all the rest of the United States combined.

The most serious photographers often find the boardwalk too challenging, as tensions flare when their big tripods block the way for birders to get past. For the long lenses, opportunities are better out along the lengthy edge of the woods or along the estuary trail that leads west from the Magee parking lot into the Ottawa Refuge. Photographers with smaller rigs or point-and-shoot cameras get superb shots all along the boardwalk, and on a really good day people are snapping pictures with their phones as the warblers come close.

Whether their focus is birding or photography or both, many of the out-of-town visitors stay for a week or more. Some come back year after year, planning vacation time to be here in early May. Friends who don't see each other at any other time of year plan to meet up on the boardwalk. I think of these annual visitors as integral members of our local family, just as much as those of us who live here all year. Some of them undoubtedly have spent more total hours on the boardwalk than I have. When I see Jack and Sue from Pittsburgh, or Brian and Jeanine and their adorable kids, or Kibby from West Virginia, or Bob (whom I dubbed "the mayor of the boardwalk") maneuvering on his electric cart and sharing his years of expertise with newcomers, I know that spring has truly arrived.

Of course, people are peeling off constantly to go to other nearby sites. During our May festival, the Biggest Week in American Birding, we make a conscious effort to reduce the crowds on the boardwalk, sending field trips out to a score of other destinations, urging visitors to check out other hot spots. But during the peak birding season, the overall welcoming spirit of the boardwalk extends out to other sites all around the region. After the season ends, we hope, some of that warmth and sense of community will stay with people for the rest of the year.

Hemingway was reflecting on his own good fortune of being in Paris as a young man when he wrote: "Wherever you go for the rest of your life, it stays with you, for Paris is a moveable feast." In a bird-watcher's view of the world, it would be possible to say the same thing about Magee Marsh.

If you want to literally feast, however, you have to go elsewhere: unless you're a bird, there's nothing to eat at the boardwalk itself. Often at the migration peak, food vendors will set up outside the visitors' center at Ottawa National Wildlife Refuge next door, a handy stop for birders on the go. Other people will fan out farther—south to Kozy Corners in the town of Oak Harbor, or east or west along Route 2 to establishments like Barnside Creamery, Porky's Pizza Trof, and Blackberry Corners.

A quiet café out in the country, Blackberry Corners is a favorite of our local crew at all seasons, and it's jam-packed with birders from all over the world in late April and May. The proprietor, Brenda Lowe, always keeps a good supply of home-baked pie on hand, and we slipped into the tradition of having a slice of Brenda's pie whenever we had something to celebrate. And what do birders celebrate most? Finding a bird we've never seen before, a new species for our life lists: in other words, a "lifer." The phrase "Lifer Pie" entered the birding lexicon, and visitors have carried it far and wide. The musician, entertainer, and birder R. Bruce Richardson came to Ohio for several spring seasons before he moved to Australia, and now many Australian birders regularly celebrate their new birds with Lifer Pie.

So as an honorary extension of the boardwalk, Blackberry Corners has touched the lives of bird enthusiasts all over the world.

For me, the Magee Marsh boardwalk in late April and May is the scene of a gigantic party — a party where all the people talk quietly, move gently, and share knowledge about the natural world. For me it's a deeply soul-satisfying experience to be there. But I know it's not for everyone. Some people, including some who love nature, will never want to go there. I respect that.

Some long-time birders in the Toledo region are still bitter about how much things have changed. They remember going to the boardwalk — or to the trail, before the boardwalk was built — with close friends and having plenty of room. It was never crowded, even on the biggest flight days. They wish they could go back to the way it was then. Some of them place personal blame on Kimberly and me, saying we brought more people here.

In a way I can see their viewpoint. Wouldn't it be awesome to have such a fabulous birding spot as your own private preserve? I live just a few miles from the Magee boardwalk, closer than practically any other birder. Sometimes, I confess, when I'm swamped with work and have hardly any time to spare, I wish that I might slip out to this site and just be alone with the birds for a few minutes. But of course during spring migration that's not going to happen.

I'll sacrifice my spring solitude because I see the good that results from the crowds. I see people greeting old friends, rekindling friendships that might have begun right here in years past. I see people coming here for the first time, gazing around in open-

mouthed wonder. I see veteran birders with years of practice sharing their knowledge with brand-new beginners. I see families
sharing the experience, and I see people coming here alone and
being welcomed by strangers. I see people arriving with mild curiosity and leaving with the spark of an intense, passionate interest. I see people arriving with a single-minded aim to add more
species to their lists and leaving with a new determination to help
protect bird populations. I see more and more variety among the
humans on the boardwalk, people of all skin colors, all ages, all
backgrounds, coming together over a shared interest.

If Kimberly and I had any kind of influence in making this happen, then, yes, we will gladly shoulder the blame.

14

The First Big Wave

Migrating birds are intensely attuned to weather. They have to be. Weather dictates their progress, and often their survival. Even a slight wind will affect their motion as they fly, because they are suspended in the atmosphere; they move in relation to the air around them, not the ground below. When they are aloft and migrating, storms can kill them, and even a mild headwind can cancel out most of their progress. So as a rule migrants don't travel every night or every day. During migratory stopovers they may wait for days, even for a week or more, for conditions to be right for their next flight.

So the flow of migration is far from uniform. On some nights and days, in a given region, no birds are migrating at all. On other nights and days, vast numbers are on the move.

Every active birder becomes a weather addict in migration season. We leave our televisions tuned to the Weather Channel or to the local news station with the best meteorologists. We obsessively check and recheck the extended forecasts. We study the weather maps, tracking the movement of low-pressure and high-pressure systems across the continent. We watch the movement of associated cold fronts and storms and warm fronts. Then, especially at the approach of peak season in May, we try to predict which nights will produce the biggest flights, so that we can plan to be out the following morning.

After a few seasons of obsessively studying weather maps, some patterns are so obvious that we see them in an instant, without thinking about them. At temperate latitudes in North America, major weather systems almost always move from west to east, so we can look to the west to see what's coming. Warm fronts and cold fronts — the places where masses of air of different temperatures come together — also move, but in more mysterious ways, and sometimes they stall in one place while other patterns of weather move around them.

Air consistently flows in a clockwise direction around an area of high barometric pressure and counterclockwise around a low. When a high-pressure area is centered just to the west of us, the wind, moving clockwise around it, will be out of the north here. After the high passes eastward, the wind will switch to the south. If there's also a low-pressure center west of us at that time, the counterclockwise circulation around it will add to the flow of wind from the south. That combination can act like a gigantic aerial conveyor belt to hasten the arrival of northbound birds — but if the low also brings storms, the rain can complicate things.

Recent years have seen increasingly variable weather events all over the globe, with greater extremes of heat and cold, floods and drought, and violent storms, all apparently linked to an overall warming of the atmosphere. Even so, meteorologists continue to get better at predicting local weather, at least in the short term. In the wildly complicated physics of the atmosphere, certain conditions tend to produce certain others, and weather scientists can run computer models to predict which outcomes are most likely for several days ahead.

Here in northwestern Ohio, as in other migration hot spots, birders obsess over the five-day forecasts and ten-day forecasts — especially toward the end of April and beginning of May, when we're impatient for the first really big wave of migrant songbirds from the tropics. There always seems to be a time in late April when it feels as if migration is behind schedule. After some tantalizing glimpses, spring seems to slow down. Even in years when warm early readings have brought full leaf-out to the trees, things cool down again. Winds are northerly for days at a time, stopping the flow of migration, and the ten-day forecast fails to offer any encouragement.

During this time, everything seems to be in a state of waiting. Local creatures are merely waiting for warmth and sunshine. After a week of cold gray skies, the first sunny day will bring out butterflies: little spring azures fluttering around the opening buds of saplings, fast-flying red admirals darting down forest paths. Sunshine will bring the painted turtles and rare Blanding's turtles up out of the marshes to bask on logs. But one sunny day won't suddenly bring out the next pulse of migrant birds, because they're not here yet. We have to wait for them to arrive from the south.

It's a tantalizing season. The stage is set, the audience is waiting, the curtains have opened partway, but the main actors have yet to appear onstage.

We know they're coming. There have been signs for weeks. After we've looked at the same bare brown woodlots all winter, there comes a day when they look subtly different. It's no detail we can see, just a collected impression of difference, a thickening of the treetops as millions of buds swell on the twigs. Within a few days after that, the edge of the woods will begin to show gauzy thin patches of color, areas like pale yellow-green clouds of smoke, just a haze of spring color. Up at the Lake Erie shore the leaf-out may be a little later — we hope it will be, to make the migrant birds easier to see — but on the drive up to the lake we can see the woods changing by the day.

Some telltale migrants hint that the first big warbler wave is imminent. Departures as well as arrivals mark the season. The big flocks of little juncos are gone, as if the gray and white feathers of these classic snowbirds had melted into the emerging green grass. A few individuals still lurk around the edges of woods, looking more furtive and uncertain than they did on the snowdrifts of winter.

At the same time white-crowned sparrows have shown up all over the region, smartly patterned birds with black-and-white stripes on their heads. Little flocks of white-crowns trip about on the ground underneath bird feeders at the Black Swamp Bird Observatory, at the visitors' center at the Ottawa Refuge, in backyards in Oak Harbor and Port Clinton. Males are practicing the songs they'll sing later on the breeding grounds in Canada, disjointed series of burry whistles and trills, providing background music for late April mornings. Their close relatives, white-throated sparrows, are also passing through. They sing a different song from the white-crowns — plaintive whistles, *Oh, sweet, Kimberly-Kimberly-Kimberly* — and they tend to stick to more heavily wooded areas. Both of these types of sparrows, white-crowns and white-throats, have spent the winter not far away, from Ohio down to the southeastern states, so they didn't need major weather systems to bring them to the lakeshore.

Chimney swifts also show up around this time. They may be anywhere, flying high above the lakeshore or swooping low over any pond, but often I see them first circling over the town of Oak Harbor, where chimneys provide their main nesting sites.

Even at a glance a chimney swift looks different from other birds. Compact and almost tailless, it has two long, narrow wings that curve back like scimitars. In flight the bird looks like a bow crossed by a short, stubby arrow, but this arrow flies forever, buoyed up by its bowed wings. Blasting through the air at high speed — the name "swift" is no accident — it alternates rapid-fire bursts of wingbeats with long, stiff-winged glides, but it can turn in an instant or hang motionless in one spot on the wind, a complete master of its element.

Swifts are the most purely aerial of all birds, spending more than half their lives flying. They have no need to pause and rest between flights, any more than a porpoise or dolphin needs to rest on the bottom of the sea. Swifts will come down for the night, clinging to rough vertical surfaces with their tiny feet — or they may not; some European swifts are known to sleep while flying.

Chimney swifts historically placed their nests inside hollow trees. As the landscape changed they adapted to using chimneys instead, and the switch is now essentially complete; they're now summer birds of towns and cities all over the eastern United States and southeastern Canada. Subsisting entirely on insects caught in midair, they must vacate the region in the colder months. They spend the winter in western South America, including the skies over the western Amazon Basin, just east of the Andes.

When they come back in spring I try to imagine their view of life, so different from ours. As they have come rocketing north, the landscape below them has changed from tropical jungle to empty farm fields and small-town Ohio. They are worldly in a way that we can never be. I'm tempted to stop strangers on the sidewalk in Oak Harbor and beg them to look at these swifts zooming and circling overhead, to understand what they are and where they've come from. Maybe I can't get every person to go out to the woods and look for warblers, but when the chimney swifts arrive, anyone can see amazing avian world travelers just by looking up from the street.

As power fliers that travel by day, chimney swifts will make their way back here even without any kind of favorable winds. They will get here even if winds and weather are consistently against them. But we are waiting for the first big arrival of migratory songbirds that have wintered in the tropics, and the majority of them are waiting for good winds to help them on their way. Watching the ten-day forecasts, feeling a little frustrated, we are waiting for conditions to line up for a spike of warmer readings and a flow of wind from the south.

A few years after I moved to Ohio, I started posting occasional predictions about the spring migration. Weather had always been a big interest of mine, and it was fascinating to see the interplay between weather events and bird movements along Lake Erie. Long discussions with Mark Shieldcastle, Kimberly, and others gave me insights into how the systems worked here. Eventually I was startled to find out that many birders were following my predictions and using them to plan their trips, so I felt a heightened responsibility to get it right.

Of course, total accuracy is impossible, because weather forecasts change. Even when everything looks perfect three or four days out, a change in the pattern can mean that the big flight arrives earlier or later than predicted, or not at all. In spring I spend a lot of time with my fingers crossed, hoping the forecast will hold up but knowing it might not.

In most springs, though, even if the flight seems behind schedule, a pattern will line up for some night in late April or the beginning of May. The local forecast and the continental maps agree: a large-scale system will bring strong warm winds out of the south or southwest overnight, with only scattered rains or none at all. When it looks that good, I'll go ahead and predict the arrival of the first big wave.

I might make such a prediction several days ahead of time, and other birders might post comments in agreement or argument. But when it comes down to the night before, we can all look at radar images and see if the flight is actually developing. A glance at the Nexrad radar pages on the National Weather Service website or at various radar apps, an hour or two after dark, will tell us whether the flight is light or heavy or nonexistent.

More and more birders are learning about radar. Every night during the peak of migration, listserves and social media sites light up with chatter about it. Experienced birders comment on the magnitude of the night's flight. Enthusiastic but less experienced birders misinterpret what they're seeing — as if a huge flight in a different part of the country would make any difference locally. Newcomers checking it out for the first time express their utter mystification: "Why are the birds flying in big round flocks?" But of course they're not; it's just that the radar beam sweeps around in circles, sampling what's present in a circular piece of the sky.

"Those circles must be more than a hundred miles across! How could those be birds? There'd have to be millions in each flock!" But in fact on a big night there are many, many millions of birds on the move above the landscape, passing through the sections of airspace sampled by the radar stations. They're mostly not in flocks; they're randomly spread out through the sky, mostly navigating on their own, all moving more or less northward but not together. Passing continuously through the cone probed by the radar's sweep, they show up as a circle, either solid or hollow, depending on the average height of their flight. In the most common graphic representation of the radar data, bird echoes show up as blue, as opposed to the green, yellow, orange, or red of actual rainstorm activity. When birders talk about "blue doughnuts" on radar, we're talking about migratory birds on the wing.

Here in the Magee Marsh region we're in one of the small gaps between the main Nexrad radar circles. One of the Nexrad sites is at Cleveland, along the Lake Erie shoreline about seventy-five miles east of us. Another is at Detroit, at least fifty miles to our north. In spring we look mostly at the radar from southwestern Ohio, near Dayton and Cincinnati. It's farther away, but in spring birds passing over that site are headed in our direction. If the circle over southwestern Ohio is lit up bright blue, with dark blue and blue-green toward the center, and if winds are from the south, big numbers of migrants are coming our way, and it doesn't matter that there's no radar image for the sky directly over our heads.

If it looks good overnight, we're all keyed up. We should be sleeping but we're staying up and looking at the weather and wind maps online, watching the radar, trying to gauge the strength of the flight.

No matter how promising it looked in the middle of the night, we can't be sure what the morning is like unless we go out there and see for ourselves. As early as we can, we head for the lakeshore. Any number of sites on the shoreline would be worth checking, but at this stage, when we've been waiting so long for the migrant wave, it seems logical to go first to the Magee Marsh boardwalk.

Turning off State Route 2 at the sign for Magee, we drive north. We pass the modest gray building of the Black Swamp Bird

Observatory, then swampy woods, then a big pond on the left that may hold a random grebe or two. We're driving slowly, alert for baby turtles or other vulnerable creatures on the pavement. Listening, too, with the windows down: are we hearing the distant sounds of birds that weren't here yesterday? The road makes a swing to run straight east, and we squint into the early sun as we pass the Division of Wildlife's building called the Sportsmen's Migratory Bird Center. We'll come back to walk the trails here later, but right now we're just eager to get to the edge of the lake.

Past the Sportsmen's Center the road curves again to arrow straight north and breaks out of the woods onto the causeway across the wide-open Magee Marsh itself. Swallows swoop and glide low over the green marsh grass, white egrets stand in the shallows, and we're tempted to stop and look at ducks or other birds on distant patches of open water. We'll be stopping anyway, because there will be other cars in front of us, and some will stop so people can ogle the baby Canada geese waddling down the shoulder of the causeway with their watchful parents. Serious birders, not so entranced by fuzzy baby geese, will wait impatiently. But finally we're across that open mile of marsh and the road turns west onto the beach ridge. Ahead of us tall trees beckon, the edge of the woodlot that holds the famous boardwalk.

Will this be one of those magic mornings when the drought breaks, when the dam breaks, when the woods are flooded with migrant birds? We have every reason to think so, but we can't be sure . . .

We can't be sure until we step out of the car at the edge of the Magee parking lot and immediately hear the rich, piping whistle of a Baltimore oriole. Somewhere up in the bare cottonwoods, a warbling vireo starts into its rambling monologue. A house wren bursts into explosive bubbling song in the understory of the woods. Turning around, we glimpse four or five small birds flitting among the opening buds of a box elder, but before we can focus on them, we're distracted by the first big flock of blue jays high overhead. Then a brilliant yellow warbler, shining like spun gold, lands in the sunlight in the nearest tree. Yes, this is going to be a good day.

Poised on the edge, I'm always torn: I want to stand motionless and soak it all in; I want to hurry up and explore, to find every bird here. But usually I begin by standing still for a minute or two, staring up at the flights of blue jays overhead.

When I first moved to Ohio, the spring flights of blue jays were among the things that surprised me most. Birders generally don't regard blue jays as migratory at all. These rambunctious, noisy, colorful jays are staples of backyards almost everywhere east of the Rockies and present year-round practically throughout their range. It's easy to make the mistaken assumption that blue jays must all be permanent residents wherever they occur. However, substantial numbers do migrate south in fall and north in spring. They often go unnoticed among local populations of jays in the lands they traverse, but when northbound jays reach the south shore of Lake Erie in spring, suddenly they become obvious.

These are daytime migrants, unlike most small birds. They seem to take off shortly after sunrise and reach the Lake Erie shoreline soon after. Anywhere along the lakefront on these mornings with southerly winds, we may look up and see long, straggling strings of a dozen or twenty or fifty or more. Long-tailed, with quick, snappy wingbeats, they look dark in silhouette except for light coming through their white tail corners and through the white trailing edges on the wings. Birders seeing this phenomenon for the first time may have trouble recognizing the birds at first, because we just don't see blue jays this way at other times of the year. Moving steadily, eerily silent, they seem filled with purpose — until we realize that some flocks are moving east along the shore, some are moving west, and some are milling around and doubling back. They're confounded by the lake, and undecided about what to do next. Their shifts in direction make them hard to count, but on some mornings they number in the thousands.

Some other diurnal migrants are moving also. A few small flocks of goldfinches come bouncing along at treetop level. Flocks of swallows are skimming low over the lake, all going in the same direction, and as the day warms up a few hawks will come by, paralleling the shoreline. But by far the biggest transformation of the day is brought by the birds that have arrived overnight.

These are the birds that bring the brightest magic, arriving mysteriously under the soft cover of night, carrying springtime on their wings.

When I call it magic it might seem like hyperbole, but that is genuinely how it feels to me. Even though I know how these birds came to be here, even though I predicted their arrival for this precise morning, it still seems unbelievable and unreal that they're actually here. This is especially true if I've made the effort to go out the day before and have those observations for a direct comparison.

Yesterday I walked the entire loop of the Magee boardwalk, and the migrants I found were sparse and predictable, much the same as what I might have seen two weeks earlier. I found only four kinds of warblers on the whole trek, and they were the expected ones: fewer than twenty yellow-rumped warblers, three palm warblers, and singles of two other species. This morning I see or hear five species of warblers in the first five minutes. I'll continue to find more different kinds as the morning goes on. Each one is a treasure, a shining gem of discovery.

Look: just above eye level, among the buds in this willow, is a male black-throated green warbler. It's so close, and so brightly patterned: glowing yellow face, black bib stretching down onto the sides of the chest, moss-green back, intricate gray and white marks on the wings. This bird might have been in southern Mexico or Central America less than a month ago, and it undoubtedly arrived here at Magee Marsh overnight.

Just a few yards farther along: here's a box elder tree in its early spring dress, pale green leaves just starting to open, flowers blooming along the branches. The flowers aren't impressive, just limp, stringy greenish strands, but they must hold some nectar or small insects or both: a Cape May warbler is methodically working over the blooms. It's a stunning bird, brilliant yellow with strong black stripes on the chest, rich reddish brown all over the face, a big white wing patch, lots of pattern crowded onto the typical tiny warbler frame. Cape May warblers spend the winter mostly on islands in the Caribbean and fly to spruce forests of Canada for the summer. During the next couple of weeks they'll be numerous here (much more so than they ever are at Cape May, New Jersey, merely the place where the species first caught the attention of a scientist), but this is the first one I've seen this year.

Birders use the term "FOY" — first of the year — quite a lot at this season, and it carries more emotional weight than the casual abbreviation might imply. First of the year! After the last one I managed to find in October, after the long decline of late fall, after the cold winter and slow spring, here is this stunning little warbler again, the first one I've seen in more than six months. I watch it eagerly, following its delicate movements with binoculars, drinking in every little detail.

But I can't linger too long, because there are so many other birds to see. Slowly I work along the edge of the woods and then onto the west entrance of the boardwalk. Crowds of people are here—some had read my predictions about this day, but many would have been here anyway—and everyone is moving slowly, speaking in hushed tones, looking around in delight.

Look: here in the bare twigs at eye level, only a few feet from the boardwalk's edge, a blackburnian warbler glows like a hot coal, a shocking, brilliant orange. It might have been in southern Ohio yesterday and in South America a month ago, but here it is yards away from Lake Erie, on its way to Canada. Over in the next tree, another Cape May warbler. Then two yellow-rumped warblers—there are many more around today than yesterday—and then a blue-headed vireo, hopping along the branches more deliberately than a warbler, the white rings around its eyes giving it a surprised look. Then a female black-throated green warbler, almost as colorful as the male, and then in the next tree there will be more surprises, and more, and more, all along the boardwalk. It's like a treasure hunt in which tiny treasures keep on coming, or an Easter egg hunt in which the eggs have hatched into brilliantly colorful creatures, moving around the trees and singing. We lucky birders are lost in wonder, surrounded with the extravagant abundance of spring.

"Nature's first green is gold," wrote Robert Frost, "her hardest hue to hold." He could have been writing about this very morning, with the pale green of opening leaves glowing in the pale golden mist among the trees. The dawn of the first big migrant wave feels like a return to the Garden of Eden. The world has been wiped clean; everything is fresh and new.

The first major pulse of migrants in this time frame usually brings numbers of Baltimore orioles and rose-breasted grosbeaks, and usually some scarlet tanagers. There's no particular connection between these birds, but all three are medium-sized songbirds (larger than warblers, smaller than robins), they're all coming from the tropics, and males of all three are colorful enough to draw attention even from casual observers.

My first male scarlet tanager of the season always comes as a shock. It's a brilliant, flaming red, glowing as if it were lit up from the inside, set off by black wings and tail. Against the pale green of small new leaves in the mostly bare branches it looks even brighter, and looks out of place, as if it had just escaped from someone's tropical hothouse aviary. Scarlet tanagers will continue passing through woodlots along Lake Erie through most of May, and many will stay for the summer in the Oak Openings region just west of Toledo, but they are harder to see in their usual treetop haunts after all the leaves come out. These earliest ones of the spring always seem like gifts for our eyes.

Baltimore orioles usually arrive in a rush during this wave. Females are an attractively bright yellow-orange, but adult males are unbelievably gorgeous, with shades of orange so deep and rich that they appear to have been melted and poured onto the birds. Their songs, too, are deep rich whistles; they sound just like they look.

If skies have been clear and winds continuous throughout the night, migrants will be mostly concentrated near the lakeshore. But if storms with heavy rain have moved through the area sometime between midnight and dawn, they bring a more widespread kind of magic: migrating birds will have come down wherever they happened to encounter the storms, so they will be spread through woodlots and backyards all over the region.

In that scenario, even people who usually pay scant attention to nature may notice the sudden influx of Baltimore orioles. And if they have any kind of bird feeder out, even the simplest and most casual sort, there's a good chance a rose-breasted grosbeak will find it. These chunky, flashy birds have an uncanny ability to scope out sunflower seeds, perhaps by following the lead of resident birds like cardinals and sparrows.

With their big beaks and with the big patches of black, white, and red on the males, rose-breasted grosbeaks seem to be decked out in ill-fitting clown suits. Their actions are so slow and hesitant that they don't seem like birds that could migrate to Central America and back. And yet here they are, looking around in sluggish surprise, as if they had not expected to get here. Because they may appear at any backyard feeder, and because they are relatively slow-moving and brightly patterned, they make good ambassadors for people who are just beginning to catch the spark for birding.

On a day like this, I can't imagine anything better that might happen in a person's life than for them to start paying attention to birds — to become aware of this magical world that exists all around us, unnoticed by many but totally captivating for those who know its secrets. This kind of spring day, with its bountiful myriads of colorful sprites just arrived from tropical shores, has to be one of the greatest gifts of life on Earth.

On days like this I want to grab complete strangers — gently — and beg them to look, just look, at this vast parade of tiny travelers ushering in the wonders of springtime. In effect, though, that's what we're about to do. The biggest, splashiest, most unusual celebration of birds anywhere in North America is starting in a few days right here in northwestern Ohio. Thousands of complete strangers will indeed be grabbed by the news, and at least some of them will be inspired to come out and look.

15

The Biggest Week

How do you become a leader? Find a parade and get in front of it.

In one sense that was what Black Swamp Bird Observatory did. In a time and place — early May in northwestern Ohio — with a huge bird migration and increasing numbers of birding visitors, BSBO established one of the biggest bird festivals anywhere.

But that flippant quip about getting in front of a parade paints a picture that's far too simple. Stating it that way conveys only part of the story and overlooks the vast amount of thought and effort that BSBO put into leading that parade, altering its course, and turning it into something that could be of great benefit to the whole community and to the birds themselves.

The basic idea of a bird festival doesn't have a long history, but it's been around for a few years. A community or a group of organizers picks a time of year when birding is good and/or when the local economy needs a boost. They set up an event lasting over a weekend, or from mid-week through a weekend, with speakers, field trips, social gatherings, and often a vendor area. People register for the festival and then take part in as many or as few activities as they like.

Some of these events are popular and successful year after year. For example, the Rio Grande Valley festival has been drawing birders to Harlingen, at the southern tip of Texas, every November since 1994. Each morning for five days in a row, vanloads and busloads of birders fan out to parks and refuges, seeking flashy green jays, elusive red-billed pigeons, and other subtropical specialties of the Rio Grande Valley. Each afternoon the birders come back to listen to entertaining programs and educational workshops by invited speakers. In the vendor hall, birding tour companies advertise trips to far-flung destinations, optics companies show off the latest binoculars and scopes, and a plethora of booths sell everything imaginable related to nature. Many experts from around the United States go back annually to serve as field trip leaders, and if you mention "the RGV" to serious birders, they'll know the event you mean.

Setting up a spring festival in northwest Ohio offered unique challenges. The South Texas organizers could have picked any dates in late fall or winter for the RGV, knowing that the noisy ringed kingfishers, stolid white-tipped doves, and all the other specialties would be in their usual spots every single day. But for migration birding in Ohio, every day is different. Some mornings bring huge arrivals of migratory birds; some bring relatively few. A random set of four or five days, picked from a calendar months ahead, might happen to fall in the lull between major waves, for disappointing results.

What was the solution? Start a bird festival ten days long. A full ten intensive days of birding and programs, the most ambitious birding event on the continent. That was the birth of the Biggest Week in American Birding.

Another challenge was the fact that so much of the birding focus had been (and continues to be) on the boardwalk at Magee Marsh. It would be tough, and pointless, to try to lead a field trip onto the boardwalk, through the crowds already gathered there. After a couple of years of trial and error, we found an approach that works well. Now every day for ten days, fleets of fifteen-passenger vans take groups out to other prime spots in the region. Some go to the Oak Openings on the west side of Toledo, seeking resident red-headed woodpeckers, blue grosbeaks, and other species seldom seen at Magee. Other vans go east along the Lake Erie shoreline to migrant hot spots that are just as good as the Magee boardwalk but not as well known.

And on the famous boardwalk itself we use a different approach. Scattered all along the mile of boardwalk and along nearby trails, among the crowds of eager enthusiasts you'll see individuals wearing bright sunburst-gold baseball caps that say GUIDE on the front and back. These people are men or women, they're white or black or brown, they range from teenagers to retirees, but they all have some traits in common: they're expert birders; they're thoughtful and patient; they love to meet absolute beginners who are taking their very first look at birds; and they are out there to help people find and identify their quarry and have a good time.

It's a point of pride to be a gold-capped guide. The bird observatory keeps a tight control on the quality of the Biggest Week in American Birding, and it doesn't just hand out that cap to anyone who asks. All the leaders and drivers on the van trips, all the official guides on the boardwalk and in surrounding areas, have proven skills and the temperament to share sightings with newcomers.

It's inspiring to see how people react when they get the gold cap. Here's a retired truck driver from Detroit who started birding just a few years ago and now has the confidence to guide others. Here's a young woman in her late teens who came up through the Ohio Young Birders Club and is now guiding for the first time. They're proud to be doing it, and you can see that shining in their eyes.

Expert birders come from all over Ohio and surrounding states to help out, but another key element has been the involvement of professional bird-tour companies. Every year up to ten or more companies support the Biggest Week by providing guides. These professionals are already skilled at helping people see birds, of course. But they also benefit: during the event they get to meet hundreds of potential clients. Kevin Loughlin from Wildside Nature Tours may fly in a dozen guides, not only from around the United States but also top professionals from Latin American countries. After people go birding on the Magee boardwalk with Glenn from Belize or with Edison from Ecuador, they're more likely to join those guides on Wildside tours to the tropics. Chris Lotz from Birding Ecotours may bring in leaders from England and South Africa, again giving them the chance to meet potential American clients. Carlos Bethancourt from the Canopy Tower, Panama, comes to the Biggest Week every year, and every year more people make plans to join him on his home turf. Rob Ripma from Sabrewing Nature Tours has shouldered the responsibility of coordinating all the field trips throughout the festival, and grateful birders gravitate to Sabrewing trips as a result. The whole arrangement is a classic win-win.

The first Biggest Week was in 2010, and in the early years our location was a challenge. Bird festivals are often headquartered at large hotels or at community centers. From the Magee Marsh boardwalk, the nearest concentrations of hotels of even moderate size were about seventeen miles to the east, in Port Clinton, and eighteen miles west, in the city of Oregon. Participants in the festival were staying in hotels throughout the region, but we needed indoor space for programs.

The visitors' center at Ottawa National Wildlife Refuge, right next door to Magee Marsh, has a meeting room that will hold eighty people. Right from the start the refuge management allowed us to put on programs there from midday into the evening. A friend who owned a hotel in Port Clinton let us use a similarly sized meeting room there. In one of the first years of the festival, before we had attracted more speakers from outside the region, I put on seventeen programs on ten different subjects, driving back and forth between the refuge and Port Clinton to give one or two every day.

The setup wasn't ideal. The wildlife refuge was great for programs during the day, but extending them into the evening and keeping the visitors' center open extra hours created very long days for the hardworking refuge staff. And neither the refuge nor the hotel had space for the social gatherings we wanted to add to the event. In an inspired moment, Kimberly went to talk to the manager of the lodge in Maumee Bay State Park, along the Lake Erie shoreline about ten miles west of Magee Marsh.

The state park was a fine birding spot, and I'd been there many times to look for birds. I hadn't seen any reason to pay attention to the Maumee Bay Lodge and Conference Center. It was a huge facility, with hundreds of guest rooms and cottages and campsites, a restaurant and lounge and store, a variety of large meeting rooms and larger banquet halls, and woodland trails right outside the doors. In other words, as Kimberly realized, it was the perfect place to host a birding festival.

We've been there every year since 2012, and it has indeed worked out perfectly. We still put on workshops and programs at the Ottawa Refuge visitors' center from late morning to early afternoon, but everything later shifts over to the lodge.

That is, if we can tear ourselves away from the birding to go there.

Birding! With a festival held at the peak of migration, those avian delights are always at center stage. In other seasons it could be different. If you go to the popular Space Coast Birding Festival in Florida in January, for example, you can take field trips to see all the wonderful local specialties and then head indoors, knowing that you're not missing anything. On the Lake Erie shoreline in early May, things change radically and constantly, and even if you bird your brains out, you can't catch it all. With so many people scouring the region, they find scarce and elusive birds, even genuinely rare ones, briefly passing through. Even as we're exploring one spot, we can't help but wonder what might be popping up in the next hot spot over.

No two of us are going to react to the same set of species. For relatively new birders, there's a real chance of seeing "lifers" — birds they've never seen before, new for their life lists. Longtime or well-traveled observers are unlikely to notch any such firsts, but we like to see anything that's rare for the local area. One year during the Biggest Week a curlew sandpiper showed up with other sandpipers in a flooded field near Toledo, and hundreds of people detoured to see it; this is a Eurasian migrant, rare anywhere in North America. Another year during the festival a neotropic cormorant, not usually found any closer to here than Texas, appeared at the Ottawa Refuge. Lesser rarities turn up almost every day during the migration peak.

During the Biggest Week there's always a lot of talk about "the K-bird"—Kirtland's warbler. This is the holy grail among warblers, by far the rarest of its clan in North America. It almost went extinct in the 1970s and 1980s, and even after a comeback its population is still only in the low thousands. Kirtland's warblers spend the winter in the Bahamas and come north in spring to nest and raise their young in scrubby jack-pine forests in Michigan, plus a few spots in Wisconsin and Ontario. Only a few are actually seen during migration every year. The Lake Erie shoreline is their only consistent stopover habitat, and even here they are very hard to find. If someone finds a Kirtland's warbler, everyone wants to know.

For people spread over three or four counties to communicate quickly about discoveries of rare birds, nothing beats Twitter. This social media app, publicly sharing brief text messages and easily accessed through smartphones, has revolutionized this kind of birding. At the time of the first Biggest Week in 2010, Twitter was still a relatively new thing, and we were the first bird festival to use it for communicating about bird sightings.

Even in that first year Twitter proved useful. Several hundred people followed our Biggest Week Twitter feed, and the handful of guides put out tweets about the whereabouts of interesting species. I was a Twitter novice, but I posted to the official feed whenever I found an uncommon bird: a black-billed cuckoo skulking through the woods at Metzger Marsh, upland sandpipers in fields along Krause Road, a hooded warbler near the small loop on the Magee boardwalk. But by the middle of the festival, everyone felt that the birding hadn't lived up to its usual stellar reputation.

Every year is different, and in that spring of 2010, the migration was not perfect for the festival's timing. A big early wave had come in around May 1, pumping more variety into the woods, but things had stalled by Friday, May 7, the first day of the first Biggest Week. The weather was unsettled and chilly through the weekend and stayed that way into the beginning of the next week, with northerly winds predominating. We were still seeing birds—more than twenty warbler species every day, and a variety of other migrants—but not in the hoped-for numbers. Birders gathering at Blackberry Corners would linger for pie and conversation, because there wasn't a strong incentive to race back out into the field.

I was writing updates on the migration almost every day for the BSBO blog: studying weather maps, talking to Mark Shieldcastle about his impressions, trying to predict when the next waves of migrants would arrive. Three days into the festival, four days, I was writing gamely about notable sightings in the area, but I still couldn't see a clear pattern for a big movement. Finally on Wednesday, May 12—the sixth day of our ten-day festival—I wrote this on the blog: "On Thursday evening, even though scattered showers will continue, temperatures will be warmer and winds are predicted to be out of the south for most of the night. Also, it appears that there won't be a lot of rain to the south of us, so migrants that have been dammed up to the south will probably be moving this direction. It's too early to say for sure, but this could be a setup for a big arrival of migrants on Friday, May 14."

You can probably imagine how I was sweating that prediction as Friday approached.

Friday morning I was out early, keyed up, anxious. We were a full week into the festival, and although people were having a good time, birding had been lackluster—good but not great. If my prediction bombed, if the flight was a bust, if nothing happened over the weekend, the ten days would pass without any big migration, and the first Biggest Week might turn out to be the last. I hadn't worked as hard on the event as Kimberly and some others, but I still had time and emotion invested in it. Would Magee Marsh live up to its legend, or would all the birders go somewhere else the next year?

I went out alone that Friday morning and drove up toward the lakeshore at Magee, but on a whim I didn't turn west to the boardwalk. Other people would be searching there—and if the day was a birdless bust, I didn't want to talk to them. I parked at the north end of the road and walked east instead, out along the trail between the beach and the scrubby, brushy thickets and scattered trees lining the north edge of the marsh.

As soon as I got out there, I could tell it was a good day. Orioles and indigo buntings hopped about in shrubs near the beach; flocks of blue jays streamed overhead. Back in the heavier thickets I could hear gray catbirds whining and chortling and the rapid songs of an ovenbird and a Wilson's warbler. I hiked rapidly east along the beach, wanting to get a quick assessment of what was around before I doubled back to the boardwalk.

Far out along the beach, I was stopped in my tracks by a birdsong coming from the right. I hadn't heard that song for years, not since the last time I visited jack-pine woods in northern Michigan, but I knew what it was. That choppy, rising chant had to be a Kirtland's warbler.

Kirtland's. The K-bird. The rarest warbler. Cautiously I maneuvered forward, peering into the thickets, and within a minute I saw it: blue-gray head and back and wings, yellow throat and chest, bold black stripes on the flanks, a classic male Kirtland's warbler.

Everyone would want to see this! But the nearest birders were at least half a mile away. I had my cell phone; should I call someone? Should I race to the boardwalk and start shouting? Should I—

Oh, yeah. Twitter.

I pulled out my phone and pulled up the Twitter app and typed it in: KIRTLANDS ON MAGEE EAST BEACH 300 YARDS EAST OF PARKING LOT KENN K

And then I waited. I had moved away from the thicket where the warbler still foraged, but I was watching, catching glimpses, and hearing occasional songs; I wanted to keep track of it until other people arrived. And soon they did. Looking back along the beach I saw an approaching mob, a hundred or more birders, some striding fast and some almost running, heading in my direction.

One great thing about Kirtland's warblers: although they're quite rare, they are not especially shy, and they like to forage in low shrubs, in the open, or even on the ground. That male Kirtland's spent the entire day within about a hundred-yard stretch of the beach. Sometimes it would disappear back into the brush for fifteen or twenty minutes while crowds waited respectfully for it to reappear. Sometimes it came out and hopped about on the sand, hopping straight toward the gasping row of delighted birders and photographers. By evening it had been seen by well over a thousand birders and captured in tens of thousands of photos.

So many other birds were around that day that most people didn't linger long with the Kirtland's. They watched it a while, then went on to pursue reports of other species popping up on Twitter. After that day there was no doubt that the Biggest Week would continue. It was a major migration day, and it would have been memorable for everyone even without the Kirtland's warbler, but I'll always be grateful to that bird for showing up when I needed it.

In the years since, one or two Kirtland's warblers have made brief appearances during the Biggest Week more often than not. The use of Twitter during the festival has become more sophisticated, with a few thousand people following at any one time and at least a couple of dozen guides sharing information. The birding, like everything else about the festival, has exploded into new territory.

Even without the launch of the Biggest Week in American Birding, the number of visiting birders in northwestern Ohio probably would have continued to increase. The local community probably would have become gradually more aware of these visitors and the birds they pursued. But the festival ramped up the increase, supercharged the pace, and gave it focus. Within just a few years a high percentage of the people in northwestern Ohio knew about this phenomenon. Often they couldn't remember the name (was that "Greatest Birding Week"?), and most were barely aware that Black Swamp Bird Observatory was responsible for the event. But the public at large knew that people were coming from out of state for some kind of bird week east of Toledo.

Furthermore, the public saw this as a good thing. And that didn't happen by accident. From the start we were determined to find a way to measure the economic impact of birding. Visitors from outside the local area were staying in hotels, eating at restaurants, shopping at stores and gas stations; surely they were putting cash into the local economy. There was no way to measure that directly, but after a few years the Biggest Week team started sending out postevent surveys to all registered participants, asking (among other things) how much they had spent on various things during their stay. Based on those responses, and on the Division of Wildlife's estimates of the total numbers of birding visitors, the team was able to calculate that the spring birding season put almost $40 million into the economy of the local area.

Tourism matters in northwest Ohio. Some businesses make most of their annual income during the three months of summer, when people flock to the Lake Erie shore. Lesser peaks involve duck hunters in late fall and ice fishermen in winter. But early May had been a slow time for tourism until the birding scene ramped up.

When you can throw out numbers in the millions and back them up, people pay attention. When you can show that seasonal restaurants are opening earlier and that hotels are booked up weeks ahead and are hiring more staff, people pay attention. Kimberly made dozens of presentations to chambers of commerce, visitors' bureaus, and local civic groups, drawing the connection between bird habitat and the spring economic boom. News media throughout the northwest quadrant of Ohio gradually came to see the Biggest Week as something to be taken seriously.

If you have seen birding mentioned on local TV news in the United States, especially in past years, you've probably seen the old approach. The fresh-faced anchor smirks at the camera and says, "*Some* people are all a-flutter this weekend about *bird*-watching!" We saw a little of that here, too, in the early years. Some journalists took the festival seriously right from the start, but others treated it as no more than a quirky novelty. The smirks disappeared, however, as the festival and its positive impact continued to grow. Now every TV news operation in the region runs multiple spots about birding during the Biggest Week, and some meteorologists describe how upcoming weather will affect conditions for birding or migration. Major stories about birding and the festival appear at the top of the front page of every newspaper in the region, including the *Toledo Blade,* the most widely circulated paper in northwestern Ohio. In 2018 the *Blade* ran more than twenty in-depth stories about birding, bird conservation, and the Biggest Week during the first half of May.

The effect has permeated every kind of media in the region. A few years in, Kimberly was out in the parking lot in front of Black Swamp Bird Observatory on a busy day when a couple of young men caught her attention: they didn't have binoculars, and they seemed to be just watching people and snickering. Of course Kimberly went over to talk to them. The guys turned out to be radio personalities from one of the local morning shows, and they had come to check out the birders so they could make fun of them on the air the next day.

Some people would have been offended, but Kimberly knows how to roll with a situation. "If you really want good material, you should go to the boardwalk to watch these birders in action. I've got a volunteer who can show you around." By sheer luck, our friend Deb happened to be at the observatory that day. Deb, a tough, tattooed machinist with memorable language, is an expert birder, often leading field trips for the Biggest Week. She's also the coolest person around, and she made the guys look at warblers and appreciate them. "Dude. *Look* at this danged thing. It's a magnolia warbler and it's *punch-you-in-the-face awesome.* This freaking little bird just flew *all the way here from Guatemala,* man, can you believe it?" When the radio personalities brought up the experience on the air the next day, they admitted up front that birding wasn't nearly as dumb as they'd expected it to be.

So on radio, television, and newspapers, birding is everywhere for the first half of May. The phrase "Welcome Birders" is up on banners along the streets in the local towns, splashed across signs in front of businesses from Toledo to Sandusky. It would be difficult for anyone in the region to miss the fact that there's some birding going on in May.

Why is all this attention such a good thing? It's not just that we like to see our names in the news. As more people come to realize that birding brings economic benefits, we gain more support for the protection of birds and their habitats.

We see the effect in various ways. In other regions I've heard people complain about lands "locked up" in wildlife areas, not producing tax revenue. I don't hear such comments very much around here. Instead newspaper and TV chiefs post editorials about how we need to "protect our bird sanctuaries" for the good of the economy. Ottawa National Wildlife Refuge has continued to buy key tracts of land in the area, and people applaud that as a good thing. Toledo Metroparks launched an ambitious project to buy one thousand acres of farmland just west of Metzger Marsh and restore it to natural habitat. When it opened as the Howard Marsh Metropark in spring 2018, political and business leaders throughout the region celebrated it as a fine addition to the warbler capital, one more destination to give visiting birders one more reason to stay longer.

And on a theme of particular interest to us, we hope that all this attention will give us more support for keeping giant wind turbines out of the most sensitive stopover sites for migratory birds. The forces pushing hardest for wind-power development don't speak any language but money, and money is just about the only argument that might keep them at bay. If enough people see that avian migration helps the local economy, the wind developers might go off to look for easier targets.

Even as the Biggest Week continued to grow year by year, we continued to be distracted by the threat of the Camp Perry wind project. Its status was still unresolved. Even though it was considered an experimental pilot project, calling for only a single turbine, we saw it as the wedge that would open the door for more. A wind turbine on a military base, bearing so clearly the stamp of government approval—that might be all it took to usher in phalanxes of bird-killing blades all along this precious scrap of remaining habitat, this last refuge for beleaguered migrants. So we waited, monitoring any news of the project and never missing a chance to trumpet the economic value of living birds.

On a personal level, though, something else about the news coverage was even better, and continues to be. It's this: local citizens hear so much about the migration that eventually they become intrigued and decide to come out and see for themselves. And if they find their way to the Magee Marsh boardwalk, where birding can be easy and spectacular even for a complete novice, they find themselves surrounded by friendly, generous people who want to show them every bird. In those surroundings, it's easy for a newcomer to get hooked on birding.

This exact thing has happened over and over. I personally know dozens of people from around northwestern Ohio and southeastern Michigan for whom a May visit to Magee sparked an abiding interest. They may never become crazed bird freaks who will cross the continent to see a rarity, but they will come out on spring mornings to look at warblers with us. Their lives have been enriched by a greater awareness of nature, and our community is richer and more varied because it includes them.

• • •

Community. That's the key word. We are a genuine community of people who love birds and nature, and we are constantly looking for ways to invite more people in. The Magee boardwalk experience is a good passive recruiter for those who happen to get there, but we use the Biggest Week as a chance to actively blast the invitation out to a wider audience.

We want our community to be defined as broadly as possible. Back in the 1990s, when I first started traveling a lot to speak to bird clubs around the United States, it became obvious to me that the birding culture in this country did not (as the saying goes) "look like America." The people I met were lovely, but they were overwhelmingly white, even in places where I knew that people of color made up a major percentage of the local population. That made me very uncomfortable. As I came to find out, the same was true for many kinds of outdoor recreation, but that was no excuse. Obviously we could not demand that anyone take up birding, but I absolutely, positively did not want us to be doing anything, consciously or unconsciously, to keep whole groups of people out.

Fortunately, everyone at BSBO feels the same way today, and we can use the Biggest Week as a positive force for change. Scattered around the United States are quite a few African-Americans who are highly skilled birders, nature photographers, or environmental educators, people who are doing amazing work, and we have tried to bring in as many of them as possible as keynote speakers, workshop teachers, and field-trip leaders. Ditto for birders of Latino or Asian backgrounds. People of color are part of the public face of the Biggest Week in American Birding, and we hope the message comes through loud and clear: everyone is welcome here.

Furthermore, the presence of so many out-of-town guides creates an opportunity to reach out to diverse communities in the nearby metropolitan area. Cleveland educator Paula Lozano and several of the professional guides from Latin American countries have led free bilingual bird walks for the Adelante Latino Resource Center in Toledo. We've been able to donate copies of my Spanish-language bird guide, *Guía de campo Kaufman a las aves de Norteamérica,* for use on these walks. Pastor Doug Gray from Indianapolis has reached out to predominantly black churches in Toledo, and he and other African-American experts have led free bird-watching sessions for the Grace Community Center while they have been here for the festival. It's too early to say whether any serious birders will come out of these efforts, but we hope that many people have gained more appreciation for birds and nature.

So we're a community, a big, sprawling, international community constantly trying to invite more people in. The Biggest Week is a party, an ongoing party spread over ten days and many venues, celebrating in a thousand ways, all loosely tied together by an interest in things with feathers.

This party starts early. Every morning before six, vans are lining up outside the Maumee Bay Lodge to take groups out for half-day or full-day guided trips. A crew from one of the Toledo TV stations may be on hand to do a live remote from the lodge, or a crew might be doing the same thing fourteen miles farther east, at the Black Swamp Bird Observatory. The observatory's gift shop, information center, and window on wildlife are not open quite this early, but they'll be opening up soon to greet the hordes streaming into and out of the road to the Magee Marsh boardwalk. In the gift shop, the effervescent Karen Z., Kimberley M., and a host of volunteers will greet hundreds of friends and give out hundreds of hugs every day. Next door to BSBO, at Optics Alley, reps from some of the world's top optics companies will be showing off binoculars, telescopes, and cameras to birders eager to check out the latest products.

Halfway back along the Magee road, the Sportsmen's Migratory Bird Center will be open all day, too, with Division of Wildlife staff and members of the nonprofit Friends of Magee Marsh greeting the public. But most visitors will go straight on to the world-famous boardwalk itself. The Division of Wildlife has a tent set up near the boardwalk's west entrance, and staffers are busy all day dispensing information, maps, and bird checklists. A few thousand people may cycle through here in the course of a day, so it's one of the division's best opportunities all year to connect with the public.

Even with official field trips taking hundreds of people to other destinations every day, even with the festival encouraging people to check out dozens of other sites, the boardwalk remains the center of the whirlwind. Birders come and go all day. The parking lot, nearly half a mile long, is mostly filled all morning, with vehicles sporting license plates from thirty states. People are everywhere. Newcomers are likely to be staring in astonishment at the bald eagles tending their nest, high in a huge cottonwood at the edge of the woods. Photographers with massive lenses on tripods stalk the edge of the parking lot, staking out spots where warblers come in to low open branches. Birders start onto the boardwalk and are usually stopped in their tracks by the first few migrants foraging nearby. If they can make it past the first knot of humans, they may be out on the farther loops of the boardwalk for two or three hours, reveling in variety and close views, until some report on Twitter sends them hurrying to their cars to race to a different spot.

Over at the Ottawa National Wildlife Refuge, next door to Magee, the action starts early. Professional staffers from other refuges have come in to help for the week, and they're taking people on tram trips through the refuge and van trips to properties usually closed to the public. At the visitors' center the bookstore, run by the nonprofit Friends of Ottawa group, does a bang-up business all day as people stream through. Many are there for talks, workshops, and programs that are officially part of the Biggest Week —a chance to hear some of the biggest names in birding as they share their expertise. Other visitors stop through the center only briefly before driving the self-guiding auto tour through the refuge, closed most days of the year but open every day during the Biggest Week.

By late afternoon the focus shifts back to the Maumee Bay Lodge for featured keynote talks, followed by a long evening social. Hundreds of people fill the lobby and common areas of the lodge. Every evening I'll see friends from around the United States and Canada, and from other countries as well, whom I haven't seen for a year or more. But the day's birding isn't over yet: around dusk, more field trips will go out specifically to look for American woodcocks. Out in the wet woods behind BSBO and Maumee Bay, those long-beaked bog-haunters are still performing the sky dance that we watched back in March, and seeing it will be a new experience for many visitors.

The intensely social aspect of the Biggest Week has become for many just as important as the birding. Even on days when the migration is slow and birding is lackluster, people may still be having a great time. In a way we're just like other communities that form around shared interests. Think about an entire weekend built around a college football game. The game itself is only a small part of the focus for most people, and they'll enjoy the socializing even if their team loses. In the community of birders it can work the same way.

A description of the social scene at the Biggest Week would not be complete without a mention of all the extras, like the trivia contest, karaoke night, tattoo contest, and birder prom. These are all part of the attempt to make the tent bigger and widen the appeal.

When the idea for the bird tattoo contest first came up, a few people suggested it would attract "the wrong crowd." One older gentleman told me, "You'll get bikers with eagle tattoos, you'll get people who aren't birders at all." My response: "What's wrong with bikers? What's wrong with nonbirders? If anyone likes any bird well enough to wear it in permanent ink — and if they're willing to come into the middle of a bird festival and hang out with us, and compete for prizes that include bird books and binoculars — we want to meet that person!"

And in fact the contest has succeeded beyond all expectations in connecting us with new friends. During the contest judging, people share not only their tattoos but the stories behind them. Not surprisingly, the decision to wear a picture on one's skin in permanent ink is often tied to intensely emotional experiences, and the stories we've heard are just as impressive as the art. These people appreciate birds in their own ways, and their reasons are just as legitimate as those of any hardcore birder out chasing Kirtland's warblers. We are happy to have them as part of our extended family.

The sense of inclusiveness and of embracing all people took another step up in about the sixth year of the festival. Our friend Deb, the tattooed machinist who had introduced the local radio personalities to birding, was ready to marry her love, Nicole, a professor of poetry at Kent State. They wanted to hold the ceremony while peak numbers of their friends were around, so why not tie the knot at the Biggest Week in American Birding? Deb and Nicole had a lovely wedding upstairs at the lodge, with views of the sunset over Lake Erie behind them. After the wedding dinner, dozens of birders who had been awake since dawn stayed up, stayed out on the dance floor, until midnight.

On the following days people went on and on about how much fun the night had been. One of our friends, Stephanie, put it this way: "We need to find volunteers to get married at the Biggest Week every year, so we can have a dance night like that!"

"You know," Kimberly said, "we *could* have a dance even *without* anyone getting married."

"Prom night!" Stephanie cried, her face lighting up. "We could hold a birder prom!"

So the next year that was exactly what happened. It was so popular that it has continued ever since. And the Biggest Week notched another first, as the first birding festival to host a birder prom.

At the birder prom in a recent year, after Kimberly and I had danced a few numbers, we stood at the edge of the room watching the crowd. I was thinking about how much the birding community has changed. Only a few years ago, a gathering like this would have been a sea of white faces, but now we see a welcome variety of skin tones. When I was in my teens and twenties I knew only a handful of active birders in my age range, and almost all were guys. Now there are large numbers of young people in the field, and more and more girls and young women are involved. Now you can hold a dance party at a birding festival and it won't be a ridiculous waste of time — you'll get lots of active people of all ages out there on the dance floor.

Look right now: it's almost ten at night, but this ballroom at the lodge is pulsing with people who have been up since dawn. More than a hundred of us are here, at least thirty on the dance floor and the rest congregating around tables or the makeshift bar. Over by the wall, volunteers running the sound system are playing oldies and current hits, filling requests or just picking out good dance numbers.

So many of our friends are here, old friends and brand-new ones. John and Tiffanie have just been voted prom king and queen by unanimous acclaim — because they showed up in outfits made of decorative birdseed bags — and they're having an encore dance. Alyssia and Raymond are cutting elegant, sweeping figures across the center of the floor; she's a field biologist, he's a tour leader, they just met tonight, but each of them used to give dance lessons, and it shows. Pastor Doug and his angel-voiced wife, LeShon, are out on the floor, too, demonstrating that devout church people can also bring out the fancy steps. Karen Z. and Kimberley M. spent the whole day working the gift shop at the observatory, but they're still on their feet; Kimberley is helping Brad with the music selections, and Karen is in the center of the floor, swaying and smiling. Paul and Rachel from Canada are off to the side, in animated conversation with Gabriel from Puerto Rico. Deb and Nicole are moving dreamily in the corner, stepping to their own beat. Erin just found out today that she has landed a job in Alaska, and she's whirling around the floor with Erich and Christina.

The song ends and the dancers pause. Some start to wander off the dance floor. It's getting late, after all.

Then the DJs spin another song.

I recognize this tune. I hadn't heard it in ages until a couple of nights ago, when three women put on a raucous, good-natured rendition during the Biggest Week karaoke event. But the DJs are playing the original version, recorded by Sister Sledge way back in 1979: "We Are Family."

It has a catchy rhythm, a good dance beat. The dancers begin to move again. Then I notice a gradual shift: people sitting at tables or over by the walls are getting up, a few at a time, and coming forward. More and more people find their place in the swaying crowd. It's starting to look like one of the most popular tunes of the night.

This is odd, I say to myself. *A lot of these young people weren't even born until ten or twenty years after that song was released. Are they reacting to the lyrics?*

Maybe that's it. "We are family," sung over and over with joyous conviction, could be striking a chord here. We *are* family, in important ways, even if we've just met.

We come from so many different backgrounds and we may have serious differences of opinion, but that doesn't matter when we're out birding together, and it doesn't matter in this room. It's such a fine thing to have an extended family based on shared interest. It's especially fine for the youngest people here, the teenagers and early-twentysomethings. They're at the age when it would be all too easy to get discouraged and drop out of birding entirely, but they won't, because they're buoyed up and supported by this community.

For a moment, at the back of my mind, a thought forms: *Oh, to be young again.* But then Kimberly looks at me and smiles, and my whole world lights up. We're young enough; we're living at exactly the right time in the development of the birding culture. We are family. To paraphrase one of the lines from the song, we've got all our sisters — and brothers, and cousins, and adopted sons and daughters — with us. This night is perfect as it is. And with the winds now having shifted around to the south under clear skies, tomorrow morning is going to be perfect as well.

16

The Impossible Peak

Daybreak is the magic time. Those last moments of night, just as we begin to see darkness lifting and dawn arriving, those are the moments when everything seems possible.

Anticipation for dawn has been building all night. We were up late celebrating with friends, and after that we were up looking at radar images online, watching the echoes of hordes of birds on the move. The blooms of blue and blue-green surrounding the radar sites on the map, growing, shifting, intensifying, told us the surge of migration was increasing.

Other weather maps added support for this reading: a warm front, a long and strong flow of wind from the south, with only a few little bands of rain showers moving through to interrupt the northward flight of millions of birds. This is just as we had hoped. In fact, anticipation for *this* particular dawn has been building for several days, as the long-range weather forecasts grew more confident that we would have perfect conditions for a flight.

We are up on the edge of Lake Erie at daybreak, on the north side of the Magee woods, shielded from the south wind, so sounds carry far in the dim light. Robins are caroling from treetops all over the woods, probably more than twenty audible, near and far, a rollicking, singsong hymn for the dawn. But we can still make out the sounds of night birds behind them. A few woodcocks sound off — *pzzeent!* — from the forest floor. A very distant screech owl gives a quavering trill. Deep in the woodlot a whip-poor-will, undoubtedly a migrant just passing through, sings its name in a rough, throaty voice three times and then falls silent.

But there are other sounds, too, becoming more obvious and insistent as the black outlines of the treetops come into sharper focus against the paling sky: light chips, lisps, and buzzes, the flight calls of small birds. These are undoubtedly warblers, sparrows, and other migrants that have just arrived here overnight. Louder liquid or burry notes are out there, too, thrushes making their flight calls over and over, even after they have landed in the woods at dawn.

As the light improves we'll start to see some of these migrants. Some come out of the sky overhead, twisting down rapidly to swoop into the shadows of the woods. Others are dark shapes flashing from one tree to another or flying just over the topmost branches, paralleling the lakeshore. Other birds will come from behind us, from the north, out over Lake Erie itself.

We have assumed for years that birds arriving from the south near dawn will drop lower and then land just before they reach the edge of the lake. More recently, studies with mobile radar units have shown what birds do if they're already out over the water at first light: they climb higher, clearly looking around to assess their location. Out over Lake Erie, if they're high enough, they can almost certainly see across to the Ontario shoreline on the north side, less than thirty miles away. But if they're still within a few miles of the Ohio shore, they don't continue on across; instead they turn back, heading for the closest land. So at sunrise, at a lakeshore location like Magee Marsh, small migratory birds are arriving from all directions, including from the north.

Their numbers build rapidly. There is so much going on here, in this zone along the lake, that it's hard to take it all in, easy to miss details even if we're paying close attention. If we're close to the edge of the woods we may see many small birds — warbler-sized — making quick, subtle movements among the foliage, at all levels in the trees. Some of these probably have come in overnight, while others may have been here for days. But other warblers are flying at treetop level, flying either east or west, and if we watch they may keep going out of sight. Many classic nocturnal migrants are known to engage in morning flights, or "redetermined migrations," flying long distances just after dawn, often in a different direction from the way they traveled during the night. Here along Lake Erie hundreds of small birds may take part in these flights, moving either east or west, roughly paralleling the lakeshore.

At the same time that these nocturnal migrants are continuing or repositioning, daytime migrants are starting up. By an hour after sunrise there may be hundreds of blue jays, or even thousands, moving high overhead in long, straggling flocks. Flocks of tiny goldfinches are easier to overlook as they move at treetop height, but dozens or scores or hundreds may move past, usually going from east to west. Buzzy or rattling notes from the flocks tell us when pine siskins are traveling with the goldfinches, as they often do. Dozens of tree swallows circle and swoop over the parking lot: they have been here for weeks and they'll stay all summer, building their nests in holes in dead trees around the edge of the swamp. But other kinds of swallows are sweeping past out over the lake, skimming low over the water, and many of them are undoubtedly still on their way north. Small groups of eastern bluebirds or larger flocks of cedar waxwings move purposefully along the edge of the woods, their soft callnotes almost lost among the other sounds of morning.

As impressive as it is to see all these birds moving, the bigger part of the story is back among the trees, not so readily visible. The woodlot here is swarming with birds, dozens of kinds that were not here a week ago, hundreds or even thousands of individuals that were not here yesterday. The spring movement has been pumping more migrants into the region, and last night's flight has pushed the numbers right off the chart.

A couple of months ago, early in the season, when migration's pace was more spread out, every new arrival was cause for celebration. I had time to savor each one: the killdeers crying plaintively over the fields, the fox sparrows rustling in the brush, each new bird a marker of the advancing season. It was as if each new character in the play had time to come out to the front of the stage, bask in the glow of the footlights, and introduce itself at length before joining the chorus at the back of the stage. Now at the peak the birds arrive thick and fast, and there's no way to pay proper attention to each kind. On this big flight day there are probably two hundred bird species within ten miles of here. I'll probably see or hear more than a hundred of them before noon. But if I tried to write about all of them, the result would be ridiculous. Peak migration is glorious, but it's impossible to describe.

Of all the migrants surging through the woods today, the tiny, colorful warblers are at center stage, the stars of the show. The second week of May is their time of maximum diversity. More than thirty-five species are possible now. We'll never find all of them on the same day, because some are quite rare here, seen only a few times per season, but finding twenty-five to thirty kinds in a day is a distinct possibility, a joyous challenge for the keenest and most energetic birders.

When I was a kid first struggling to learn about warblers, I had a vague notion that all of them flew south in fall to a hazy distant land called "the tropics." Now, after many trips throughout the American tropics, I've seen most of these birds on their wintering grounds, and I know that they separate out at that season. Nashville warblers and Wilson's warblers are all over Mexico during the winter months. Magnolia warblers and hooded warblers are common in southeastern Mexico and northern Central America, while chestnut-sided and bay-breasted warblers are mostly farther south in Central America. Black-throated blue and Cape May warblers mainly go to islands in the Caribbean. Blackburnian, blackpoll, and Canada warblers spend the winter in South America. No two species have the same exact distribution, in winter or summer or during migration. It's odd and wonderful that so many of them can be seen in the same place on a day like this.

They come north by various routes. Warblers and other migrants arriving in eastern North America from the tropics follow three basic routes, differing in how they get past the open waters of the Gulf of Mexico. Vast numbers come pouring straight north across the Gulf, taking off from the region of the Yucatán Peninsula and powering across the water to arrive along our Gulf Coast anywhere between Texas and Florida. Some species—especially those wintering on Caribbean islands, but also some arriving from South America — enter the United States primarily through Florida, skirting around the Gulf on the east side. Others go around the Gulf on the west side, through Mexico and Texas. This is a logical route for many that have spent the winter in Mexico, but there are some that come from as far away as Panama or even South America and take the long overland route all the way around the Gulf. This is true for mourning warblers and Canada warblers and may help explain why they are among the later warblers to arrive in the north.

Once migrants on these three routes enter the United States, they spread out widely. Blackpoll warblers that have arrived by way of Florida may angle westward, aiming for Alaska, or north-northeast toward Labrador, or anywhere in between. Wilson's warblers that have come through Texas may aim northeast toward Maine. Blackburnian warblers that have come straight across the Gulf may fan out widely toward the northeast or northwest. All of these routes cross and merge, and large numbers of birds from all three pass through northern Ohio, obliterating any idea of flyways or of gaps between them.

Because the warblers are coming from such diverse winter quarters and traveling by different routes, their arrival here is far from uniform or even. Every day some kinds are unexpectedly numerous while others are oddly scarce, and that's one of the delights of going out to check on each day's surprises.

Today it's clear that enormous numbers of magnolia warblers must have been moving last night. They are everywhere along the edge of the woods, everywhere along the boardwalk, hyperactive little birds of yellow and gray and black, with a white band across the tail flashing when they fly. Blackburnian warblers, too, are prevalent, the males with brilliant orange throats, females with softer yellow-orange. Chestnut-sided warblers, with their yellow caps and white bellies, and bay-breasted warblers, uniquely patterned with reddish brown and pink and gray, are also numerous. We keep seeing these four species, over and over, but there's a generous sprinkling of other kinds as well, keeping us on our toes.

It's a game, an addictive game, watching for those movements and raising binoculars again and again to see which warbler will be next. Here's another magnolia, and another chestnut-sided, and another magnolia, but then the next one is a blue-winged warbler, the first one we've seen in several days. Then two more blackburnian warblers, then a bay-breasted, then another magnolia, then suddenly a female cerulean warbler with her soft shades of greenish blue. Then a yellow warbler, two magnolias, a stripy black-and-white warbler crawling along a branch, two chestnut-sideds, then a yellow-throated vireo to remind us that warblers are not the only birds on the move. It's a treasure hunt with living, moving treasures, and we just can't stop looking.

There is so much going on today. Migratory birds have been flooding into the region in successive waves over the last few weeks. Although most of those individuals have continued on toward the north, some have lingered, continuing to pump up the variety. On each big flight day it feels as if we've hit the peak of the migration, but then the next wave hits and more birds come in.

Sharply patterned white-throated sparrows and white-crowned sparrows forage quietly on the ground inside the woods, joined by a few shy, buffy-brown Lincoln's sparrows. They'll all go on toward Canada soon, but for the moment they're still here. Tiny, whiny-voiced blue-gray gnatcatchers arrived in April, but a few are still flitting through the branches today. Brilliantly hued scarlet tanagers and Baltimore orioles aren't as obvious now that the leaves are fully out, but they're still here, popping up as flashes of rich color. Gray catbirds and house wrens have returned from the tropics to spend the summer here, and they're everywhere near the boardwalk—the catbirds flipping their tails and posturing and making weird catcalls, the little brown wrens fussing and bubbling over with an excess of energy.

We can't be looking in every direction at once; we can't possibly see everything happening on this day of movement. If we're out on the edge, looking toward Lake Erie, we might see flocks of golden plovers or the colorful sandpipers called dunlins flashing past. These smartly patterned shorebirds are pouring through the region now, on their way to Arctic tundra. If we went to shallow impoundments on the refuge or flooded farm fields along the roads, we might see a dozen or twenty different kinds of shorebirds. If we moved out into the open and watched the sky, we might see birds of prey: broad-winged hawks sailing high overhead, Cooper's hawks powering over the trees, zippy merlins showing off their speedy falcon flight. But it's so hard to tear ourselves away from the woods on a day like this.

Late in the morning near the east end of the boardwalk, I'm talking to a friend, another very experienced birder. Three strangers passing by recognize us, and they stop to talk. They're almost giddy with delight: they've never seen anything like this, they can't believe their good fortune in being here for this day. As they're walking away my friend asks me quietly, "Don't you envy them? Wouldn't you love to step back into their shoes, to see this for the first time?"

Out loud I don't answer, but I'm thinking, *No, actually, I don't envy them. I'm terrifically happy for them, but there's no reason for envy. My amazement at this scene has not faded. Every year, every big flight, every time I learn more about what we are seeing here, I'm more completely filled with a sense of wonder. And I'm glad our new friends here are now feeling that same wonder for themselves.*

If an astronaut walked past you on the street, you wouldn't know. Other than a certain confidence in his or her step, perhaps, there'd be nothing to suggest that this person might be different. Unless you knew the name, unless you had seen a picture, you would not realize that this man or woman had climbed into a metal canister and ridden a fountain of fire up out of the atmosphere to the emptiness of space. You wouldn't guess that this traveler had blasted beyond the bounds of all normal experience and had survived to return to the humdrum street, to walk among those who had never traveled at all.

It's the same with migratory birds. Some undertake journeys that defy all imagination, but those extraordinary travelers look utterly ordinary at first glance. Unless we know their names, we might see them on a spring morning and pass them off as nothing special.

This morning at Magee, among the abundance of other birds, we're seeing the first major push of blackpoll warblers. Females are drab greenish gray with lots of streaks; not many are here today, as they tend to arrive later in the month. Adult males have black caps (hence the name) and white faces, and at a glance they might look like chickadees. That's ironic, because chickadees are nonmigratory, hardly going anywhere, while blackpoll warblers are among the most astonishing and extreme of all migratory birds.

Watch this male blackpoll warbler as it hops along the outer twigs of a maple, disappearing behind leaves and reappearing again. It looks attractive enough—small, compact, smartly patterned in black and white, with yellow feet for an accent of color. It also looks perfectly at home in the maple. But it wasn't here in Ohio yesterday, and it's sure to be gone by next week. Blackpolls perform some of the longest migrations in the warbler family. They spend the winter in South America, mostly in the Amazon Basin, including well south of the equator in Brazil and eastern Peru. Their summer range stretches across the boreal forests of northern Canada and far west into Alaska. A blackpoll that lands on the Lake Erie shoreline in Ohio in May has probably flown more than three thousand miles from its wintering grounds already, and it may fly another three thousand miles before it arrives at its nesting territory.

Consider how improbable this journey is. The blackpoll warbler normally weighs about half an ounce. Fattened up with fuel for migration it may nearly double its weight, reaching almost an ounce, or about as heavy as a good ballpoint pen. This blackpoll we're watching now started gorging to build up its fat reserves in March, somewhere in the Amazon jungle. In early April it started north, in a series of nighttime flights. It may have paused for a week or two on the northern coast of Venezuela or Colombia before setting out across the water, flying hundreds of miles, even as much as a thousand miles, north across the Caribbean.

There's a good chance this blackpoll warbler paused in Cuba or the Bahamas and stopped again in Florida before continuing north. Flying overnight when skies were clear, covering two or three hundred miles in a night, then pausing for a few days in some unfamiliar place to build up strength for the next nocturnal flight, it made its way to northern Ohio. Today it's with us here, part of the avian mob at Magee Marsh. By the end of May it will be somewhere in northern Canada or Alaska. In the space of a few weeks it trades rainforest giants along the Amazon for spindly spruces at the edge of the Arctic. On the way it flies six thousand miles, navigating through heat and wind and storm, stopping over in a dozen alien lands, evading countless dangers, pushing on with single-minded purpose to reach the breeding grounds.

What do you think about that? Aren't you impressed? You should be. But actually that's a trick question, because this bird's spring migration is hardly the most impressive thing about it. This spring journey is a walk in the park compared to the flight that it survived last fall.

Seriously. The flood of blackpolls that sweeps north through Florida in spring is reduced to a trickle in fall migration, even though the total population is higher at that season, swelled by all the young birds hatched during the summer. Why aren't the blackpoll warblers coming through Florida in any numbers in fall? Because most of them are farther east, out over the open waters of the Atlantic.

Blackpolls that nest in Alaska or western Canada in summer don't fly straight south in fall. Instead they fly east or southeast across Canada. They dip into the northeastern United States — sometimes in September or early October we see large numbers in northern Ohio, hugging the edge of Lake Erie — as their route takes them east to the Atlantic Coast. Then a blackpoll may linger near the coast for days, feeding and fattening and waiting on weather, until that night when sunset brings clear skies and steady northwest wind. As darkness falls the tiny bird takes off, rising rapidly, arrowing out over the water and heading southeastward into the empty night.

Probably, mercifully, the bird has no way of marking time comparable to ours, and no visual map of its route. It isn't thinking about the fact that it is taking off from coastal Massachusetts on a Sunday night. When the sun comes up on Monday, with nothing visible below but ocean waves out to the horizon in all directions, it won't think about the fact that there's no land ahead for the next two thousand miles. The warbler will just keep flying all day Monday and all night Monday night.

Dawn on Tuesday brings an unchanged scene: nothing but water, the deep blue of midocean water, out to the endless horizon. Sometime Tuesday morning the warbler might see the islands of Bermuda off in the distance, but unless the weather is turning bad, the bird isn't likely to detour to a stop there; it just keeps flying, beating those tiny wings, a speck of life in the vastness of the sea and sky. And it continues on its course, still moving southeast, all day Tuesday and all night Tuesday night.

By Wednesday morning there's a different feel to the air, more warmth and more humidity. The warbler has been aiming southeastward this whole time, but now the trade winds are coming in from the northeast and pushing the bird more toward the south. During the day on Wednesday it might see some of the islands of the Lesser Antilles down below, Martinique or Barbados or one of the others, but again if the weather's good it probably won't come down. Wednesday night, though, during the night, it may be dropping lower, feeling depleted, its energy mostly gone. When first light on Thursday reveals land coming up ahead, the northern coast of South America, the warbler is ready to land, to pitch into the first tree that rises out of the tropical mist.

Again: this is a bird with a body just a little larger than your thumb. Weighing almost an ounce at the beginning of its flight, it's now exhausted and emaciated, down to less than half an ounce. Sunday night to Thursday morning. Four nights and three days in the air. Eighty hours of flying. More than two thousand miles. Hundreds of thousands of beats of its small wings. Think about it.

As a test of endurance, as a physical ordeal, it's both miraculous and monstrous.

Nothing in the human experience can compare to this. And that's especially true when the blackpoll is a young bird, making the flight for the first time. Any comparison that we try will fall apart. Think of Ferdinand Magellan in 1520, attempting to be the first to sail around the world. Picture him surviving the brutal trip through the straits at the southern tip of South America and then heading out across the wide Pacific — but imagine that Magellan is not on a ship but rather is swimming, pumping with his own arms and legs, out into that vast sea. That might be a parallel to the first southward flight of a young blackpoll warbler.

Human explorers through the ages have drawn courage and inspiration from examples set by earlier travelers. Written histories and oral traditions have served to pass down legendary exploits from the pioneers. Astronauts today may look to the examples of John Glenn or Sally Ride. Sea captains of recent centuries might have absorbed the legends of Francis Drake or James Cook. Magellan, on his voyage of circumnavigation, was steeped in the proud history of earlier Portuguese explorers. Norsemen plying the icy North Atlantic in their longships a thousand years ago probably drew strength from repeating the tales of earlier Viking expeditions. Humans of all stripes, boldly going where no man has gone before, thrive on stories of others who have done the same.

Of course, traveling birds have no language to pass along any verbal history. From our viewpoint it might seem that they're cast out there on their own, specks of life against the sky, flying alone into the unknown. And to some extent that's true. But they have their own traditions and unspoken legends, and these are handed down more directly, generation to generation, in the blood. Every long-distance migrant is the direct descendant of champions.

A harsh equation of death is what keeps the whole species strong. Blackpoll warblers will not build a nest and raise their first brood until they are one year old, and to reach that opportunity they will have to run a gauntlet of extraordinary challenges. Born in a land where they could not possibly live through the winter, programmed to travel to wintering grounds a continent away, they must endure the monstrous marathon of the overwater flight to South America at the age of three or four months. If they can survive the winter in the tropical jungle, they must then fly back north across the Caribbean — in a series of flights measured in the hundreds of miles rather than thousands — and work their way north, evading predators and dodging obstacles, heading for the boreal forest. Only if they make it back can they even contemplate the next challenges: finding a mate and raising a brood of young.

Those who succumb to the dangers of migration will never breed. The genes of weaklings are never passed to the next generation. Every baby blackpoll warbler in the nest has the blood of heroes pumping in its veins; every one of its ancestors was an astonishing champion, going back thousands of generations. That is the epic legend the bird carries on its journey, not in words but in its heart.

It's almost impossible to translate this into human terms. It's very uncomfortable and awkward even to make the attempt. Just try it. Imagine an evil dictatorship in which no one was allowed to have children until they had performed extraordinary physical feats of skill, strength, and endurance. Imagine a tyranny in which all young people were put through brutal trials, tests in which the penalty for failure was instant death. Only the physical superheroes would survive to raise families. Within a few generations, heredity working as it does, fewer weak individuals would be born, and all the people on the street would be sculpted like gods.

Of course we recoil in horror from such a scenario, and we should. Human culture is not so simple. Physical strength is just one of many potential attributes of a person, and not the most important. We have so much more to gain from a wide array of creative minds — Stephen Hawking, Steve Jobs, Stevie Nicks — than from any hypothetical race of muscular robots. And every individual has the right to live his or her own unique life without passing anyone's tests or trials.

But for the long-distance migrant birds, the scenario I just described is a fairly accurate reflection of reality. Every blackpoll warbler in the woods at Magee this morning wears this same invisible badge of distinction, this same history. The strong and graceful fliers we see are the product of a system that has killed billions of the less strong and less graceful before they had a chance to breed. These little pagans live in a harsh and merciless world, but they fly through it with a confidence that is beautiful to see, and every day that they survive is its own small miracle.

I use the term "miracle" here intentionally. For many people it reflects some phenomenon they assume they'll never see, like walking on water. But back up for a moment: consider the water itself. Isn't it remarkable? Isn't it absolutely phenomenal that the right combination of two common gases, hydrogen and oxygen, could produce this precious liquid, this water that sustains a world of life? And then consider the act of walking. Consider the idea of a living creature making the decision to go somewhere, sending a signal through its nervous system to move muscles and lift bones and flesh to perform this action, to move legs in a co-ordinated way to walk forward, a seemingly simple motion that is really so complex.

Walking is a miracle. Water is a miracle. We don't have to combine them to achieve something wondrous. Every little bird in the woods today is its own living, breathing miracle, whether it's a chickadee that survives extremes of winter and summer or a look-alike blackpoll warbler that survives a flight from Brazil to Alaska. We are surrounded by miracles on all sides, every day, if only we open our eyes and notice them.

17

The Parade's Gone By

Then one morning, without fanfare or prior notice, the white-crowned sparrows were gone.

We had been so happy to see them when they first arrived. The white-crowns had descended in a rush in late April, just before the main push of warblers. Undeniably elegant, trim gray-and-brown birds with snappy white-and-black head stripes, they were suddenly everywhere. Little flocks of white-crowns hopped and foraged around the edges of woods and hedgerows, around the parking lot at Magee Marsh, around the outskirts of Oak Harbor, rummaging in leaf litter on the ground under bird feeders. For more than three weeks they had been with us, a reliable presence. On sunny mornings males would perch up in the shrubbery to sing short, breezy songs, whistled and wheezy. But they weren't singing to establish local territories or attract local mates. These birds were just passing through, heading for the Canadian taiga up by Hudson Bay.

I knew that, of course. I knew they were just transients that would be leaving soon, but I had gradually paid less attention to them as the full flood of arriving migrants built up in May. They had been around yesterday and I'd hardly given them a second look. Then last night skies were clear and winds were calm, and this morning there were no white-crowned sparrows under the feeders at the house. One or two might have lurked in thickets near the bird observatory, but the flocks were gone. Their voices were missing from the morning chorus.

Today there's a different feeling in the air. I had been so focused on the migration that I hadn't consciously marked other changes in the season; but now, in the third week of May, the light is different, the sun higher in the sky, trees almost at full leaf-out. It's getting warm toward midday, and there's a haze over the land that makes it seem warmer than it is. If I didn't know better, I could look around and believe it was summer already.

Of course the spring migration is still in full swing. Up by the edge of the lake there are still plenty of warblers in the woods, and there are more to come. The specialties of late May have only begun to arrive. Typical late migrants like Wilson's, Canada, and mourning warblers are still building up in numbers, while red-eyed vireos and certain thrushes and flycatchers are approaching their peak flights. The sought-after and elusive Connecticut warbler — much more reliable here in Ohio than it ever was in Connecticut — will pass through during the last week of May. It will lurk quietly through the thickets, and birders will come back to Magee Marsh to try for it, some after multiple unsuccessful attempts in the past.

So, yes, migration is still going on, but it feels different today. The white-crowned sparrows are gone. So are the juncos and kinglets and other early-spring birds. There are no more silent flocks of blue jays flying high along the lakeshore, no random gatherings of flashy scarlet tanagers or rose-breasted grosbeaks. The warblers and other migrants in the woods are more hidden now among the luxuriant foliage. Even for those of us who are actively looking, the migration has become more obscure.

The ranks of visiting birders have thinned as well. Numbers stayed high for the first few days after the end of the Biggest Week, and even now a few hundred birders remain in the general area, but they're not as concentrated. Of the tour leaders, optics dealers, and other vendors, most had to leave almost as soon as the festival ended, going on to other birding events. Of my hundreds of other friends who visited, many were here for only part of the festival. Some I saw only briefly in passing, or our paths didn't cross at all.

With so many of my friends visiting the area at once, I never feel as if I've had enough chance to connect with them all. We'll say hello early in the week, and then the time for a full conversation never materializes. Heidi and Eric from Colorado, Carlos and Jenn from Panama, that family from Saskatchewan, those two couples from Nevada, the grad students from Vermont—they were all here this year and I wanted to talk with all of them, but it never happened, and now they're gone. Melanie from New Hampshire, those brothers from Illinois, Jonathan from Israel—I expected to catch up with them on the boardwalk or at the evening socials, but it never happened, and now they're gone, too. I said goodbye to a handful of people when I knew they were leaving, but most just disappeared when I wasn't looking. Just like the migratory birds, they departed on their own schedule, without notice.

I know that people have their busy lives to lead, and I accept that they have to go. With the birds, though, I often find myself wishing they would just stay. Or maybe it's not a wish so much as a completely irrational sense that I've somehow let them down by letting them go.

The great flights of ducks that came thundering into the open lake and thawing marshes back in March—I was so thrilled by their arrival, but then I was off looking for migrant songbirds in the woods, and the duck flocks dwindled and disappeared. The shy fox sparrows with their rich colors and rich songs, the flighty little kinglets fidgeting and flitting in the trees, the bands of rusty blackbirds filling the swamp with a creaky chorus—I had welcomed them all when they swept onto the scene in early April, but then I was looking past them, watching for warblers, and they drifted away. The white-crowned sparrows with their smart and snappy pattern, showing up alongside the first big warbler wave—I had celebrated their arrival at first and appreciated their reliable presence, but then gradually paid less and less attention to them. And now they were gone.

The annual disappearance of the early migrants bothers me more than it should. It touches me at a gut level, like the deep regret that comes from losing a friendship through neglect. Today I feel a need to grab the spring migration with both hands, to hold it a little longer, so I drive up to the boardwalk at Magee Marsh. Because of the concentrating effect of the lake edge, the migration remains obvious here long after the birds have become too scarce to notice over most of the landscape. In other words, most of the birds have gone on north, but of the ones that linger, a high percentage are right here.

Today the boardwalk is pulsing, vibrating with American redstarts. These active warblers, flashing patches of orange or yellow in their wings and tails, are typically among the later spring migrants.

Several times I'm able to stand in one spot and see three or four without moving my feet. And at this point in the season, seeing even one bird is an accomplishment, since the leaves are so thick.

So many of the birds around today are females or young males. I'll see dozens of redstarts, and almost none will be the striking black-and-orange adult males. With most of these migrants, the adult males move north earlier, on average, hurrying to claim the best summer territories. Most of the singing is done by adult males, so there is less birdsong now than there was two weeks ago. Birds of various species just appear randomly from behind the foliage . . . one Wilson's warbler here, one female black-throated blue warbler over there, slipping out onto an open twig and then vanishing again.

So we have to sense, rather than see, that there are a lot of birds here. If the foliage now were as it is in late April, sparse and thin, this would be a day to make beginning birders gasp with delight at the abundance of birds. As it is now, beginners would miss most of these hidden birds. Birders with more experience will see a handful of migrants and sense that more are present — hearing songs filtered through heavy foliage: high thin zips of blackpoll warblers, sibilant chants of redstarts, short phrases of red-eyed vireos, all sounding distant.

Out there in the midday heat of late spring, a new feeling washes over me. I'm filled with a desperate longing to stop the passage of time — to back it up a few days to the heart of the bird festival and then to live in the moment, to live in *that* moment, forever. To be in that perfect time when I'm with my lovely Kimberly and all of our friends are around, all of us celebrating the dazzling peak of spring migration. To grasp that moment when a few of the birds of winter and early spring are still lingering and all the migrants from the tropics have arrived in a rush, creating that glo-rious sense of diversity and abundance, the sense that anything is possible in the perfection of springtime.

Time won't stop. I know that. It's a tired cliché to say that time is like a river flowing inexorably down to the sea. But is it really like a river? If we watch the flow of a river, we'll notice places along the banks where the current doubles back, eddying and circling. A stray leaf floating on the surface may be swept into one of these eddies and just circle there, turning slowly, while the rest of the current moves downstream. Could there be eddies like this in the flow of time? If I could, I would tuck into some obscure spot near the bank and just turn circles in this hidden backwater, letting the current go on by while time stands still in this one spot, this per-fect moment in May.

Even if I could, of course, it's too late. The main part of the mi-gration has gone by already and now the season is rocketing to-ward summer.

Time is accelerating, not standing still. Everything is growing in the woods and fields, branches spreading, shrubs sprawling out, vines climbing trees, every twig bursting with flower or leaf. As we blast into the heat of summer, abundance rules. Life is every-where, on extravagant display, from fireflies to butterflies, baby birds to baby foxes. Uncut fields turn into thickets, woodlots into jungles. If this abundance continued unchecked for a few more months, Ohio would look like the rainforests of Borneo.

Of course it won't continue unchecked. Before the middle of summer we've already passed the longest daylight of the summer solstice, and days are beginning to grow shorter again as Earth starts to tilt away from the sun. Temperatures, trailing behind the position of the planet, eventually will drop with crushing finality, as winter puts an end to summer's abundance and the land sinks into uneasy sleep.

I'm still coming to grips with the winter here after living for years in Arizona, where winter was hardly more than a rumor. The Arizona climate was popular for retirement communities, and I wonder now if there were subtle, hidden reasons for that. Did retired people simply want to avoid cold weather? Or were they getting away from the concept of winter, the very idea of it? After all, the change of seasons and the arrival of winter are like reminders of mortality. In Arizona there was seasonal change for naturalists who went out to seek it, but it wasn't apparent if you just looked out the window. It would be possible there to live in a state of suspended season, to pretend that each day would be like the one before, unchanging and unending.

To live here in northern Ohio, of course, forces you to accept the reality of winter, even if that reality is changing. If you're a birder in northern Ohio, you embrace winter as the precursor to spring. Even in the depths of winter you're confident that springtime will come like a resurrection, bringing waves of beautiful migratory birds flooding northward across the region.

But if you're paying attention to bird conservation issues, your confidence may be shaken. Will the birds come back after all? Can we take it for granted, or will there come a year when the migration dwindles away to nothing?

Threats to the migration loom larger and larger. Just as relentless as the flow of the river, just as blindly inexorable as the flow of time, the wind industry is still out there, just over the horizon. Its proponents are constantly pushing to erect more huge towers with deadly blades, even in the most sensitive wildlife habitats. We continue to monitor the news about plans for commercial-scale wind farms in central Lake Erie, in north-central Ohio, in eastern Michigan, marching closer and closer to the region we are trying to protect.

But in the midst of these ominous signs, we received news that was as encouraging as it was surprising: the plan for the "experimental" wind turbine at Camp Perry, right next door to our most treasured habitats, had been officially canceled.

The news came at the end of the spring migration season in 2017. The American Bird Conservancy and Black Swamp Bird Observatory had filed a lawsuit months earlier against the Air National Guard, claiming that the wind-turbine experiment at Camp Perry would violate aspects of the Endangered Species Act and the Migratory Bird Treaty Act. We were prepared to hang in there for a long fight. But by the end of May we heard from our friends at ABC that a resolution was in the works. And in June the attorneys representing our case received formal notice from the National Guard Bureau: the Camp Perry wind project would not move forward.

In the end it worked out just about as well as it possibly could have. Did we force the Air National Guard to cancel the plan? No, of course not. No one forces America's military to do anything. All we did was to present it with detailed information about the potential impacts of the wind-power experiment. On that basis, ultimately its officials concluded that the honorable thing would be to stop the project, so they did. Officials at Camp Perry didn't hold a grudge; within a few months some of them were reaching out to BSBO to talk about positive connections.

Our congresswoman, Marcy Kaptur, had promoted the wind-turbine project with great enthusiasm at first, when consultants had told her it wouldn't harm birdlife, but later she had listened to our concerns. After the Camp Perry project was taken off the table she didn't miss a beat. She ramped up her promotion of solar power and continued her warm support of the bird observatory and of bird conservation in general.

So our victory in the case was something we could celebrate, a success with no serious downside, at least not immediately. We had stopped one turbine in a bird-sensitive zone, and perhaps sent a message to the wind industry that this was a challenging place, best to avoid.

Of course, nothing exists in isolation. The threat posed by wind turbines in stopover zones was just one of the many threats faced by migratory birds. Ironically, during the months after we celebrated the end of the Camp Perry project, the United States suffered some of its most damaging and extreme weather events in history. Major drought across the western states led to a horrific fire season, with almost 10 million acres burned. California suffered some of its worst firestorms, with dozens of people killed and billions of dollars in property damages. Hurricanes devastated huge swaths of Texas and Florida and brought widespread destruction to Puerto Rico. Going on into the following winter, many eastern cities experienced record cold and massive blizzards in early January, followed by record warmth in February, while Alaska remained oddly warm and Arctic sea ice fell to record lows.

Among the diminishing ranks of those still denying the reality of climate change, each of these events is viewed as an isolated case, an anomaly. For those who have actually studied the science, the view is different and more nuanced. No single event, it's true, can be stated conclusively to be the direct result of climate change. But the trend to more and more frequent violent storms, to greater extremes of heat and cold, drought and flood, is exactly what was predicted as a result of overall warming temperatures. When you break record after record, something is wrong. When "the storm of the century" starts arriving almost every year, things are seriously out of balance.

Year by year the evidence becomes more ironclad: human activity is contributing to climate change, the effect is accelerating, and we're not doing nearly enough about it. Nothing about this should be political, yet people keep fighting about it, wasting precious time.

In the meantime the great worldwide systems of bird migration are at risk. The timing and routes of these avian journeys are dependent on weather conditions at multiple locations. Changes in climate may mean these patterns of travel cannot continue. This is especially true for the birds that migrate the farthest, pushing the limits of what is even possible. At the same time, some of our most ambitious attempts to halt the advance of climate change, by striving for renewable energy, can be deadly for the same long-distance travelers. The migratory birds are caught in the middle. What can the future possibly hold for them?

18

Pagans of the Sky

Tonight they are on the move.

It's the end of May, almost three weeks past migration's peak here, and most of the birds of passage undoubtedly have already passed through. But tonight's conditions are perfect for a big flight. The national weather map shows a low-pressure area centered over southern Missouri and a strong high over the central Atlantic Seaboard; in between them, a corridor of warm air runs all the way from the Gulf of Mexico to the eastern Great Lakes, right over the Lake Erie shoreline in northern Ohio.

An hour after sunset I pull up the Nexrad image and I can see blooms of blue circles exploding around most of the radar sites in the eastern half of the country. They're only modest rings of color around the southernmost sites, but here in the upper Midwest they are major, growing, with dark blue and blue-green and green developing in the centers, clear signs of heavy avian traffic. Even if most migratory birds at these latitudes have already reached their breeding grounds, many millions are still moving to areas farther north.

At any point during the season we can guess which kinds of birds are creating those anonymous radar echoes over the Midwest, based on what we know about timing of migration. Early on, in March and early April, many of the nocturnal migrants would have been sparrows — fox sparrows, song sparrows, and more — and the rest would have included hermit thrushes, golden-crowned kinglets, winter wrens, and other odd early birds. Going on through April, the diversity would have swelled along with the sheer numbers flying, as more warblers, vireos, wrens, and others joined the parade. By early May there might have been two hundred species moving on a big night, a dazzling array of tiny travelers, with many warblers, tanagers, orioles, buntings, thrushes, and others reaching peak passage. But now we're beyond that point, and the variety of migrants is diminishing again.

Earlier today I went out to the Magee Marsh boardwalk to assess the current state of the migration. The scene is far different now than it was in the second week of May. There are fewer birders now — I saw only a few dozen — and there is much more foliage, with every tree and shrub and vine in full leaf-out. There are fewer warblers now and they are foraging at all levels, from the leafy treetops to the dense green thickets near the ground, making them harder to spot.

As I walked around today I was thinking how wonderful it is, how reassuring, that migratory birds are predictable in their timing. The prophet Jeremiah noted this first: *Yea, the stork in the heavens knoweth her appointed times; and the turtledove and the crane and the swallow observe the time of their coming.* Today, more than 2,500 years later, we have more data points to confirm the premise.

Every kind of migratory bird passing through Ohio observes the time of its coming.

At the peak of the warbler flight in early May, it might have seemed as if all three-dozen-plus of these colorful creatures were random and interchangeable, all equally likely or unlikely, so that pure chance would dictate which warblers we would see on a given day — like twisting a kaleidoscope to get a beautiful but completely random pattern. But of course that isn't the case. Yellow-rumped warblers were everywhere on May 1, but today it would have been surprising to find even one. Palm warblers mostly come through in the early part of the flight, magnolias peak in the middle, blackpolls are mostly later. The patterns are well established. Today I knew I was likely to find Wilson's warblers and Canada warblers, because they're typical of the latter part of the flight, and I did see several of each. A couple of mourning warblers were out there as well, hiding in dense brush piles, and a few American redstarts — all females or young males, flashing yellow instead of red-orange patches in the wings and tail, because the adult males have already gone through. These were all as expected for the season.

A few shy brown thrushes lurked in the shadows near the boardwalk today, too. I saw a Swainson's thrush and heard a couple more, and saw three gray-cheeked thrushes; usually the Swainson's are more numerous, so the ratio was a surprise. These were all on their way much farther north, with the gray-cheeks possibly going beyond tree line in northern Canada or Alaska, or even heading on across the Bering Strait into Siberia. Numbers of red-eyed vireos were around, too, moving deliberately through the higher foliage, and they would be going on to forests across the temperate latitudes of Canada.

During my hike of the boardwalk today I had some of my first mosquitoes of the season; they're mercifully scarce at the peak of the warbler flight in early May. The woods have far more flying insects now, so the flycatchers are finally coming through in force. Flycatchers, which feed on small insects caught in midair, move through northern Ohio mainly in the last half of May. They're mostly drab birds, wearing tones of gray and olive, and most easily recognized by voice. Right now, at the end of May, willow flycatchers are arriving and setting up territories in scrub-shrub thickets near Lake Erie, while their lookalikes, alder flycatchers, are just passing through.

Today along the boardwalk I heard and saw several alder flycatchers, and hearing them took me back to my first visit to Alaska, when I was eighteen. I had hitchhiked up the Alaska Highway and gone to the central part of the state, and when I camped out near lakes between Fairbanks and Denali, I heard alder flycatchers every night. They sang their short songs incessantly, a burry *ffrree-beeeo!*, throughout the long twilight, even after the thrushes stopped singing and after the sun set at midnight. They would start up again before three in the morning, before the sun came up to end the short subarctic night. To me their song became the emblematic sound of those northern woods and of my teenage freedom, and I love hearing it now, years later, from migrating birds in the Midwest.

Tonight I am still thinking about bird sounds. After looking at the maps of current weather, looking at the bursts of bird echoes lighting up the radar, I go outside to listen for the nocturnal flight calls of migrants overhead.

It's a clear night and the south wind is steady, with no noisy gusts. As my eyes adjust to the darkness I can see more and more stars spread across the heavens. Mostly, though, I'm listening to sounds of the night. Toads are trilling softly in the grass, crickets are rasping, and a very distant bullfrog grumbles for a minute. But there are other sounds, avian sounds, from high above.

A soft, liquid note, *hweep,* comes down from the sky, and a few seconds later it's repeated, fainter now, as the bird moves away. It's the night flight call of a Swainson's thrush. Three minutes later I hear another one, and then the nasal *veeyr* of a gray-cheeked thrush. A while later there's another gray-cheek, then the sharp buzz of an indigo bunting, and later another Swainson's thrush. In between, a scattering of light lisps and chips are undoubtedly the notes of warblers.

Listening to these magical sounds in the night sky, I start to wonder about the birds I'm *not* hearing. For example, there have to be red-eyed vireos going over, but I haven't heard one yet. There have to be many small flycatchers among the birds creating the blue circles on tonight's radar, but I'm not hearing a sound from them.

Why? According to the people who have studied the subject the most, even though vireos and small flycatchers are traveling at night, they rarely make any kind of nocturnal flight calls.

But again, why? The more I consider it, the stranger it seems. Alder flycatchers, for example, overlap in range with both Swainson's thrushes and gray-cheeked thrushes at all seasons. They all can be found in western South America in winter, especially just east of the Andes in the upper Amazon Basin. They all spread across boreal zones of Canada and Alaska in summer. They all migrate north relatively late in spring, and they all take off shortly after sunset and fly strongly north through the dark skies. But those two thrush species make frequent, distinctive callnotes as they fly, while the alder flycatcher is mostly or entirely silent. Why?

Why? I find myself asking that question more often these days. The more I learn about the when, where, and how of bird migration, the more I wonder about why it should be so.

Why do crows start moving north across the frozen landscape in the middle of February? Why do some sandpipers, coming from South America, get here in March, while others don't arrive until May? Why do blue jays migrate in the daytime while scarlet tanagers travel at night?

For that matter, why do we have such a beautiful, abundant variety of birds performing these migratory flights across the landscape? Why do more than twenty kinds of ducks pass through these marshes, all of them striking and unique, instead of just a few generalized, adaptable species that could fulfill every duck role? And the warblers, the colorful little gems that brighten the woods in May—why do we see such a dizzying, dazzling diversity of different kinds?

These are the questions that fill my mind as I stand out under the stars, listening for the voices of tiny travelers overhead.

Purely in terms of physics, Earth could function all right as a lifeless rock. It could spin through the void of space for a few billion years until its gravitational dance around the sun comes to a fiery end. It could exist with nothing moving on its surface, ever, besides the impacts of meteorites and cosmic debris. But instead this rock is wrapped in nurturing blankets of air and water, covered with the most incredible complexity, seething with motion, brimming with a fabulous abundance and diversity of life. Everything on this planet is more wonderful and amazing and beautiful than it would have to be.

Many people will credit this abundance and wonder to an all-powerful creator. I can't argue, as long as the definition is kept wide open. Of course, many will take it a step further and claim all credit for their own particular god or gods. Humans crave certainty, I suppose, even if we have to seek it out in obscure places and then sometimes talk ourselves into believing it. Among all the thousands of different religions embraced by humans in the past and present, many people are absolutely certain that their own belief is the only true one and that all others are wrong. Maybe a few of them happen to be right. I can't claim to know.

What I do know is that I'm filled with awe and reverence when I look at the natural world. And it's not a first flush of wonder that fades after I learn more facts. Everything, everything becomes more astounding the more we look at it. Everything. Peer into a microscope and we discover that a drop of pond water contains a whole world of little things going about their busy lives; study the science and we learn that each of these invisibly tiny creatures is made up of cells, and those cells are made up of atoms and subatomic particles far too small for our microscopes to discern. Peer into the most powerful telescope and we discover that out beyond the faintest stars in the night sky, whole galaxies spin in the darkness of space, and others beyond those, on and on, world without end.

Viewed at any scale, from small to large, close to distant, the universe is far more complex than any human intellect could grasp. In the brief blink of my own life I have chosen to focus on these remarkable creatures called birds and their travels across this one planet. The subject is still too vast for me to comprehend, but it's a manageable little fragment of the infinite number of vast subjects out there. Even in looking at bird migration, each new fact leads not to a more complete picture of the whole but to more questions. And so it is with every aspect of science. The more I learn, the more I am overcome with an intoxicating sense of the wonder and magic of it all.

If all of this came about by chance — if we are having this experience called life, in this astonishingly diverse and beautiful world,

merely because of random accidents of physics and chemistry—
then we are insanely lucky. If, instead, this is part of the plan of
some supreme being, then we are incredibly blessed. Either way,
I will revel in the wonder and beauty of it all for as long as my life
lasts. If some all-powerful, all-knowing, all-seeing force is watching over us, then she or he or it must know that I am grateful, and
that I am filled with reverence for all of creation.

I have come to realize that this is part of what drives me: this
sense of reverence for the abundance and diversity of living things.
I want to see it, learn about it, immerse myself in it, and then do
what I can to protect it. My desire to preserve the patterns of bird
migration is not just a cold scientific calculation to maintain func-
tioning ecosystems—it's more of a spiritual calling.

Is there a danger that the phenomenon of bird migration might
disappear completely? I don't think so. It's under threat, especially the patterns that create the most remarkable long-distance
travels, but I have hope that we can preserve these as well as the
shorter migrations. During my travels all over the world, I've been
awed repeatedly by the astonishing resilience of life. In the harsh-
est conditions, in the most unlikely places, life finds a way.

Besides, the ability to move around with the seasons is such a
basic element, practiced by so many kinds of creatures, that it could
be considered an integral part of life on this planet. Birds are not
the only migrators. Herds of caribou walk hundreds of miles across
the arctic tundra twice every year, and herds of wildebeest thunder
north and south through the Serengeti. Some whales swim from
Mexico to Alaska, or from the Caribbean to waters near Greenland,
or from the equator to the edge of the Antarctic. Certain bats fly
from Canada to Central America, and others migrate across Africa.
Bluefin tuna swim from spawning grounds in the Mediterranean

or the Gulf of Mexico out to cold waters of the North Atlantic. Some trout, salmon, and other fishes glide down rivers to the sea, then fight their way back upstream in the same rivers to spawn. Butterflies and dragonflies may migrate thousands of miles, with some dragonflies even crossing the ocean from India to Africa. Even a milkweed plant or a dandelion reaches for mobility for the next generation, with seeds adapted for being carried on the wind. It's a whole world in motion in myriad ways.

Right now, somewhere high overhead, a gray-cheeked thrush gives its vibrant note. Staring up at the sky brimming with stars, I try to imagine what the thrush would look like: a small bird flying with strong, quick wingbeats far above the ground, arrowing toward the north, confident in its single-minded purpose. As I look and listen I hear the voices of other thrushes, other birds, drifting down through the dark night.

In this moment it seems wholly appropriate that I'm looking into the enormous vastness of space, seeing light from stars that are untold trillions of miles away, while I listen to the voices of these tiny specks of life. The birds and the stars are impossibly far apart, but they are part of the same world.

These migratory birds will inspire me and fill me with wonder for as long as I live. They practice no religion, but they are buoyed up and carried along on their journeys by what seem to be infinite levels of faith. They live the briefest of lives, but they are bound to eternal things. They are out there now between the heavens and the earth, legions of travelers flowing strong and deep through the night, beyond all understanding, beyond all imagination, filling the sky with life.

ACKNOWLEDGMENTS

In a way I've been working on this book for most of my life, so my first debt of gratitude is to people all over the world who have studied bird migration for the last couple of centuries. I've lost track of the scores of books and thousands of technical papers about the subject that I've read, but they all contributed somehow to the account in these pages.

Aside from reading, some of my strongest influences have come through deep conversations about migration. Early discussions with Scott B. Terrill, Susan Roney Drennan, and Victor L. Emanuel were pivotal for me. More recently, Peter P. Marra helped me to see some aspects of migration in a whole new light. Regarding weather's effects, I learned a lot from Paul Lehman, David La Puma, and Paul Hurtado. Special thanks to Pete Pokrandt and the rest of the staff at the Department of Atmospheric and Oceanic Sciences, University of Wisconsin–Madison.

In this book I've tried to illuminate the whole worldwide phe-nomenon of migration by taking a deep dive into the details of one region. For expertise on northwestern Ohio, including all aspects of natural history and human history, Mark Shieldcastle was an amazing resource. Historian and author Jim Mollenkopf shared his extensive knowledge of the Great Black Swamp. Others who went out of their way to help me understand the region included Tiffanie, John, and Delaney Hayes, Paula and Tom Bartlett, Tom Kashmer, Randy Kreager, John Simpson, and David K. Welles, Jr.

Of course I received help from many other people during the course of this project and I can't begin to thank them all, but I must single out Mike and Sue Blakely, Jen Brumfield, Patrick Czarny, Bob Fay, George Fenwick, Ashli Gorbet, Doug and LeShon Gray, Laura and Jason Guerard, Robert Hershberger, Ryan Jacob, Ken Keffer, Ethan Kistler, Greg Links, Jeff Loughman, Paula Lozano, Ron Miller, Barb and Dan Myers, Deb Neidert, Barb Padgett, Mike Parr, Steve Pollick, R. Bruce Richardson, Rob and Stephanie Ripma, Paul Riss, Nicole Robinson, April and Jeff Sayre, Ben Warner, Bob and Kim Wistinghausen, Anna Wittmer, and Brian Zwiebel.

The actual writing of the book isn't the fun part, but several people made it a better experience for me. My dear friend Karen Zach reached into her endless well of creativity to help me figure out the structure of the story. Wendy Strothman, my longtime friend and agent, gave expert guidance (as always) on how to distill a vast subject down to its essential core.

It was a pleasure to work again with the professionals at Houghton Mifflin Harcourt. Lisa White, one of the finest natural history editors anywhere, has improved every book I've written since 1996, and she worked her magic on this project as well. Liz Du-vall, with her peerless eye for detail and clean phrasing, polished up the final text. Others at HMH who played key roles included Bruce Nichols, Katie Kimmerer, Beth Burleigh Fuller, Chloe Foster, Brian Moore, Liz Anderson, and Taryn Roeder. My sincere thanks to all.

The late Dr. Michael Hutchins left an indelible mark — a good one — on conservation efforts in Ohio and around the world. Without his efforts, the story told here would have been different. Another person who touched every aspect of this story is the remarkable Delores Cole. A genius behind the scenes, fiercely shunning the limelight, she did much to put the bird observatory and the Biggest Week bird festival on solid organizational ground. I would like to dedicate this book to Michael Hutchins and Delores Cole.

Finally, there's no way to adequately thank my wife, Kimberly. If you read the book you'll get some glimpses of her, but if I accurately described how wonderful she is, you'd think I was writing fiction. Trust me, she's more amazing than I can describe, and more than you can imagine.